A GUIDE TO
STUDENT-CENTRED LEARNING

A GUIDE TO STUDENT-CENTRED LEARNING

DONNA BRANDES
and
PAUL GINNIS

Basil Blackwell

First published 1986

Reprinted 1986 (twice), 1987, 1988, 1989

Published by Basil Blackwell Ltd
108 Cowley Road
Oxford OX4 1JF
England

ISBN 0 631 14933 3

British Library Cataloguing in Publication Data

Brandes, Donna
A guide to student-centred learning.
1. Activity programs in education 2. Project method in teaching
I. Title II. Ginnis, Paul
371.3 LB1027

ISBN 0-631-14933-3

Typeset by Freeman Graphic, Tonbridge, Kent
Printed and bound in Great Britain by
Dotesios Printers Limited, Bradford-on-Avon, Wiltshire

"I know I cannot teach anyone anything, I can only provide an environment in which he can learn."

Carl Rogers

CONTENTS

ACKNOWLEDGEMENTS

Many people have contributed to the writing of this book. The names of those who offer 'reflections' in Section 2 appear at the end of their contributions. In Section 3, some of the activities and games are not our own. We would like to thank the following for their ideas and creations:

Jill Baldwin; Colin Baldyga; Peter Beckhelling; Rhoma Bowdler; Martyn Briggs; Kay Chaffer; Peter Connah; David Greer; Yvonne Hanson; Keith Hardwick; Carol-Ann Heeks; Jackie Jones; Tim Jones; Di Kemp; David Lambourne; Edward Lear; Marian McFall; Malcolm Peters; Eva Ross; Eric Sant; Chris Traxson; Sally Tweddle; Jacky West; Maggie Whitely; the Core Group; *Active Tutorial Work*; *New Games UK*; and anyone else, whom we have been unable to trace, whose work is reproduced or reflected on these pages.

We also thank Martyn Briggs and Ron Peck for their delightful illustrations.

Contributions which could not be made with pen and paper have been enormous, and we are grateful to:

Ruth, Clare and Steven Ginnis, who loved and encouraged us and gave us, without complaint, time to work and write together; Sudhiro, who generously supported us; the Core Group, who were at the heart of the project and whose work enriches this book; Chris Lea, for helping us to get started, and for his unwavering commitment and encouragement; David Settle, for his constant inspiration and care; Keith Dennis, for encouraging the work at Queensbridge and for his vision of how a good school should be; Roger Brewster, for helping the methods to take root at Queensbridge; the students and staff of Queensbridge School, including 5B and Tech 1, for their cooperation, readiness to experiment and willingness to change; Philip Swan and Peter Hewitt, who put up with things not being done, or did them themselves; the Heads, staff and students of other Birmingham schools who were involved in the project; Kathleen Meacham, who typed the manuscript, for her dedication and commitment to completing it on time: Yvonne Hanson, who gave us the peace and quiet of her home to work in; Becky Higgins, for her determined optimism, cheerful support, and photocopying.

(Chapter 1 and part of Chapter 3 were adapted from Donna Brandes' thesis *An Illuminative Evaluation of an Alcohol Education Programme*, 1985.)

FOREWORD

This book describes a development which is at the cutting edge of change in education.

The last two years in Birmingham have been an important time for innovation through our TVEI project and it was this initiative which provided the opportunity and means by which work on student-centred learning could take root and grow.

Society as a whole is becoming more questioning, more challenging. Participation is becoming the norm of our culture. Schools will have to reflect these moves, and this will manifest itself through the ways in which learners and teachers learn together.

As a measure of its commitment to these developments, the Birmingham LEA has recently submitted proposals to the Manpower Services Commission for funds to support teachers in their personal and professional development, focusing on a move towards a more student-centred approach.

Donna's and Paul's work, as reflected in this book, is a touchstone to accelerate changes already in train. It is both a record of that change and a resource to sustain it in the future.

In their introduction, Donna and Paul tell us how they met along the continuum – the one to reinforce the experience of 26 years' teaching and the other to experience change in himself and his students. The great value of this book is that it describes learning observed in teacher and student alike.

John Crawford
Chief Education Officer
Birmingham

June 1985

A note to teachers . . .

Because of TVEI our brief for this seven month contract in Birmingham has been to work in secondary schools; the book reflects this concentration.

This does not alter the fact that these methods have been used *successfully at all age levels*. The challenge to primary teachers is to read and absorb the theoretical aspects of this book, and to adapt the activities for their own needs.

Young children are capable of making decisions and choices, taking responsibility, and owning their learning. In fact, without adult interference, that is exactly what they do!

Similarly, the principles, strategies and suggestions found in this book apply to tertiary eductation and many can be put to direct use; others can be adapted with a little imagination. They may complement experiential, active learning styles and philosophies already practised.

This symbol appears in the margin throughout the book to indicate passages and sections of key importance.

STOP
Do not pass page one!
Go directly to INTRO.

INTRODUCTION

We cannot claim ownership of the term 'Student-Centred Learning'; it was invented by Carl Rogers (Rogers 1965). We have experimented with terms such as 'Active Learning', 'Participatory Learning', and others that we devised ourselves. However, we have chosen student-centred learning because it is graphic; it describes exactly what we are hoping to achieve, that is, a system of providing learning which has the student at its heart.

A system of providing education which has the student at its heart

There is a continuum of teaching styles which extends from:

Traditional (didactic) ⟷ Student-centred (participatory)

Most teachers are already familiar with traditional methods, having been taught that way themselves, and trained in methods and techniques which are variations on the didactic theme. This style, which still makes up the bulk of teaching in British schools, seems to be concerned primarily with the transmission of knowledge and skills from the expert-teacher to the apprentice-pupil. The cognitive and practical domains tend to be emphasised much more than the affective, while the authority to make and carry out decisions is placed almost entirely in the hands of the teacher. Learning is, to varying degrees, passive. Obedience, reward and punishment are features of the teacher-pupil relationship, while mistrust, conflict, even fear, are often accepted as part and parcel of the system.

Many teachers are not familiar with alternative teaching styles. At the same time, they are searching for a way of working with their students which will be more satisfying and create closer relationships.

In this book we hope to provide the means by which you, the teacher, can move along this continuum and discover a much wider range of styles to choose from. Like any other teacher, you will want to operate at a point where you feel comfortable. We would simply encourage you to explore and experiment with non-didactic methods so as to increase your awareness of alternatives and make the process of self-discovery more complete.

Our dilemma: we do not claim that the student-centred approach is the only effective way to teach; different styles may be appropriate in different situations. However, we are undeniably and incurably *biased* and want you to be convinced of its value. We do not intend to present traditional styles here; you already know about those. What we are offering is a wide spectrum of alternative ideas, theory, experience, activities and suggestions. We hope that in the process of reading you will find yourself embarking on a course of personal and professional growth. We are asking you to take a hard look at your own teaching practices. If you are happy with what you see, read on anyway, just for the fun of exploring new territory. If, on the other hand, you think there is room for change in your attitudes and methods, then we hope this book will turn out to be what you have been looking for.

Self-concept

We are not blind to a social climate which tends to depress the self-concept of kids* through, for example, poor employment or career prospects. While this is not a 'do-goody' book, one of the most valuable aims of, and arguments for, a student-centred approach is that it can have a tremendously positive impact on self-esteem and mitigate the damage being done elsewhere.

We believe that every human being has the right to achieve his or her full potential – 100%, and that a student-centred approach to learning helps to make this possible. Students are encouraged to participate fully in, and take responsibility for, their own learning; each individual is valued and trusted. Such an approach will, we believe, move the student towards self-fulfilment by enhancing self-concept and at the same time facilitating the release of potential. These beliefs are not abstract theory but are founded on solid experience where they have been rigorously tried and tested.

For Donna, these ideas are irreversible truth. After being taught in a student-centred way for 21 years, through a series of fortunate circumstances, and after teaching this way herself for 26 years, she no longer needs to prove to herself the validity of these concepts.

For Paul, who was taught almost entirely by didactic methods and who had become dissatisfied with them in his own teaching, there was a dramatic conversion. The need for change had been building up and suddenly the means were provided. So Paul, although he has experienced moments of doubt, has, in the few short months since the project began, witnessed remarkable changes in himself and his students.

Intentions of the book

This book is intended for all educators and group leaders, not just for classroom teachers. We intend to combine theory and practice; the practice stemming from our own experience in training and in

* We have searched our souls and the dictionary looking for the proper title for our protagonists; we find 'children' and 'pupils' denigrating, 'teenagers' too narrow, and 'youngsters' or 'young people' condescending. We feel that 'students' is the respectful term for people in school, and we use it that way. 'Kids', however, is what they call themselves and each other, and what we teachers often call them in casual conversation, so we feel comfortable using this term.

classroom use. So this is not a 'How-to-do-it' book; it is a 'How-*we*-do-it' book. We are not presenting our experience in order to set ourselves up as models to be emulated, but to ensure that all the ideas are rooted in reality, and therefore are entirely possible and usable.

Section 1

The first section presents the theoretical background, and has three chapters:

Chapter 1 is an exposition of the principles of student-centred learning, in contrast to traditional methods. We draw upon an extensive body of literature to show that student-centred learning is a widely accepted approach, with a long history.
Chapter 2 Here we offer basic group work skills, and apply them to the classroom. This chapter is not an analysis of group dynamics and how to influence them; we want to avoid manipulation. There is no substitute for profound training in group work skills, but this chapter will open doors and provide a substantial guide to what may be unfamiliar territory.
Chapter 3 This looks at ways of initiating change towards a student-centred approach, in the classroom and the system.

Section 2

The writings in this section have been collected from educators and students during the Birmingham project. They ground the theory and methodology which we are advocating in real experience. They reflect the frustrations and successes of people who have been taking risks in trying ideas which are new to them. There is feedback from students who describe their responses to a style of learning which is a radical departure from their previous experience. Many readers may be able to identify with the feelings expressed.

Section 3

This is a compendium of activities, ideas and examples of good practice invented by educators and students, mostly from Birmingham, but also from other parts of the country. These activities are included, not only to be used as they appear, but also to be adapted for use with other topics, age groups and settings. Most importantly, they aim to encourage teachers and group leaders to invent their own.

Basic assumptions

When introducing student-centred learning with a group of educators, we operate in the same way that we would with students or any other group or individual. We work with a set of assumptions which are not only inherent in what we do and say but are also openly expressed to the group members, and form part of a verbalised agreement between us. The assumptions stem from the works of Carl Rogers and others, who have tested them and recorded the results on a regular basis over the years; we have also tested them and are able to sustain them on the strength of our experience. We assume that:

- '. . . the (person) has all the tools needed to make any personal changes needed or wanted.' (Van der Riet et al 1980, p. 71)
- we can purposefully and yet with integrity adopt a stance of unconditional positive regard for the person, to which the person may, sooner or later, respond with trust.
- the person has a willingness to change and grow, indeed a desire and a need to do so, and at the same time she has resistance and fear about changing; these two factors are equally acceptable;
- the person is in charge of herself, is fully responsible for her own behaviour, can participate or not, as she chooses;
- '. . . if we can provide a certain type of relationship, the other person can discover within himself the capacity to use that relationship for growth, and change and personal development will occur.' (Rogers 1961, p. 33)

These assumptions operate as our ground rules, and we discuss them openly in our work.

A new orthodoxy?

One of our great fears in producing this book is that we might be creating a Frankenstein, a monster which will grow out of proportion and reproduce hundreds of cloned classrooms, with all the kids playing the same games, and all the teachers parroting the same alternative phrases. We have already had experience of this. In a school in Leicester, for example, when we started playing 'How do you like your neighbour?' (Brandes and Phillips 1978, p. I. 128), a boy shouted, 'That's not how you play it!'

At one school, where we had worked with about a dozen of the teachers, a lad who had apparently had contact with a number of those teachers said 'Please, Miss, I'm getting sick of these Alternative Learning Styles. Can't we have a real lesson?'

It would be sad if teachers simply *adopted*, without *adapting*, the strategies, techniques and activities suggested in this book. In essence, student-centred learning is not a bag of tricks; it is about attitudes and relationships. For the teacher who is beginning to make the transition to a student-centred approach, there may be a period of inexperience, when she may want to lean heavily on ideas already established. Gradually she may begin to take more risks, and develop the ability to respond to challenges and think on her feet. With increased confidence and experience will come the possibility of inventing, not just adapting, ideas, and encouraging students to improvise and create their own learning experiences.

When the fundamental principles of a student-centred approach have been internalised by the teacher, each day in school can be fresh and new, and unpredictable.

Section 1

UNDERSTANDING

1 THE TEACHER'S CHOICE

The comfort of tradition

Although student-centred methods have been around for at least 2000 years, we are introducing them here as if they were something new. What is it about the traditional methods that keeps them dominant after all this time?

Many teachers say that they still find didactic methods safe, natural, comfortable and appropriate. One of the aspects of these methods is that they are subject-centred. Hargreaves has described the subject-centred teacher

> The teacher's authority ultimately rests in the authority of his subject. For such a teacher his subject expertise is absolutely central to his identity. He thinks of himself not as a teacher, but as a mathematics teacher, or a history teacher and so on. (Hargreaves 1982, p. 195)

When subject syllabuses are heavily laden with facts which must be memorised, it is easy to understand that teachers feel comfortable in the role of the expert, handing out information. Even if a lesson goes badly, there is at least the feeling that some information has been imparted, and some materials left behind. As Bennett (1976, p. 46) puts it, 'It is probably no exaggeration to say that with a more formal structure somebody is almost certain to learn something along the way'. If it goes well, the lesson may appear very slick and impressive, the teacher's expert image is enhanced and a strong impression of that part of the syllabus may be engraved on the students' memory.

There is a legacy of didacticism, and a model of pouring necessary information into empty vessels. A creative traditional teacher may effectively use many different sources of information and means of communicating ideas: slides, video programmes, contacts within the community, media resources and a wide range of other materials. These are, however, controlled by the teacher who decides when and how they should be used within the framework of a predetermined syllabus. In schools, colleges and other educational settings, teachers often feel restricted by time allocations, curriculum content, spatial arrangements (tiered lecture halls and formal classroom organisation) and by the expectations of pupils, students, parents and staff. We live in a hierarchical society, organised so that those who know tell those who do not know, and thereby maintain and enhance their own status, while passing on accumulated wisdom and experience.

> Teachers are qualified in their subjects; they *know*; and they are not satisfied until they have told their pupils what they know. In the jargon of the educationists this is the 'transmission' model of teaching: the function of the teacher is to impart knowledge to (in this respect) ignorant pupils, and the most obvious way in which to achieve this is by telling. (Hargreaves 1982, p. 200)

The most obvious way is not always the most effective, nor is it necessarily the way in which knowledge will be deemed relevant and will be retained by the learner.

An alternative approach

> I shall only ask him, and not teach him, and he shall share the inquiry with me: and do you watch and see if you find me telling or explaining anything to him, instead of eliciting his opinion. (Socrates c.400 BC)

There are many phrases which refer to the alternative approach that we are advocating:

Student-Centred Learning (Rogers)
Enquiry (Socrates)
Experiential (Dewey)
Humanistic (Weinstein)
Confluent (Brown)
Androgogy (Knowles)
Progressive (Bennett)
Active Tutorial Work (Button)
Participatory Learning.

While these different descriptions are not completely synonymous there are certain common themes which connect all of these ideas.

> If one attempts to formulate the philosophy of education implicit in the practices of the new education, we may, I think, discover certain common principles amid the variety of progressive schools now existing.
>
> To imposition from above is opposed expression and cultivation of individuality;

> to external discipline is opposed free activity;
> to learning from texts and teachers, learning through experience;
> to acquisition of isolated skills and techniques by drill is opposed acquisition of them as a means of attaining ends which make direct vital appeal;
> to preparation for a more or less remote future is opposed making the most of all opportunities of present life;
> to static aims and materials is opposed acquaintance with a changing world. (Dewey 1938, p. 223)

Bennett (1976, p. 38) has contrasted the two approaches in the following way:

	Progressive	Traditional
1	Integrated subject matter	Separate subject matter
2	Teacher as guide to educational experience	Teacher as distributor of knowledge
3	Active pupil role	Passive pupil role
4	Pupils participate in curriculum planning	Pupils have no say in curriculum planning
5	Learning predominantly by discovery techniques	Accent on memory, practice and rote
6	External rewards and punishments not necessary, i.e. intrinsic motivation	External rewards used, e.g. grades, i.e. extrinsic motivation
7	Not too concerned with conventional academic standards	Concerned with academic standards
8	Little testing	Regular testing
9	Accent on cooperative group work	Accent on competition
10	Teaching not confined to classroom base	Teaching confined to classroom base
11	Accent on creative expression	Little emphasis on creative expression
	We would add:	
12	Cognitive and affective domains given equal emphasis	Cognitive domain is emphasised; affective is neglected
13	Process is valued	Little attention paid to process

It should be remembered that we see these two approaches as opposite ends of a continuum; they are not the only two styles available. Many teachers would be unhappy to place themselves in either camp, feeling that they operate somewhere in between.

Perhaps a closer look at some of the main principles of student-centred learning will be helpful.

The learner has full responsibility for her own learning

> I know I cannot teach anyone anything, I can only provide an environment in which he can learn.
>
> (Rogers 1965, p. 389)

The ownership of learning is with the student. The teacher acts as a facilitator and a resource-person. Students are responsible for choosing and planning the curriculum, or at least they participate in the choosing. Learning is self-initiated, and often involves the processes of enquiry and discovery; the learner is also responsible for evaluating the results. A difficult concept to grasp, at first, is that each individual is 100% responsible for his own behaviour, participation and learning.

The subject matter has relevance and meaning for the learner

This can be accomplished in part by having the students choose their curriculum. In sectors of education which have no required syllabus, there is little problem in achieving this, as the major limiting factors would be the subject area, the previous experience of the students, and their stated needs. Activities can be designed so that all of those factors are taken into account. 'Learning which is meaningful and relevant depends partly on what is taught, and partly on how it is taught.' (Weinstein 1970, p. 21)

Much of the learning process is aimed at helping the learners to identify, clarify, and deal with their own concerns. If this is true in a classroom or course, there is likely to be little difficulty with student motivation, which, in turn, tends to reduce the problem of control. There is little for students to resist as they are doing what they have chosen to do.

As Postman and Weingartner put it:

> Good learners seem to know what is relevant to their survival and what is not. They are apt to resent being told that something is 'good for them to know' . . .
> (Postman and Weingartner 1969, p. 31)

The teacher who works with a participatory approach enters into a dialogue with the students in which their needs, as related to the topic at hand, are uncovered and stated.

> The most important single factor influencing learning is what the learner already knows. Ascertain this and teach him accordingly. (Ausubel 1968, p. 171)

Involvement and participation are necessary for learning

> In fact, learning is the human activity which least needs manipulation by others. Most learning is not the result of instruction. It is rather the result of unhampered participation in a meaningful setting. Most people learn best by being 'with it', yet school makes them identify their personal cognitive growth with elaborate planning and manipulation.
> (Illich 1971, p. 44)

The constraints of the punishment/reward system of teaching, so familiar to most teachers and learners, do not apply when the learner is personally involved. The rewards of working through a process together and finding new questions or answers on the other side are exciting in themselves. Intrinsic rewards are derived from the fun of learning, of discovering, of challenging or questioning, of becoming competent in new areas and of completing self-initiated tasks.

Praise and blame or negative criticism from the teacher are also out of place in this new context; the learner is as involved in evaluating as she is in planning and participating.

If the learner is fully involved, he does not have to seek outside approval; in fact, as Hargreaves points out below, approval-seeking behaviour negates 'unhampered participation'.

> I want to suggest, then, that the majority of pupils become addicted to the teacher's approval during the process of formal schooling. When they learn, it tends to be as a means of obtaining approval rather than as an end in itself. Indeed, paradoxically, the pupils' desire to obtain approval

> may subvert the learning process. Approval-seeking may become a *substitute* for learning . . .
>
> (Hargreaves 1972, p. 200)

Neill discusses the same issue in relation to compelling a child's attention:

> When we consider a child's natural interest in things, we begin to realize the dangers of both rewards and punishment. Rewards and punishment tend to pressure a child into interest. But true interest is the life force of the whole personality, and such interest is completely spontaneous. It is possible to compel attention, for attention is an act of consciousness. It is possible to be attentive to an outline on the blackboard and at the same time to be interested in pirates. Though one can compel attention, one cannot compel interest. No man can force me to be interested in, say, collecting stamps; nor can I compel myself to be interested in stamps. Yet both rewards and punishment attempt to compel interest. (Neill 1962, p. 17)

The sort of lively true interest that Neill describes is what is really meant by participation. When everyone in the learning group is awake, alert, interacting and yet acting individually, there is involvement.

Approval *does* have its place in the student-centred classroom, but it is not related to the quality of academic work; the student will feel good and satisfied when he has assessed his own achievement. In place of the old right/wrong, approval/disapproval system, students receive acknowledgement from the group, including the teacher, for what is considered to be positive behaviour in this context; that is, for participating, for completing tasks, for acting responsibly, for sharing, and for creative efforts. People seem to need appreciation and acknowledgement. Yet even that is external. The most nourishing and motivating reward is that of *internal* satisfaction. Appreciation and satisfaction together produce an interaction which enhances self-esteem.

The dialogue that takes place between all of the learners, including the teacher, is one of the sources of excitement within a participatory environment.

> Finally, one of the most crucial ways in which a culture provides aid in intellectual growth is through a dialogue between the more experienced and the less experienced,

> providing a means for the internalization of dialogue in thought. The courtesy of conversation may be the major ingredient in the courtesy of teaching.
>
> (Bruner 1971, p. 123)

The relationship between learners

Dialogue itself is not enough, nor is interaction; the *quality* of that interaction is also crucial. Rogers (1961, pp. 39–40) describes the helping relationship as one in which 'at least one of the parties has the interest of promoting the growth, development, maturity, improved functioning, improved coping with life, of the other'. Thus, one of the goals of student-centred education is to enable people to make their own choices.

The person in the helping role may have advantages of experience, position, or advanced knowledge over the learner, but one of the aims of working together is to equalise the relationship. The way that the helper talks, listens, and *is* in the relationship gives the learner the message: 'You are in charge of yourself in this relationship'.

The teacher becomes a facilitator and resource person

Neville Bennett argues that:

> . . . to teach well informally is more difficult than to teach well formally. It requires a special sort of teacher to use informal methods effectively – one who is dedicated, highly organised, able to plan ahead and willing to spend a great deal of extra time in preparatory work.
>
> (Bennett 1976, p. 160)

This makes the methods we are advocating seem very demanding; however, as we will show later, time and energy spent on this sort of preparation will be more than repaid in other ways.

Indeed, the participative approach *will* require of the teacher some qualities and skills which perhaps may differ from those demanded by didactic methods. She must have a degree of sensitivity and perception in order to clarify and identify student needs. She will need to be capable of divergent thinking and considerable resourcefulness to find the materials requested by students, which cannot be predicted in advance. Tact, skill, humour, and a willingness to take risks, are needed to facilitate interpersonal communication in a participatory setting. But the most essential requirement is a willingness on the part of the teacher to share himself without imposing. All of his expertise, knowledge, attitudes, training, are the resources he has to offer the student, and they must be offered in a context of availability not of insistence; the student may freely accept or reject the offerings (Rogers 1961). The reverse of this is not true, however, in regard to students' offerings; the cliché phrase 'all contributions will be gratefully accepted' is adopted by the teacher as a matter of policy. The students' contributions, and the students themselves, are accepted in an atmosphere of unconditional positive regard and are individually and collectively valued. Some contributions will be viewed as being more useful or pertinent at a certain time; all are acknowledged in a positive manner.

The phrase 'unconditional positive regard' is Rogers' way of saying that the teacher prizes the student in a total way, not a conditional one, an 'outgoing positive feeling without reservation, without evaluation' (Rogers 1961, p. 385). In an atmosphere where the teacher displays this behaviour, it is usually reciprocated by the students and this tends to enhance their self-esteem, cooperation and productivity.

The learner comes to see himself differently

The learner sees himself differently as a result of the learning experience

This method of learning is designed not only to enhance knowledge, but also to bring about changes in the learners.

Rogers (1965, p. 280) suggests that the learning process which takes place in client-centred psychotherapy could be adapted to apply to student-centred education:

> The learner comes to see himself differently . . .
> He becomes more self-confident and self-directing
> He becomes more the person he would like to be
> He behaves in a more mature fashion
> He adopts more realistic goals for himself
> He changes his maladjustive behaviour
> He becomes more open to the evidence, both to what is going on outside himself, . . . and inside himself.

The learner experiences confluence in his education

Student-centred learning is *confluent*; the affective and cognitive domains *flow together*. While he is thinking, the learner is also feeling; while he is feeling, he is thinking.

In a traditional mode, it is the cognitive aspects which are emphasised and developed, while affective learning is given very little attention. A student-centred approach encourages students to understand, and be able to deal with, their own and others' feelings. Feelings arising out of the cognitive content are explored, along with emotions generated by social interactions. Since attitudes and values arise out of both cognitive and affective learning, they too are investigated and given space to develop.

Confluent education could be achieved if two integrated aims were fulfilled:

1 If affective learning were included in the *content* of the curriculum (as in Active Tutorial Work, and as in Personal, Social and Moral Education, but across all subject areas);
2 If the very *process* by which learning is achieved were confluent; that is attention were paid, at all times, to both cognitive and affective development.

Some major points in the debate: Didactic v. Participatory Methods

What about experience?

One of the most common arguments against student-centred methods is that they require learners to 'reinvent the wheel'; some kinds of knowledge are proven and tested and it is a waste of time to discover them again.

> A school is . . . a place where the massed wisdom of the ages is passed from one generation to the next, and where youngsters are taught to think in a logical and systematic fashion. (Rafferty 1969, p. 70)

Rhodes Boyson puts it even more strongly in one of the 'Black Papers':

> Discovery methods though useful in stimulating the mind are dangerous if people grow up thinking that they can in their life-time discover what it has taken 10 000 years of human history to achieve. Men are arrogant to believe that this can be achieved for its only result would be to revive the Dark Ages. People must learn the theorems of Euclid and the grammar of a foreign language. Traditional methods of study are generally short cuts to knowledge. Many new methods have been introduced as experiment for experiment's sake and to help bored teachers, not bored children. (Rhodes Boyson 1969, p. 161)

Proponents of participatory methods do not claim that the massed wisdom of the ages should be ignored, nor that a student in a progressive learning environment would not come across Euclid in his reading; it is the way in which this happens that is being questioned. Phrases like 'People must learn . . .' and 'Youngsters are taught to think . . .' are translated into 'People may decide to learn when they see that a piece of learning is relevant', and 'People learn to think things through for themselves'. The idea is that the learner will be exploring the wisdom that has been passed down, when it is relevant to his own present needs, when it fits into the framework of what he wants to know. The teacher is there to provide resources when they are relevant, i.e. when the student has discovered the need for them. However, as an equal member of the group, the teacher can also offer suggestions or introduce new ideas when she feels it is appropriate.

Right and wrong answers

Participatory activities, to an extent, do away with what Glasser (1969) calls 'the certainty principle': the idea that there is a right and wrong answer to every question. This raises another major objection, which is often stated as 'But there *are* right answers. Paris *is* the capital of France, and Tokyo is *not*.' The answer to the objection lies in the basic aims: what do we want the student to take away with him? If it is simply, and only, the right answer, then we can give it to him, or someone else can state it, and he can remember it as long as he needs it, and reproduce it in an exam or repeat it in his own lectures. In student-centred learning the aim is to equip the student to find out for himself what the capital of France is, and to be able to find out the answers to such questions, to understand the difference between the 'knowledge that' and the 'knowledge how', and furthermore to ask and to explore questions like 'What makes Paris uniquely French and Tokyo uniquely Japanese?'.

One of our own favourite maxims is 'A good teacher soon renders herself obsolete'. This is a source of some discomfort to people making the initial transition to this way of thinking. A new type of reward has to emerge for the teacher; she will learn that she is valued for her skills as a resource person and facilitator, rather than as a giver of knowledge.

New teaching skills

Bennett's argument, quoted earlier, about the higher degree of dedication required of an informal teacher, is frequently used against participatory methods. As he puts it (1976, p. 161), 'How many teachers do we have who could meet these specifications?'

Bantock in the 'Black Papers' was also concerned with whether or not teachers could handle such approaches competently:

> . . . used incompetently . . . they are probably more disastrous to learning than an exclusive reliance on the old formal methods. These methods, with their permissive atmosphere, in the hands of incompetent teachers are enervating and time wasting. (Bantock 1969, p. 116)

We would reply that in the hands of an incompetent teacher, *any* method would be boring and unproductive. However, what Bantock says is worth noting; it is true that there are not many teachers who have achieved competence in the new methods, as the necessary skills and practice are seldom offered in their training. Should we then discard the new methods, or should we produce a greater number of teachers who are capable of using them effectively? Obviously, we prefer the latter course of action.

It is true that new skills are difficult to master. For the teacher, adopting new methods may mean changing old assumptions and former attitudes, and developing strategies which are different from the familiar, comfortable ones to which he is accustomed. Far from being a drawback, this can be considered an advantage of using new methodologies. The teacher may be stimulated and excited by the prospect of her own personal growth, which can either be constrained and limited, or extended each day that she is teaching. Stenhouse points out that if the teacher is a learner each day of her classroom life, her growth, both intellectual and emotional, can be stimulated; she can even rejoice in being overtaken and passed by the growth of her students, because she has provided a positive environment for learning.

> A good classroom, by this criterion, is one in which things are learned every day which the teacher did not previously know. (Stenhouse 1981, p. 37)

Stenhouse also says that the teacher should not be expected to accomplish all this on her own:

> Cooperative and well-organised effort is needed, and teachers working cooperatively together have the same right and need as other professionals – such as doctors or engineers – to have access to consultancy and to draw on research. (ibid., p. 25)

The charismatic teacher?

Some critics of participatory methods argue that the approach is reliant upon a charismatic teacher in order to work successfully. The idea is that an ordinary person cannot be trained, or cannot learn through experience, to be skilled in this work of interaction; that a good teacher has something special which is innate – the 'born not made' argument. As Peters says:

> Nevertheless there is something distinctive about the charismatic leader which he shares in an exaggerated form with other 'natural' leaders who exercise authority in virtue of personal claims and personal characteristics . . . because he is a special sort of person. (Peters 1959, p. 16)

We would argue that participatory learning depends upon mutual respect between teacher and learner. This sort of respect does not depend only on expertise; it depends upon human interaction characterised by trust and high regard. Neither is it dependent on the charisma of the leader, but rather upon that leader's skill in communication, and this can be learned. In fact, what a teacher may need is in-service training in communication and group work skills. It is of prime importance that the teacher addresses the group with respect and an attitude of interest and caring, and that the teacher and the group listen to each other. This is related to the principles of andragogy (peer-teaching) outlined by Knowles (1970, p. 41) and one of the statements he makes seems extremely relevant here:

> The behaviour of the teacher probably influences the character of the learning climate more than any other single factor; however, the teacher conveys in many ways whether his attitude is one of interest in and respect for the students or whether he sees them essentially as receiving sets for his transmissions of wisdom. The teacher who takes the time and trouble to get to know his students individually and who calls them by name (especially by first name) obviously conveys the first set of attitudes. But probably the behaviour that most explicitly demonstrates that a teacher really cares about a student and respects his contribution is the act of really listening to what the student says.

It is equally important for students to listen to each other; in fact later, in another context, we describe how one class of difficult students was transformed (in terms of their behaviour in our class) just by learning Active Listening skills.

Charisma is a distinct advantage in most professions, but it is a gift, and ought to be regarded as a bonus, whereas the skills discussed above can be classed as necessities, and can be learned.

Reactions of colleagues and students

Another negative point frequently raised is that the progressive methods create suspicion and cynicism among teachers' colleagues. This point ought not to be regarded lightly; it is of serious concern to teachers, most of whom care very deeply about what their colleagues think of them. Often their career advancement depends upon the high esteem of the rest of the staff.

> Teachers naturally make judgments on the professional competence of their colleagues, but they are rarely discussed openly . . . Reputations are common knowledge but they are transmitted *sotto voce* in the channels of staff

> gossip . . . Relations between colleagues in school are characterized by sensitivities in matters of competence . . .
> (Hargreaves 1982, p. 205)

An innovator who dismisses these concerns will find himself facing increased resistance to his innovations. Part of the training for future use of an innovative programme such as this one ought to be in developing skills which would equip educators to talk with people who are suspicious. Cynicism can be overcome with communication if the communication is a genuine two-way exchange of understanding. Cynics are sometimes speaking out of fear or misapprehension; they need to be heard and answered, or sometimes just heard. Another way of dealing with cynicism is to point to successes, as in the following letter from a teacher who was newly involved in participatory learning:

> . . . The response from my classes to the Waiting Game and to 'Confluent Education' in general has been fascinating to observe. The initial suspicion and general 'this isn't English' attitude has given way to cooperation, enthusiasm and genuine discussion (as opposed to a rather fake question/answer routine). Interestingly, although I've spent less time 'teaching' them than the rest of our Department, one member of staff did comment on the large amount of work they seemed to get through. They seem to work together much better and actually said that they enjoy English rather than endure it! . . .
>
> I think I'm winning my 'battle' with the new approach – mainly because the children and their work are my best adverts and other classes are beginning to enquire of their chums what it is that they are actually doing!

As for anxieties expressed by students, the teacher can listen to these and accept them. Holt says:

> It might be helpful, if we feel comfortable doing it, to say to the students that we understand their scepticism and suspicion, and the reasons for it, and are sympathetic rather than hurt or angry. (Holt 1972, p. 89)

This does not mean that the teacher can never express his opinions, just that he also listens to the ideas and worries of the students, and takes time to explore and clarify problems until they feel satisfied.

Not permissive!

An issue which causes some educators a considerable amount of anxiety is that progressive education often seems to be synonymous with permissiveness; we quoted a similar concern of Bantock's earlier in this chapter. Teachers imagine scenes of wild chaos, uproar and confusion. As Glasser points out:

> For most students who have not done well in school, permissiveness is destructive. Ultimately it generates antagonism and ridicule toward those who unrealistically administer without rules. (Glasser 1969, p. 200)

Permissiveness is a very unpopular word with us; we throw away the word permission, and substitute responsibility. This is true at all levels of education: who are we to give permission to, or indeed to take away responsibility from, the students?

In fact, the ground rules are just as firm in a progressive learning milieu as in a traditional one. The differences are in who makes the rules, how they are implemented, and in the kinds of rules they are. They are generated by students and teacher (or group leader, or lecturer) together, and they refer to a way of working together which gives everyone opportunities to participate or not, to be heard, to make choices about the curriculum, to pay attention to each other's needs. The ground rules are negotiable, and are used as foundations, or reminders, not as sanctions.

Fallibility

If the teacher cannot assume the 'fountain of all knowledge' or expert stance, the students will not respect him; so goes another fear that teachers sometimes express. The idea of saying 'I don't know' in response to a student's question is anathema to some teachers, who feel very uncomfortable if they are not in possession of all the facts related to a subject they are presenting. This sort of incompleteness is referred to by some as poor or sloppy teaching.

Abercrombie, writing about group teaching in higher education, states:

> We assume that one of the main aims of education should be that of encouraging autonomous learning, and that consequently the relationship between teacher and pupil

needs to be that of cooperators exploring knowledge (rather than that of givers and passive receivers of information) . . .
(Abercrombie 1979, p. 46)

Theory X and Theory Y

What McGregor (1960, pp. 39 and 48) has written about management and motivation may also be applied to theories of education.

Theory X Assumptions about Human Nature	**Theory Y** Assumptions about Human Nature
The average human being inherently dislikes work and will avoid it if he can.	The expenditure of physical and mental effort is as natural as play or rest.
Because of this characteristically human dislike of work, most people must be coerced, controlled, threatened, in the interest of organisational objectives.	External control and threat of punishment are not the only means for bringing about effort toward organisational objectives. Man will exercise self-direction and self-control in the service of objectives to which he is committed.
The average human being prefers to be directed, wishes to avoid responsibility, has relatively little ambition, wants security above all.	Commitment to objectives is a function of the rewards associated with their achievement. The average human being learns, under proper conditions, not only to accept but to seek responsibility. A high capacity for imagination, ingenuity and creativity in solving organisational problems is widely, not narrowly, distributed in the population. Under the conditions of modern industrial life, the intellectual potential of the average human being is only partially utilized.

Here too we would like to imagine a continuum:

Theory X ←——————————→ Theory Y

A teacher does not have to choose between one end of the continuum or the other; a move towards student-centred learning will probably include a move along this continuum towards Theory Y at the same time.

No compromise

Our bias has been stated; and we are not attempting to compromise when we say that there is no single method of learning that is better than all the others. There are those which are most appropriate to particular tasks in particular contexts. In our work together we have tested the methods clustered around the student-centred end of the continuum. We want every teacher reading this book to understand that these methods will suit *any* learning milieu and *any* age group. This bold claim has been proven time and time again, and has been found to hold true in the Birmingham project, out of which this book was born. If you doubt that the student-centred approach we are advocating will work in your situation, rather than dismiss it at this theoretical stage, we simply ask you to continue reading this book, and as you go along, to look for the points of contact between this way of working and your own subject.

Student perceptions after one term of the new methods

> This is a good class, which is a responsible one, and a hard working one. The pupils trust each other and rely on the teachers if any difficulties crop up. Fourth Year Students

> I liked the way we could choose what we wanted to do.
> Third Year Student

> As we worked in groups, I felt disappointed at first, but after working with my group I felt very responsible for the work we were to present. It made me feel as if I was experiencing something totally different from what I have experienced in my last four years at school.
> Fourth Year Student

> It took a lot of practice, but it turned out good.
> Third Year Student

2 GROUP WORK SKILLS

Introduction: ownership, responsibility and power

The question of ownership is at the heart of student-centred learning. The word is familiar enough, but the concept as we define it may need a little explanation.

If you win the pools, you may go out and buy a new Porsche; you are then its proud owner. When you have paid off your mortgage, you will experience total ownership of your house, maybe for the first time. If you write and publish a song, you own the copyright of the words and music. This is *not* the way we are using the term ownership.

There is a similar concept of ownership in education which refers to a student's right to own, for example, her own assessment. This would mean that she has a right to decide what is written in her profile or report, to veto sections of which she does not approve, and to take it away with her and use it as she wishes. Again, this is *not* the full meaning that we ascribe to the term.

Just as a person can own a house and not live in it, maintain it or improve it, so a student can 'own' a profile and choose to do nothing with it. Likewise a man can own a car, drive it to death, never have it serviced and ignore the spreading rust, and would not be called a responsible owner. Our use of the term ownership refers not just to the moral or legal right of possession, but to the motivation for care, maintenance and development of that which is owned.

Possession + responsibility = ownership

To own something, to us, means to accept full responsibility for it.

A student who owns a profile, in our terms, will firstly negotiate about it with her teacher, make sure it is kept up to date, add to it, discuss it with her parents, and then use it to her advantage by taking it to interviews.

Similarly, a student may be constantly getting into trouble for coming to school late. We may say the student has a problem with punctuality. Indeed, logically, it *is* the student's problem. *He* is the one who is late and *he* is the one who attends late detention at the end of every school day to make up for lost time. Yet he may not see it as *his* problem. He may blame the alarm clock, his mother, the buses, or the school for starting too early! If he really owned this problem in our terms, he would accept responsibility for doing something about it. In this situation, rather than punish the student for being late, it may be more useful for someone in the school to counsel him in such a way as to help him take ownership of the problem.

In many schools, the ownership of learning belongs initially to the teacher. The teacher writes or decides on the syllabus, chooses the methods, selects the resources, creates the exercises and tasks and decides when, where, how and even why things are to be done. Some see the teacher's authority consisting in these functions. Take them away and it is feared that the teacher's power, reputation and position will collapse like a house of cards. Again, there are those who feel that the teacher's autonomy and professionalism are derived from the expert execution of these tasks; without them, the job would lose status and credibility.

Those who wish to defend the teaching profession at a time when it is under threat in various ways, do so by defending the role which teachers have traditionally fulfilled and which is therefore assumed to comprise the teacher's expertise. Any move to transfer ownership from teacher to student is likely to be met with fierce resistance because it may be perceived as a threat to the profession as a whole. Indeed, our proposal is a radical one and calls for a redefinition of the teacher's role, which is, in essence, what this book is about.

The group work skills described in this chapter encourage and enable the movement of ownership from the hands of the teacher to each individual student and to the group as a whole. We have found that the teacher does not lose her own power or control in giving away ownership; in fact they are enhanced. In scattering the seeds of responsibility more widely among the group, the levels of creativity and energy are exponentially increased.

There are two parts to the process of handing over ownership:

1 The teacher learns to accept and internalise the idea that the students have the right to own their own learning. If you have difficulty accepting this premise, ask yourself:

- Whose names appear in the mark book and on the exercise books, folders, display work, reports and examination certificates?
- Who is writing, asking and answering questions, going home with the homework?

- Whose future do we often claim will be affected by their performance in school?
- Whose development are we aiming to promote?

The realisation that students own their learning can come as a liberating experience. One teacher described how

> '. . . it suddenly came over me. Light dawned and I saw clearly for the first time that I need not make myself responsible for their work. I knew that as long as I imposed tasks, enforced deadlines and assessed the quality of work done, I was actually preventing the students from taking responsibility. I was keeping them dependent on me, and that was often keeping me tense, worrying about their progress and lack of cooperation. In this moment, a great weight lifted from my shoulders. It was not that I no longer cared; rather, because I cared, I wanted them to be independent, responsible learners, growing up as human beings, not automatons.'

2 The teacher enables the students to accept that ownership, to understand and appreciate what ownership of learning means. It is that:

- each person in the group is 100% responsible for his/her own behaviour;
- each person in the group is 100% responsible for how the group progresses.

When the student perceives his own need to take responsibility, the transfer of ownership can begin. The student who is late for school will somehow have to become aware that he needs to change, and that only *he* can make the changes; no-one else can do it for him. After the perception of need, a period of transition may be required in which the students begin to take hold of responsibility and wake up to the idea of organising their own learning. It is not a sudden leaping out of bed and running round the block full of enlightenment; rather it is hearing the alarm, groaning, yawning and stretching, turning over just once more and then finally making it out of a comfortable bed and standing on their own two feet.

It is generally accepted that the teacher has the power to make and enforce decisions and exercise control, rather like a policeman has the power to enforce the law of the land and make arrests. It is power invested in the office or job, not in the person. Out of school or out of uniform, the person does not have the same powers. We

There is another kind of power in the classroom – that of creative potential

would like teachers to get away from resting on this job-related power which is wielded over students and which may alienate or demotivate them.

There is another kind of power in the classroom – that of creative potential. This is not related to a job or status, but is inherent in every human being. Teachers and students alike possess it. In a traditional setting this power is released only in a limited way, through strict, predetermined channels, and this may breed frustration and encourage students to create a whole range of cunning, subversive activities which are the cause of so much classroom confrontation. In the worst kind of didactic teaching, there is deliberate suppression of these creative powers which may be seen as a threat to the central task of 'learning'. Teachers who operate within a traditional framework may feel that their own creativity is being stifled too as they sit down to mark yet another set of books.

Student-centred learning is about opening the cage door and releasing this creative power. Yes, there is a risk involved, not knowing where it will go or what it will do; but more than likely at first it will need coaxing out, like an animal which has been in captivity for too long. Handing over responsibility and ownership to the student is not dangerous; it simply sets him free to use his creative powers, or not to use them, as he chooses. It is only granting him his human rights.

Each individual has enormous creative potential. Put a collection of individuals together and you multiply the potential. This is real power! Power to do and to achieve, power to solve problems, change things, overcome difficulties, power to learn. Once released, this collective creative power can replace the single-handed, status related power of the teacher as the means of control within the group.

This chapter describes the way in which you can begin to hand ownership of learning over to the students and release their creative power.

A student-centred classroom

Imagine that you have been invited to visit a well-established student-centred classroom. What follows is what you might see and feel – a collage of your impressions. Of course, by the very definition of student-centred learning, every classroom will be different. This is just one example.

The first thing you notice is that you do not immediately see the teacher. You then realise that she is seated in the circle with the rest of the group. You are welcomed by one of the students and invited to join the circle; a chair is brought for you.

One of the other students tells you that they are preparing to work on a project in small, self-selected groups, and shows you the brainstorm of ideas which has just been completed on the blackboard. The teacher asks the students what deadlines they want to set for themselves and a spokesperson from each group responds with a different date and plan. One group shows the rest a board game which they had designed and produced themselves as their last project. Everyone applauds and then the teacher asks for feedback in the form of two questions: 'What things do you like about it?' and 'If it were to be done again, what improvements would you make?' Various answers are given to the two questions, but none of the comments is derogatory.

What you are feeling is a sense of warmth and an all-pervading air of positive cooperation and trust. (This is on a good day!) You also notice that not all comments are directed through the teacher, but that people tend to look at, and listen to, the person who is speaking. People are speaking spontaneously without raising their hands and without interrupting. Some people are participating more than others.

One of the students says 'There are only 35 minutes left; can we get started?' The teacher asks if there is anything else that anyone would like to say first. There being no response, she nods and everyone leaves the circle.

There is a sense of purpose as students get out the materials and start to work together. Everyone seems to know where he is going and what he is intending to do. You notice that people seem to be doing a lot of different things, and that students seem to go to each other for help and to the teacher mainly for advice on materials and sources of information: they have access to the cupboards, shelves and the stockroom. A student walks up to the teacher and says 'I'm just going to the Woodwork room to turn this piece of wood on the lathe'.

There is a good deal of talk and laughter and general buzz; all of it seems to contribute to an atmosphere of getting things done.

A girl walks into the classroom. It is quite late, the period is half over, and she says 'Sorry Miss, I was late back from Community Service'. She sits down – in her group with her coat on – and starts work.

One lad seems to be daydreaming. No-one says anything to him for a long time. Then, one of the other boys says 'Come on, we said we'd get this finished today'.

A girl by the window says 'The bell's gone.' People begin packing up at their own pace. One lad dashes out of the door, saying 'I've got to see Miss Roberts. 'Bye.' Another says to the teacher 'Can I come back to your office with you to get my Duke of Edinburgh's Award book?' Others put things back in the stockroom. People say to you 'Goodbye. Thanks for coming.'

While the teacher is talking to one student, another comes up and puts her arm round the teacher's shoulder while she is waiting to speak.

You drift out of the classroom, talking to one of the students.

In this cameo of a fully functioning student-centred classroom the students are initiating and directing their own work. The teacher is simply making things possible. She is an enabler, a facilitator, who sets up the structure for efficient group work and supports the students by her positive regard for them, and by offering guidance and help if invited.

It is very different from the tightness of a traditional lesson and many teachers who normally operate at the didactic end of the continuum find it hard to see how ownership and responsibility can be handed over without creating anarchy and chaos. There was neither anarchy nor chaos in the class we just described – true, there was noise and movement, but only in pursuit of specified goals and within a structure accepted by the whole group. *Student-centred learning is controlled and purposeful.*

Even if this is accepted in principle, many teachers still feel that *they* could never achieve such a situation with *their* kids. Two points need to be remembered:

1 Change does not happen overnight. It may take time for a teacher and a group of students to learn how to work in this student-centred way.
2 Strategies and techniques which give structure and bring control to the group can be learned. In-service training is important and the teacher can experiment by trying out student-centred activities and patiently practising them until they feel comfortable and natural.

In the next section we describe basic management strategies which can form the foundation of a student-centred classroom.

Classroom management strategies

1 The circle

Our experience has been that if we ask a group of kids what they think is the point of the group sitting in a circle, they will list some or all of these advantages:

- we can all see each other, and hear each other
- we can make eye contact
- we are all equal
- the teacher visibly becomes a member of the group
- it's easier to concentrate and listen to each other
- there are no barriers between us
- we feel like a group
- we can speak to each other more easily.

There are two disadvantages which also need to be mentioned:

- students may feel exposed, and therefore shy, at first;
- in some rooms, it may be difficult to rearrange the furniture.

Another important feature of sitting in a circle is that the strategies which people employ to escape from boredom or tension are no longer possible to use without being noticed. For example, it is very difficult to talk to your neighbour, doodle, eat, sleep, daydream or do your homework, when everyone in the group can see you. This is an advantage in that it reduces such distracting behaviour, but it can also cause some initial discomfort.

The aim is for the circle to be a safe place, where people can speak freely, express their opinions, share their feelings, and contribute *or not* without fear of ridicule, and with a sense that there are no right or wrong answers.

2 The round

A round is a time when each person in the circle has an opportunity to make a statement about whatever the group is discussing. One person starts, and the turns move round the circle; no one may comment on what anyone else says, and this includes the teacher. Anyone can say 'I pass', when it is her turn.

For example, in a traditional classroom, when a film is to be shown, the teacher may say something like: 'Now, we are going to see a film about Tanzania, and I want you to notice the Ujaama system, the emphasis on practical skills, and the idea of education for self-reliance.' . . . In student-centred work, the teacher may say 'Here is the film you wanted on Tanzania; we can show it as many times as you like. After we've seen it the first time, we'll do a round of "What I noticed in the film was . . .".'

The aim of the round is to provide a structure within which everyone has a chance to say something, but is not forced to do so. All ideas and opinions are valued equally. When rounds are first introduced, many people may say 'I pass'. Initially, no comment should be made about this, as the choice must be free; but, if it continues to be a problem, the group may need to discuss it together. Usually the number of passes decreases, as the students realise that they can speak freely without fear of ridicule from teacher or peers.

The round may often be a good way to start a lesson; it provides 're-entry'; in other words, the group gets to know each other again, and establishes the feeling of safety in the circle. A good round to do in this situation would be 'The best thing that happened to me this weekend was . . .'. The round can be used at any point where there needs to be an expression of opinion, or feedback, or planning, or evaluation. So, at the end of a lesson, the class might do two rounds: 'What I didn't like about this lesson . . .' (Resent) and 'What I liked about this lesson . . .' (Appreciate). It is a good idea to do the negative round first, leaving the class with a positive feeling.

Remember, the freedom *not* to participate is extremely important in establishing trust. It is also important that no-one is interrupted, and that no-one, including the teacher, comments, positively or negatively, on anyone else's contribution while a round is in progress.

3 Listening skills

One of the keys to effective group work is the skill of active listening. In Section 3 you will find a series of exercises designed to practise the skill. Here we want to describe its uses and values. Active listening consists of:

- looking at the person who is talking
- sitting quietly with him
- doing nothing else but listening
- responding to him naturally with your own gestures and expressions
- reflecting back the essence of what you just heard him say
- asking no questions
- making no comments of your own.

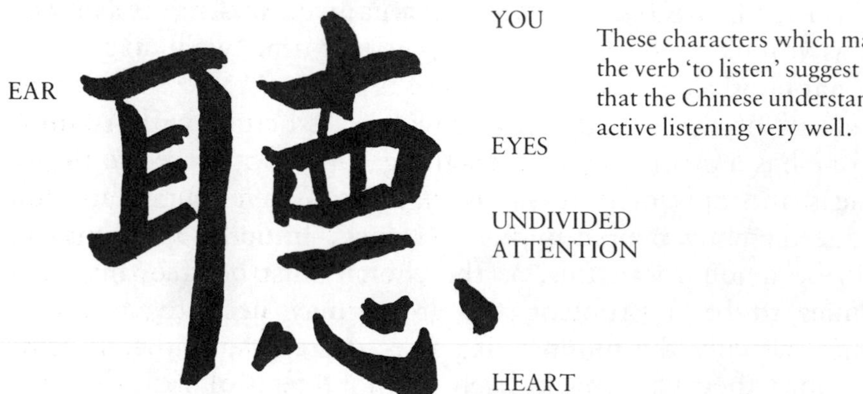

These characters which make up the verb 'to listen' suggest that the Chinese understand active listening very well.

Not listening is much more common in our society than listening. Think of your own communications with people. When was the last time someone:

- interrupted you
- took over the conversation you had started
- switched off while you were talking

- fidgeted around, looked at her watch, edged towards the door
- changed the subject
- answered with an inappropriate response
- could hardly wait for you to finish so he could speak again?

Do *you* ever do any of these?

One of the ways to show someone that you value them is to give them the gift of your full attention when they are talking to you. It is also a fundamental group work skill: if the whole group is listening to each other, there is an atmosphere of cooperation, consideration and mutual regard. Time is saved as clarity is improved, and therefore productivity is increased. If what the teacher is doing is just listening, she does not need to be agreeing, disagreeing, arguing, praising, blaming; therefore she can take a neutral role which enables other people to express their opinions. It stops the group placing responsibility on the teacher for the way things go. It can defuse an aggressive situation, allow someone to explore his feelings in depth, and bring the best out of people, in the sense that if they are being listened to they are more likely to contribute.

We have seen classes transformed by listening skills; that is how crucial it is to the introduction of group work. The development of listening skills need not be a protracted process. For example, in a fifth year remedial class, the communication was so bad that no-one could finish a sentence without being interrupted or put down. The teacher could not give a simple instruction and complete it; the battle for attention was going on all the time.

The teacher played a game called Control Tower (Brandes and Phillips 1978, p. 39), which involved one student travelling blindfolded through an obstacle course, guided only by the voice of another student at the other end of the room. The obstacles were the rest of the group, who stood motionless and quiet. Several people had turns at being the 'Aeroplane' and the 'Control Tower'. In a circle, the group then discussed the purpose of the game, and realised that its success had depended upon clear verbal communication from one student, and on careful listening from the other, made possible by the silence and stillness of the group. The teacher then asked the students to compare this experience of the game with what normally happened in the class. The realisations which followed seemed to generate a desire for things to improve in the class.

The teacher then suggested an agreement that from now on in the group everyone would look at, listen carefully to, not interrupt, and not put down, the person who was talking. Everyone agreed eagerly and at the beginning of the next lesson remembered the agreement and carried it out with only the occasional reminder. From time to time, the group mood was more unsettled, and at these times we found that an additional strategy was helpful: it is the old idea of the conch, from *Lord of the Flies*. A pen or other suitable object can be used, and only the person with the object in his hand can speak. People reach for it when they want a turn.

Listening skills represent a necessary step in the effective functioning of a group; the step is towards self-responsibility. Listening is the oil in the machinery which enables all the various activities of group work to operate smoothly. We would go as far as to say that efficient and productive group work will probably not take place until listening skills have been firmly established. They have the highest priority on any agenda for introducing a participatory, student-centred approach.

4 Brainstorming

There are four main purposes in Brainstorming:

1 To generate a large number of ideas quickly.
2 To encourage creativity and lateral thinking.
3 To involve the whole group.
4 To demonstrate that people working together can achieve more than the individual can alone.

It is a good idea to teach the process for fun the first time it is introduced, without any particular aim in mind other than to learn how it is done. So, the teacher might say 'Give me as many ideas as you can for ways in which the building we're in could be used . . . I'll write them down as fast as you give them to me. Nobody should comment on anyone else's ideas. Just keep the ideas flowing . . . There's no need to put your hand up, just shout them out . . .'

The teacher writes them down in no particular order, just scattered over the board or flip chart. This way, there is no priority or ranking of ideas, and suggestions quickly become anonymous, emphasising corporate creativity. The teacher can throw in ideas of his own, and if people begin to make comments, remind them just to keep the ideas coming without comment. If the flow begins to dry up, don't panic, or take over; just wait patiently. Often there is more to come, and the silence proves to the kids that you really are handing responsibility over to them. If they do not generate the ideas, you will not rescue them. So a pause is not only acceptable; it may be crucial. It will be difficult to establish brainstorming as a modus operandi for your class if you insist on jumping into every silence. There will come a point, however, when the tide of ideas is finally stemmed, and it may take some experience before you can easily recognise when this point is reached.

In this first practice brainstorm, when the contributions have come to a natural end, it is important to take time to discuss the process; but do it by *asking them*. 'What did you notice? . . . What was I doing? . . . What happens if we start talking and making comments and jokes about what people say? . . . Would you have thought of so many ideas if you were working on your own?' Allow enough time for a thorough discussion of the process, because it is likely to become a normal and important part of your daily activities.

Brainstorming is very useful in a variety of situations; for example, it is a feature of the problem-solving process. It is an exciting way to introduce a new topic, or revise an old one. In the process of evaluation, you can brainstorm 'What's good about what we've been doing?' and 'What needs improving?'. Brainstorming is also a very good way to set up an agenda for a meeting or group work session.

When a brainstorm is completed, it may be helpful to group the ideas into categories, or to put them in some order of importance; the group is then in a better position to make decisions and choices.

It is important to get across to the group that you are going to take seriously whatever it is that they say. We feel that the best way to do this is to write down absolutely everything they say, and censor nothing, even if it is silly or 'rude'. We have found that when the students realise that we are actually recording everything, they soon stop saying 'silly' things.

Underlying all the purposes of brainstorming there is one fundamental aim: the enhancement of self-concept. It is not magical, it is not a panacea, but it *is* a very subtle and effective method. The fact that all contributions are accepted and anonymous, that no one is excluded or evaluated, that most of the time the teacher cannot even notice who is participating, all add up to a positive feeling in the group. The message to each person is: 'You are valuable; you are equal with everyone else. You are being heard.'

5 The waiting game

One of the most common mistakes that teachers make is to take responsibility for getting the kids to be quiet. There is a lot of shouting and hushing on the part of the teacher; this causes increasing noise, impatience and tension. It is one of the most wasteful activities, in terms of time and energy, that a teacher could engage in. It says to the students 'I am responsible for getting and keeping you quiet. You are not able to do it yourselves.' The teacher is creating an unnecessary confrontation, which can become a battle of wills, and which is, inevitably, a win-lose situation.

You can create the impression for yourself that the kids are your enemies, and this may colour your attitude for the whole lesson. Some people walk around in this mood all the time; you can see them yelling and pointing fingers in the corridors. Every kid is on the opposing side. The students pick this up and see the teachers as enemies, which encourages sneakiness, deception and a constant desire to 'put one over'. It becomes a vicious circle.

An alternative strategy is to play the Waiting Game. It is very simple, and consists of just sitting quietly until you have everyone's attention.

You start by telling the class that you are not going to fight to get their attention, and that you will wait as long as it takes for everyone to settle down. They should be able to recognise the times when you are playing it, because you will be sitting quietly doing nothing. Your demeanour during this time is important; it would not be appropriate to scowl, tap your foot, or appear impatient, self-pitying or resigned. You can use the time to relax, take some deep breaths, think about your shopping list, or the World Snooker Final you saw last night. It is no good pretending to be patient; it has to be a real feeling within you. It may be difficult at first to remain patient, in which case you can remind yourself that your overall aim is to encourage them to take responsibility for themselves, and that no other priority is more important.

We have found that once students understand that we are playing the Waiting Game, others soon join in, it spreads, and we begin to have peer pressure on our side. We do not play the Waiting Game all the time; if students are very involved in something else, we may have to call them together. Also, not being saints, we sometimes lose our patience, or have a need to act quickly, or even to shout a command if there is an emergency. But, in general, the Waiting Game provides us with a calm, relaxed, positive frame of mind, and takes a lot of the stress out of the classroom.

6 Ground rules

Again, student-centred methods are not permissive! They have structure and limits. In any student-centred group it is important to develop and establish ground rules near the beginning. The ground rules constitute the method of control.

How ground rules are established

After a group has been working together in a student-centred way for a while, it may be appropriate to elicit the ground rules from the students, to reach agreement about them and to write them up so that they are established. Sometimes the appropriate moment arises out of a comment made by a student or an event in the classroom. For example, a probationary teacher, let's call him Steven, had begun to introduce student-centred methods in his third year class by the use of several activities such as rounds, brainstorming and games. At the end of the first session, the group played Control Tower and then went home. At the beginning of the next session the class did a round of 'How I feel about what we did last week'. Joe said 'That game was good because we stuck to the rules we had learned during the lesson.' When asked what these were, he replied 'We listened to each other, kept still and did not interrupt. Because of this cooperation everyone was able to hear and succeed with the game.' In effect, Joe had just 'written' some of the ground rules. This was the moment to record the 'new rules' as the students saw them.

So, while engaging in introductory activities, the group actually experiences the ground rules in practice before they are asked to define them. What is wanted is a set of rules which will create and sustain the friendly and cohesive atmosphere in which student-centred learning can be effective.

Now you may well ask 'Why do it this way round when you could then be accused of being manipulative by setting up the ground rules you want and subtly planting them on the kids?' Our answer would be that we do not advocate manipulation and the antidote to it is honesty. So we would say to the kids at the outset 'After you have experienced some student-centred methods, we will define the rules that make them work and you can add any others you want and perhaps subtract some, but there is a bottom line.' Many students are sceptical about the ground rules working; they do not believe that other class members will listen to each other and stop making sarcastic comments, but when the teacher has suggested it and they have tried it, they begin to believe that it is possible. The students need to experience a wider range of learning styles before they can choose which ground rules they wish to establish.

Now, back to the moment when the rules are to be developed, whether that moment arises naturally in the group's development or whether the teacher chooses an appropriate moment to discuss the issue. What is the actual process; what does the teacher say? Something like:

> 'If you think back over the activities we have been doing, what rules would you say have been operating?'

The students will obviously have a variety of answers, and all of them may be written up on the board or flip chart. The students can then be encouraged to think of other rules which they would like to initiate. All of these should be listed as well. Then the process of prioritising, negotiating and selecting can take place.

The teacher does not disappear from the scene; she is there to offer guidance and new ideas to try. Also, every teacher comes into the room with a set of values, and it is hypocritical to pretend that they are not there. In a student-centred setting, however, these values will not just be imposed autocratically on the group. There is negotiation, there is flexibility on many points, but there will probably be a bottom line beyond which the teacher is unwilling to go.

For example, we do not believe in punishment, so we would have to say at the beginning that we would not support any rule which involved punishment. We would be happy to negotiate about other questions, but we would not be willing to budge on that one. It is crucial for the teacher to tell the truth at this stage, and to allow free discussion of the points which concern the students.

What we would hope to substitute for the discipline/punishment system would be self-discipline and constant support from the group.

A possible set of ground rules

Beware – this is not a perfect set, nor a desirable set, but just a possible list of rules that a class might produce. Please do not use them as a model, or attempt to imitate them; they are here as an example only.

- We listen to each other.
- We respect each other's ideas and values.
- We take responsibility for ourselves.

- We avoid punishment.
- Participation is optional.
- It is OK to make mistakes; they are valuable learning points.
- We keep our agreements.
- We avoid hurting each other, verbally or physically.

How the ground rules are maintained

Since punishment is avoided, how then are the rules maintained (please notice that we did not say 'enforced')? Initially, patient reminders come from the teacher; and the ground rules are visibly posted at all times. They constitute a contract between group members, and therefore a consensus must have been reached before they are finally written up. Eventually, group members will begin to take responsibility for pointing to them, and for reminding each other.

7 Sabotage

Even in an excellent student-centred atmosphere, kids are not saints. Some of them have been used to getting attention by behaving negatively: that has been the only time when anyone paid attention to them. The concept of sabotage can be quite useful in counteracting this problem and; it can be introduced through playing the game Sabotage (Brandes and Phillips 1978, p. 519). Through the discussion that follows, students can explore their own behaviour and see that they can enjoy themselves more by taking part in the events of the group than by trying to destroy them subversively or blatantly. At first it may be the teacher who points out that sabotage is happening; later, kids begin to use the concept themselves, and to remind each other. In fact, there soon develops considerable peer pressure not to sabotage; the burden of discipline has been lifted from the teacher and placed where it belongs, on each person present. In this way all behaviour problems become group problems. The teacher no longer shoulders sole responsibility for the students' behaviour and discipline any more than he does for their learning.

8 Assertiveness

In bringing about these changes, the teacher is almost certain to encounter resistance and lack of comprehension, as well as considerable difficulty in remembering to do them herself. It is not rash to predict that everyone involved will make lots of mistakes in learning about the new ground rules. Many teachers use aggression to get their rules enforced; others, we have noticed, are non-assertive and one can hear the doubt in their voices when they say 'Please sit down?????' wondering 'Are they going to do what I tell them?????'.

Assertive behaviour on the part of the teacher consists of *reminding* people of the ground rules, and doing so without sanctions or punishment; this reminding rests on inner strength, on confidence that the rules have been fairly established by agreement, and that people in the group will support each other in remembering to stick to those contracts.

If faced with a particularly awkward or resistant student, group or, for that matter, colleague, parent, member of the public . . ., the teacher may find it helpful to follow this procedure, commonly taught in assertiveness training:

1 state your point of view or request;
2 actively listen to the other person's viewpoint, reflecting back the essence of what is said without comment or criticism, thus acknowledging that you understand their point;
3 calmly restate your point of view or request;
4 actively listen as before;
5 restate your position;

and so on . . .

This 'broken record' technique is assertive, not aggressive. There is no confrontation because you are not expressing your disagreement, or arguing back. You are simply accepting the opposing viewpoint as a valid one *and* repeatedly stating your own. This process ensures that you actually do listen to the other person, which in the normal style of argument often does not happen. The conversation is less likely to end in a stalemate because the other person has been heard and valued, and feels able to concede a point without losing face.

9 Games

The reader may have noticed by now that games and structures are used as basic tools for this brand of group work skills. The activities that we are describing have definite aims and purpose; they should not be seen in isolation, but as part of an overall campaign to introduce group work. They are very much part of an initial phase, while ground rules are being established and trust is being built.

Once a class is working well together, there is not the same need for games, and you can turn to the academic work with greater success. At any time in a group's development, however, you may decide to return to the games to re-establish the ground rules, enhance cooperation and trust, or to enliven the proceedings.

The value of games

They can:

- provide a structure to lean on
- initiate group work skills
- defuse tension
- build trust and sensitivity
- enhance self-esteem
- provide opportunity for everyone to participate (or not)
- enhance academic achievement
- break down teacher/student and student/student barriers
- promote good communication
- improve group functioning
- increase self-disclosure
- increase concentration
- encourage creativity and lateral thinking

A number of games are described in Section 3 of this book and much larger selections can be found elsewhere (e.g. Brandes and Phillips 1978; Brandes 1984).

10 Open discussion

The process which traditional teachers call class discussion is often not a discussion at all. The Oxford Dictionary defines 'discuss': 'to examine by argument or debate'. More often, a 'discussion' consists of the teacher asking questions, calling on certain students to answer, and remarking on which responses are right or wrong.

Even in lessons where there is room for students to argue or express opinions, the exchanges are usually referred through the teacher, and monitored and controlled by him; in other words, they are teacher-centred or teacher-led discussions. The big problem then is how to retain the interest of those class members who are not involved with the teacher at any given moment.

A student-centred discussion would probably be student-originated; it might stem from a student's disagreeing with a point in the work. Characteristics of an open discussion would be:

1 The teacher has no investment in how it turns out; she is not trying to prove anything.
2 Students are encouraged and not forced to participate.
3 They can speak to each other without referring to the teacher.
4 The teacher does not have to jump in and re-motivate or clarify.
5 If participation becomes unequal, students could use the 'conch' or magic pen, or The Token Game (p. 261).
6 Students could also choose to bring the discussion to an end.

11 Affective learning skills

A classroom is never an emotional vacuum; at all times people are experiencing feelings. All human beings are capable of a vast range of emotions. Imagine a continuum from mild annoyance to extreme rage; at some time in your life you will probably have known every shade in this spectrum. Imagine a similar scale between slight satisfaction on one extreme, to ecstasy on the other. Some people carefully avoid the extremes of the emotional range, preferring to live within a safe and comfortable band of feeling. It could be said that, usually, the school system is geared to limiting emotional experience to these accepted and 'mature' confines of behaviour.

We could contend that it is not dangerous to allow people to experience their feelings, and that, on the contrary, it is important that students learn to understand their own and other people's emotions, and to be able to deal with them.

In a traditional setting, if a student arrives in a bad temper he may be asked to stand outside until he has calmed down; thus we give him the message that being angry is abnormal, it is not socially acceptable for him to feel that way, and that he is in some way inadequate, a lesser person, for losing his temper. We exclude him from the company of his peers, at a time when he may well need their support.

In a student-centred climate, the teacher could recognise his need by allowing him to stay, asking other students to listen while he talks about it if he wants to, or by letting him be alone if that is what he wants. Some teachers even have a punching bag, a large cushion, or a soft toy that can be hammered or kicked when someone is angry.

There may be times when the teacher is aware of a general mood or undercurrent in a group. Perhaps one of their number has just been suspended from school, and people are incensed at the injustice of it all. Rather than pretending that the vibes are not there, and just ploughing through the work, the group could choose whether or not to take some time to discuss the matter and air feelings. Active listening could be the key, allowing the teacher to avoid taking sides. If she joined sides with the headmaster, she might end up sermonising, which causes resentment and turns people off. Nor is it advisable to win popularity with the students by taking their side. A better position for the teacher is neutrality, and that is best achieved by listening. Furthermore, listening prevents the possibility of misinterpreting the mood, which could very easily happen if the teacher assumes that she knows what the students are feeling and why.

So, it seems important to acknowledge that feelings exist, and that valuable learning can be gained from spending time exploring them. Tanzania is not *always* more pressing than the immediate emotional needs of the students.

Sometimes, social skills are taught as a separate curriculum component, and role play is used to recreate situations from which learning can arise. This can be unnecessarily artificial; real life situations occur daily; it is just that they may occur during maths or physics, rather than during the form period or social education lesson. The teachers of those subjects may feel that it is the job of pastoral staff to cope with students' feelings, and that they themselves have neither the skills nor the time to give attention to them. We have already said that we believe that time spent on affective learning is valuable; we would also suggest that teachers could become skilled in these areas, that it should be an integral part of their initial training and in-service provision. Self-awareness, interpersonal skills, assertiveness training and basic counselling skills ought to be components of teacher preparation.

There are two kinds of inherent affective elements in academic subjects:

1 The feeling content of the subject itself, for example, in maths, the beauty and symmetry of geometric shapes; the relationship between mathematics, art and music; the immutable laws which govern nature, and all of our lives.
2 The attitudes and values of the students and the teacher towards the subject. Some of us hate maths; others love it. The differences are worth acknowledging and exploring.

Perhaps the most important point to be mentioned here is that, through affective learning, we can open the door to peak experiences. Think about the high and low points in your own life: birth, marriage, death of loved ones, a moment of attunement with nature, a shared delight in music, whatever comes to mind when you look back over your life so far. Surely school ought not to be a time when only the narrow band of 'safe' emotion is explored? We can make available the feeling of profound satisfaction with a job well done, the disappointment of a task not completed, the joy of discovering something new for ourselves, on our own, the anger when we read about injustice . . . All of these, we believe, make the classroom experience richer, and the big bonus is the opportunity to share these feelings with our peers and our younger and older friends in school.

12 Telling the truth

The concept of telling the truth seems obvious and simplistic; it isn't. In fact, from our experience of INSET, it appears to be one of the most difficult ideas for teachers to grasp. Not that teachers tell lies, but in many cases they have been trained not to share with students what is going on in their minds or what they are feeling.

We have met teachers who have among their natural assets a delightful sense of humour, but who have been told in no uncertain terms: 'Never smile until Christmas', or in some cases '. . . Easter'! Others believe, as we have mentioned before, that they must always speak in stern and formal tones when addressing students in or out of the classroom.

What we are suggesting is that teachers who are confident enough to be themselves in the classroom, and not pretend to be anything else, who treat students like fellow human beings, who are clear, precise and honest in sharing their perception of the truth at any given moment, these teachers are likely to achieve warm and trusting relationships in their school life.

An example: suppose you complete the reading of this book, and you decide that you are going to experiment with some of the ideas or activities. Instead of 'figuring out' how to convince the students that this is a good idea, or just going in and starting to play a game, tell them the truth; which would mean saying something like:

'I've been reading a book on student-centred learning, and I've come across some ideas which seem exciting to me. I'd like to experiment with some of them, and then ask you to tell me what you think about them. Is that all right with you?'

Or, another example,

Teacher: 'Look, I have a dilemma here. On the one hand, I'd like to have us all look at each other's completed projects: we've been working on them a long time, and we ought to celebrate. On the other hand, we need to get started on the next topic, and we're running out of time. What do you think we should do?'

In other words, what we are suggesting is not merely that a teacher should build trust by avoiding any type of lying, but that she be *pro-active*, that she come forward and tell the truth about what is underlying her choices and actions.

13 Ask them

Here we have yet another key, or underlying necessity, to establishing student-centred methods. *Stop making decisions by yourself: ask them.* Some of the questions which teachers usually answer by themselves, and which we are suggesting should belong to the students are:

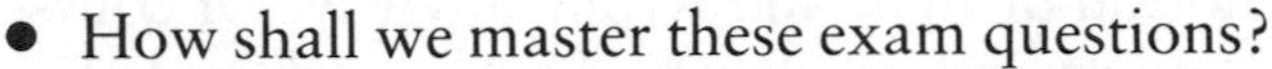

- How shall we master these exam questions?
- What do you think ought to be the deadline for this task?
- Who wants to be the first to volunteer to explain their project?
- What should we do about this problem?
- What shall we do next?
- What are you feeling upset about? Do you want to talk about it?
- What could we (you and I) do that would help you to get to school on time?
- How can we help the people in the class who are not feeling safe enough to participate?

BEWARE! There is no point in asking these questions of the students if we are not prepared to pay more than lip-service attention to their answers. The other half of asking them is listening to and acting upon their answers. The spin-off effects of this can be increased trust and improved self-concept. The students can come to believe that you value their opinions, and that you recognise their right to take responsibility for themselves.

14 Valuing mistakes

In traditional classrooms, the wrong answer is anathema, and mistakes are aberrations quickly to be corrected, and often to be condemned or ridiculed. It seems as though, if a student says that swans are white birds, he must immediately be told that some are black, or he will spend the rest of his life suffering under a misapprehension. Yet some scientists and philosophers take a different view of mistakes. Karl Popper (Magee 1982) wrote that if you want to prove that all swans are white, you do not look for sixty million white swans, you search for the black one, the exception, the oddity. You attempt to refute and disprove your own theories, you search rigorously for your mistakes and misunderstandings, and you even celebrate them. They are learning points of a high order.

If a child says to us 'two and two are four', we grin and agree. But if he says 'two and two are 22', we smile condescendingly and let him know how wrong he is. There are other possibilities: we could say 'Show me', or we could say 'Take these oranges and prove it', or we could say 'Perhaps in some cases that is true, see if you can find such a case'. Or we could ask a class 'Does anyone have a different opinion?'

If we let mistakes stand and be aired, we are not damning the student to a whole life of wrongness. In fact, it can be useful to do away with the whole notion of right and wrong anyway. Of course exams ask for right answers, and the thrust of an exam-based class will have to be the mastering of the information, the facts. But in classroom conversation, an ethos of exploration, of lateral thinking, of endless possibilities, can be much more productive than a search for correctness.

Wise men through the ages have said that the more we know, the more we have to acknowledge that we do not really know anything. Philosophers in the West since Descartes have grappled with the question 'How can I be certain of anything?' In the fields of science and technology, new possibilities every day deny old truths. If the sharpest minds across the centuries have struggled to open our perceptions and to broaden our potential by abandoning concepts of Rightness and Wrongness, we sometimes wonder how teachers can dare to claim the ultimate wisdom for themselves.

Direct communication

The manner in which people talk to each other in the group is crucial. It can either destroy or build trust; it can enhance or diminish self-esteem; it can foster or prevent open communication.

What we would be aiming for is communication characterised by respect and positive regard; any form of verbal abuse would definitely be *out*. All kinds of honest statements, whether negative or positive, can be expressed so that they are neither saccharine-sweet nor destructive and hurtful.

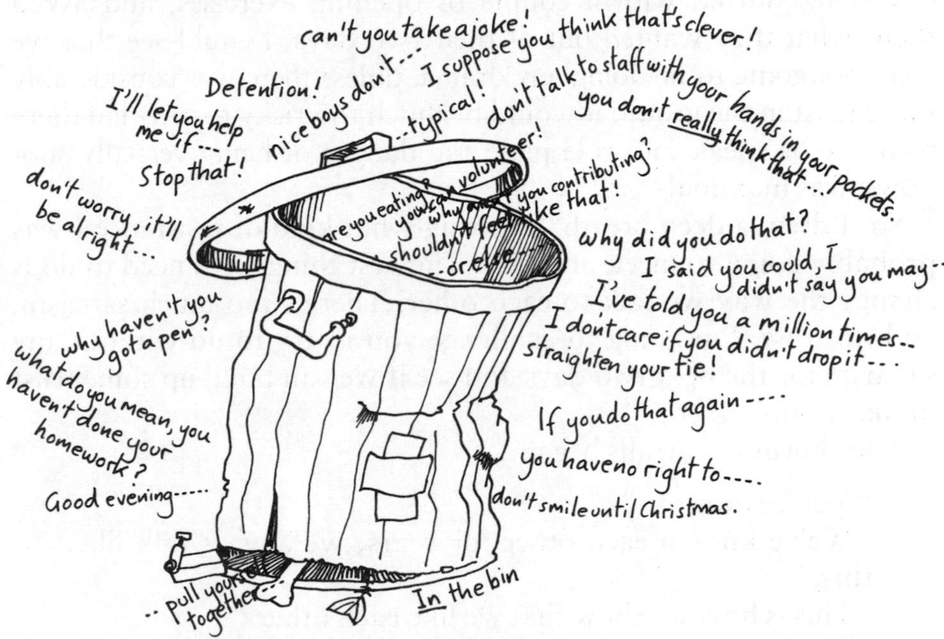

Clean up your language . . . get rid of the rubbish

Sarcasm

Sarcasm is one of the all-time great destroyers of trust. It is indirect communication; it often says the opposite of what it means, and people on the receiving end are often confused as to what is intended. It is argued that sarcasm is harmless amongst friends who are used to that sort of playful banter. But we contend that there is always a risk involved; you can never really know whether the other person has been hurt or not, because we have been trained and conditioned to be 'good sports', to laugh whether we feel like it or not, and to join in the repartee.

This is a true story:

There were 20 Geordie lads coming to me for a two-day Drama course. They were doing Art, and their teacher wanted them to work together better, to communicate with each other. This was my task.

As they entered, and I observed the way they interacted, the first thing I noticed was the devastating comments they made to put each other down. The repartee was typical of the Geordie pub culture, which is very concerned with machismo, and in which the Sharp-Tongued-Wit is King.

Having started with a couple of opening exercises, and asked them what they wanted out of their two days, I could see that we were not going to be doing any drama, unless there was considerably more trust in the group; it would be much too risky for any lad there to move or speak in a role play; the danger of being verbally shot down was maximal.

So, I drew a deep breath, knowing what kind of resistance I was probably going to meet, and said 'The first thing we'll need to do is change the way we talk to each other. There's too much sarcasm, and no trust. I'm going to challenge you to try to do without any sarcasm for the next two days and see if we can build up some trust in this group'.

The chorus of catcalls began:

> "You're too soft!"
> "We've known each other for years; we always talk like this."
> "This is how we show that we like each other."
> "You have no sense of humour."
> "All Geordies talk like this; you just don't understand."

The lads were very incensed; I had hit at behaviour that was habitual, and which had always been part of their survival tactics. They were very sure they could not do without it. (If I can step aside from that incident for a moment, I'll just say that no matter what group I've been in, teachers, social workers, married couples especially, if I've made some challenge, I've had the same responses; this is not exclusively a Geordie phenomenon . . .)

I gave the lads my reasons once more, assured them that I did indeed have a sense of humour, and that I was sure they would find plenty of things to laugh about without putting each other down. I repeated that I didn't want to argue about it; I was making a challenge, asking them to try it just while they were with me, and to see what would happen . . . finally they took up the contract.

We got down to work on some communication and listening exercises and, for the next few hours, all jokes were met with snide remarks like 'That's a no-no, you're a nasty boy!' or 'Oh, Spotty, you're not supposed to be sarcastic, ha, ha, ha!'

But after a while they had dropped it, forgotten about it, and got involved in the work we were doing. There was a palpable change in the atmosphere, and by the end of the second day, we were engaged in some good drama work. But that is not the real point of the story.

The feedback session at the end of the last afternoon was very serious indeed and, at the time, it was so poignant that I had tears in my eyes. The lads were saying things that they had never said aloud before, so they told me. One boy said:

> "I never know where I stand with anyone. I can't tell if they like me or not, because secretly I think that if they liked me they wouldn't talk to me like that."

Another lad, very small and quiet, said:

> "Almost all the time, my feelings are hurt, but I can't show it. I spend most of my time covering up how I feel. No-one knows what I'm really like, because I always laugh and answer back."

And so it went; they had a lot to say about it.

Later reports from the art teacher said that they had kept away from the repartee within the art room, but that out at the pub or in the Tech., they had to go back to it in order to survive.

Since that event, my crusade against sarcasm has been even more unrelenting. I can remember telling a married couple I knew very well that, since they were asking me for advice about their marriage, I would tell them one thing; they were too sarcastic with each other. They replied with exactly the same phrases that I always hear, especially the one about 'This is how we show we love each other'. It did not give me any pleasure at all when they told me two years later, as they were getting divorced, that I had been right, and that the put-down comments were funny when they knew they loved each other, but when the relationship was faltering the jibes turned sour and began to hurt.

I know for myself that I enjoy a good exchange of wit, and that repartee is very seductive; I get drawn in and begin to enjoy it, until I remember what I am doing.

The bottom line for us is that teasing, banter, wit at someone else's expense, and sarcasm, are all indirect forms of communication. They often mask unexpressed hostility, and prevent clear messages from being received.

Sarcasm involves a risk of hurting the other person and destroying their trust in us; it is a risk we are no longer prepared to take, either personally or professionally. But, above all, it is a subtle and aggressive weapon that teachers use against children who would be in severe trouble if they answered back, and are therefore defenceless. It is a form of bullying that is no less damaging than the cane and just as cruel.

What sarcasm and banter do is to drive true feelings deeper and to discourage honesty. Students have often said to us that their reluctance to participate at first in rounds or other activities is due to the fear of being put down or laughed at. A teacher could measure the degree of trust in a group by the freedom of speech which exists; if students feel free to say whatever they think and feel, and to say it in a manner underpinned by positive regard, then a very high level of trust has been established.

Language changes

Language can reflect the extent to which a person is assuming responsibility for himself; even minor changes can make a difference. For example, in polite society people tend to disown a statement by saying 'One often finds it embarrassing to say what one really thinks'. This generalises a personal feeling, which saddles the rest of the population with an idea which perhaps does not apply to them, and also allows the person making the statement to evade his ownership of the problem. Another way of hiding is to say 'You know how it is; you often feel shy in that situation'; not only does this transfer responsibility, but also it makes it more difficult for the listener to have and express his own feelings if they are not the same as the speaker's. A third evasion is to say 'We all feel that the meetings are too long', without consulting the rest of the people in the group. Such a statement puts pressure on the rest of the group to agree, particularly if it is said by an influential member, and so again blocks direct communication.

In group work, we encourage people to speak for themselves, saying 'I feel embarrassed when I say what I really think,' 'I feel the meetings are too long, and I want to know if anyone else agrees with me.' In making such statements, the speaker accepts full responsibility for her own feelings, and allows other people to do the same. In a classroom, owning feelings in this way can help to build trust, and can also break down the hierarchy of influence, so that those students who have in the past been very quiet and afraid to speak for themselves can begin to feel less threatened. This concept applies to the teacher as much as to the students; it is all too easy for the teacher to hide under phrases like 'In this school we . . .', or 'Our policy is . . .'. The teacher will be able to set an example by sorting out her own language first.

Other language changes can similarly facilitate the building of trust and sharpen the awareness of responsibility (for further reading see Passons 1975). Here are some examples:

a Change 'Can't' to 'Won't' in any sentence, and see what happens, e.g. 'I can't tell you what I really think' becomes 'I won't tell you . . .'.
b Change 'but' to 'and' so that the second half of the statement does not cancel out the first, e.g. 'I need to stay and finish this, but I want to play football' changes to 'I need to stay and finish this and I want to play football'.
c Change passive voice to active, e.g. 'This always seems to happen to me' to 'I do this frequently'.
d Get rid of blaming other people for the way you feel, e.g. change 'You make me angry' to 'I feel angry when you do that'.
e Avoid the word 'Why?'; it produces rationalisations and intellectual explanations, or defensiveness:

Teacher: Why did you throw that egg at the window?
Student: I dunno . . .

or Teacher: Why did you throw that egg at the window?
Student: Well, it wasn't my fault. I was just passing by and I saw these guys with a bunch of eggs, and I just sort of picked one up . . .

or Teacher: Why did you throw that egg at the window?
Student: It wasn't me, miss . . .

So, what do we put in the place of 'Why?' A statement, rather than a question, can often be much more effective.

Teacher: I'm concerned because I've got a report on my desk which tells me that you were seen throwing eggs at a window yesterday. I'd like you to tell me about it.
Student: Who says I did it?
Teacher: I'm not concerned about whether you did it or not; in fact you were seen doing it. I'd like to discuss with you what you could do about it.

Another way to disown responsibility is to use the word 'try'; not try as in 'try on some clothes', or 'try out a new piece of behaviour', but try as in 'I tried to do my homework'. Any person who has ever had a weight problem knows the difference between 'No thanks, no cake for me. I'm sticking to my diet', and 'Oh well, just a little piece, I'm trying to stay on my diet'.

Here is a simple exercise to illustrate the concept to a group:

Leader: Try to pick up that chair.
Group member: *(Picks it up easily.)*
Leader: No, don't pick it up, TRY to pick it up.
Group member: *(Struggles with chair, doesn't manage to pick it up.)*
Leader: What did you notice?

Part of responsible behaviour is to do with making agreements and keeping them. Again the teacher's integrity is on the line here: if she says 'I will have these papers marked by Monday', then she is not talking about 'trying' to have them marked; no excuse or reason will convince the students that they are going to keep their agreements, if the teacher does not.

Words like 'should', 'ought' and 'have to' also take responsibility away from the student. Doing things because we ought to do them is truly dutiful, and also joyless. Doing things out of choice and wanting to is rewarding. So, the teacher can experiment with another substitution of language:

not 'These papers should be done by Tuesday'

but 'Let's agree about when the deadline for these papers will be'.

Agreement, negotiation and choice tend to produce positive results which feel satisfying; duty tends to produce grudging compliance.

Another point about communication seems to be worth mentioning. We have found that when a group is first introduced to the idea of circles, rounds and working together, students still address their comments to the teacher. They usually look at the teacher and begin with 'Miss' or 'Sir' or the teacher's name. It is a habit which could be broken by the teacher frequently reminding students to look at and address the whole group. If this does not work, the teacher could sit out of the circle or 'disappear' temporarily.

Support v. rescue

Handing over responsibility to students requires them to be confident enough to accept it. In order to build this confidence, the teacher will need to avoid rescuing them every time the going gets a bit rough. For example, we have seen the following interchange taking place on many occasions:

Teacher: Right, we need a volunteer for the next exercise . . .
Students: *(Stony silence.)*
Teacher: Come on, you lot, let's get going, who's going to volunteer?
Students: *(Looking at floor; no answer.)*
Teacher: Right then, Clare, we'll start with you!

In most cases, the teacher intervenes in this way because he cannot stand the silence; the students are very aware of this, and they know that if they wait long enough they will be rescued eventually, so why should they bother to take the risk and volunteer? We suggest an alternative interchange:

Teacher: We need a volunteer for the next exercise.
Students: *(Stony silence.)*
Teacher: (Waits patiently, feeling confident that the students want to get going as much as he does.)
Students: *(Looking at the floor; no answer.)*
Teacher: Well, I see that no-one wants to be the first to volunteer. Shall we move on to something else, or what do you recommend we could do about it?

In this way the teacher indicates that he is there to support the students in accomplishing the task in hand, and that he is not there to rescue them or relieve them of their responsibility.

Acceptance

Many children go through school, and through their home lives as well, feeling that they have 'got it wrong' or that they can never get it right. They may grow up still feeling this way. We do this to kids by perceiving mistakes as failures and every answer or every action as being either right or wrong. And often by our standards, as parents or teachers, they don't *do it*, or *be it*, the way we think they ought to. In other words, we are forever evaluating them and finding them somehow wanting. Then we tend to label them, saying 'You're thick', 'You're naughty', 'You're a troublemaker'. These sorts of labels are surprisingly adhesive, they stick around for a very long time and tend to reinforce exactly the behaviour we want to change.

While it is true that there are actions and behaviour that are absolutely unacceptable to us, and there is no use pretending that they are not, the students themselves, as people, must feel our acceptance and our love, in short our unconditional positive regard, if we want them to trust us.

Conditional Regard	**Unconditional Positive Regard**
You're been a very naughty boy today. I don't like you when you act like that.	I like you, and right now your behaviour is unacceptable. I don't want you to stand on my desk.

This positive approach says that the person is always OK, but that sometimes his behaviour is not OK. It allows the person to move and to change the behaviour, knowing that he himself is accepted.

In a classroom characterised by this kind of regard emanating from the teacher, a reciprocal positive feeling tends to build up, so that an atmosphere of acceptance and cooperation exists. Sometimes when a group is functioning in this way, a feeling of trust becomes so solid that it is evident in every word the students say to each other; you can 'feel it in the air'; it is almost tangible.

Our experience has been that, in such an atmosphere, good relationships among all members of the group begin to thrive, and discipline problems begin to disappear.

At the same time, in such an atmosphere, the teacher can feel free to be 100% himself or herself. Time and again, teachers will talk to a friend in a warm and friendly manner, and then turn around and speak to kids in a cold and stern tone of voice, fearing that otherwise the kids will take advantage. Positive regard breeds respect and love, so that the teacher can speak the same way as she speaks to friends, can laugh, play games, interact with the students in a loving way, and without any risk of losing control. Love, and not fierce aggression, is the most powerful natural asset that a teacher can have.

One expression of affection is touching, which is quite a controversial issue in a classroom. It is difficult to choose what to say about this subject, because it is not something which can be prescribed, and it must come naturally if it is to mean anything. Some teachers feel quite at ease putting an arm around a student's shoulder, or being leaned against; others feel this as an invasion of privacy. There are those who feel that it can be misinterpreted or that it can lead to casual and informal attitudes which in turn lead to lack of respect, or a weakening of discipline.

Emphasising again that we want people to feel comfortable, we just want to say that touching can break down barriers and build trust within the group. If you allow a student to touch you, you are

Keep your distance

indicating your acceptance of him as a person; if you actively resist being touched, you may be sending a message which says 'You and I have to be separate; you must keep your distance'.

Many of the games which are used in group work involve touching; the intention is to break down barriers between students, another step towards encouraging the group to work at full capacity.

Imagine your classroom being like this:

> The first bell rings in the morning. The students come in a few at a time, stopping to give you a warm hug or a kiss on the cheek as they enter, and then going to their seats or to the circle. Some kids who aren't in your class pop in to give you a hug and then go off to their own lessons –

How would you feel about such a scene? . . . This is how it used to be for one of us, and to us it meant that the students were happy to be in school, and genuinely, warmly, glad to see us. The teachers did not initiate this; the boys and girls started it themselves, spontaneously.

If you like the sound of that, and you want it to start happening in your classroom, you could encourage it through games, or simply begin by putting a hand on someone's shoulder when you want to. After all, are these students human, as we are? Are they one with us, or are they part of another species further down the evolutionary ladder? On the other hand, affection cannot be faked, and the kids will certainly know if you are uncomfortable, or if you don't mean it.

Products

Syllabus and exams

When student-centred methods are introduced to a new group, one of the first things which is usually said is, 'Well *of course* you can't do this with an exam subject.' This dictum is often stated as fact, with no room for argument. It tells us that we *cannot* do something which we have already been doing successfully!

In our experience, exams *are* passed through these methods, moreover other kinds of learning take place at the same time, which are very valuable. These include the ongoing personal and social development of the students, which actually enhances their ability to pass exams, but which is often pushed aside in the pursuit of academic achievement through didactic methods.

We traditionally view external exams at 16 (and also for some at 18) as the climax of a student's school career. Parents, employers, most students, and many teachers, seem to place great value on cognitive development – the accumulation of knowledge which is eventually sufficient to pass the all-important exams. However, this apparent success is usually achieved through a narrowing of the child's educational experience:

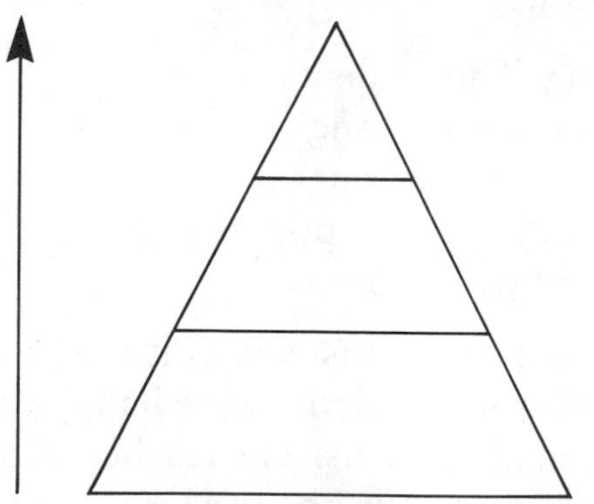

'peak of success': external examinations

often narrowed down more and more to didactic teaching style and cognitive development

forced to choose options at 13

broad-based primary education; often includes personal and social development

By contrast, a confluent view of education would look like this:

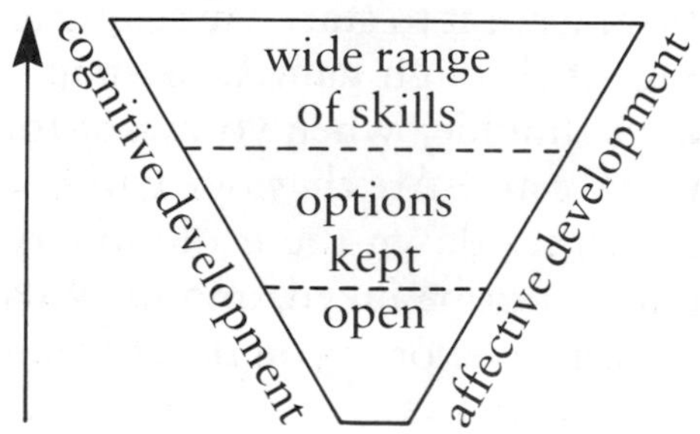

broadening experience, preparing for adulthood, development of the whole person

very limited experience in a small child

All aspects of a child's development would be given equal emphasis.

Although we feel strongly, and many educators would agree, that abolishing the exam system would be the greatest liberating move for education this country could make, this is *not* the case we are making here. Rather, we wish to demonstrate that student-centred methods can operate successfully within the system as it exists.

So, how would you approach an exam syllabus in a student-centred way and what would be the advantage? The two key words are again ownership and responsibility:

- Who sits the exam?
- Whose career will be influenced by the outcome?
- Who gets the exam certificate?

Ask yourself these questions and notice where you feel the weight of responsibility lies. It is one thing to accept logically that the students own their exams; it is a more difficult thing to let them take ownership, especially as there are many pressures on teachers to accept responsibility for students' performances: parental expectations, judgment of colleagues, students counting on you to pull them through, your own prestige and satisfaction, or a feeling of 'it's too late to change now'.

We are not suggesting that you should not care whether they pass or not. Of course, your relationship with the students involves deep concern. It is a subtle shift of stance from '*I* will get *you* through this exam if it kills me' to 'I will do everything in my power to enable *you* to own and pass this exam yourself.

We are in a dilemma here for, while we are suggesting that the students are responsible for devising their own ways of absorbing the required information, we do not want to be accused of being unrealistic. So the following are ideas which have been devised by students. We hope that you will give them the opportunity to solve their own particular problems themselves.

The *first* step in passing ownership over to the students is for them to become thoroughly familiar with the syllabus. Make a copy for everyone. Ask them to read it through, discuss it with other students, conjecture about which parts will cause them trouble and which they already feel they have mastered. Do not lie awake at night thinking of clever strategies for 'covering' the material. Ask the students how they want to take charge of it.

At first there may be resistance as they are not accustomed to making these sorts of decisions. So, the *second* step is to allow plenty of time for the students to say how they feel. Let them know what you see as the benefits of working this way, e.g. if they take charge of the information, they will understand it and remember it, not just for the exam, but beyond it. Furthermore, they will know that they can organise and assimilate information for themselves and that they can encourage and assist each other. Also, it can transform a potentially dull syllabus into an exciting and creative experience. It communicates to each student that he is a responsible and valuable person, capable of learning for himself. Moreover, a tremendous amount of time can be saved as students may decide to divide the tasks and share the information with each other.

A *third* step could be similar to this true experience with a fourth year RE group. The students looked at the syllabus together, and decided to tackle the next three topics, which were: church activities and functions, church architecture and design, and Christian symbolism and church decoration. They decided to divide into three self-selected but balanced working parties, and made a contract with each other that at the end of four weeks they would supply everyone with written materials which thoroughly covered each topic. The working parties set themselves up in different areas of the room and organised their work so that everyone had a task. The teacher took each group to see what resources were available within the department, and only made suggestions when asked. He also provided spirit duplicating masters and offered to make copies of their materials.

The groups set to work and not only used the departmental resources but organised two visits to contrasting church buildings, and an interview with a local Methodist minister. One group organised a questionnaire on church activities and sent it out to 17 local parishes. The replies were collated and a summary of the information was incorporated in the information pack that they presented to the other students. At the end of the four weeks, a total of 40 information sheets had been prepared by the students and shared with each other.

Just to make sure that the information had actually been assimilated, the teacher gave oral quizzes, across the groups, and was impressed with the amount of accuracy of detail that the kids had mastered. An evaluation revealed that the students had found this approach rewarding, stimulating and effective, a view that was confirmed by many of their parents at the next parents' evening. The final comment was: 'Sir, we're shattered. You teach us for a few weeks now, and give us a break!'

As for other approaches, we have seen students take old exam papers, practise writing answers and criticise each other's work. Sometimes they agree to divide into pairs and quiz each other on the different sections. Often they create mock exams.

People's styles of learning differ; some people remember more easily if they can argue and talk through information; others prefer to do it on their own. Why should we force them all into the same mould of learning when this approach can provide each individual with her optimum method?

Other kinds of products

We have addressed the problems of exams and syllabus coverage first because they are the ones that seem to produce the most doubt about the efficacy of student-centred methods. When the group is not restricted by a prescribed syllabus, a much more diversified range of products is possible. Here are some examples of work done in the Birmingham project, in the space of just a few weeks:

a video feature film
a dance drama
visual display materials
a news programme on cassette
a mobile
glove puppets
advertisements for products invented by students
models
a board game
a filmed quiz programme (similar to *Mastermind*)
a newspaper
a thought-chain garland (a logical sequence of thoughts, made into a paperchain)
written projects in folders

Students who had previously not been successful at writing are now achieving finished work of which they feel proud and are seeing themselves as creative, productive people. The only limits on creativity are the imagination of the pupils and the willingness of the teacher.

Resourcing

A student-centred approach to learning has implications for departmental and school resourcing policies. One head of department explained how he used to spend the minimum on reprographic and consumable materials. The students got through about one and a half exercise books a year and, with enough file paper for special display work and fifth year projects, that was just about all the stationery he needed to order. The bulk of his allocation went on sets of textbooks, filmstrips, posters and a few artefacts. The department was considered to be well-resourced; the stockroom shelves were full; there was an impressive collection of audio-visual materials and posters covered the walls.

Half way through an academic year, he began to adopt a more student-centred approach, and soon found that the students needed lots of folders, file paper, drawing paper, coloured paper, sheets of card, sugar paper, sellotape, glue, crayons, felt pens, scissors, spirit duplicator carbons and masters, photocopying paper, audio and video tapes, stencils, strings, staples, pins, clips, labels, tags . . . even wood, felt, aluminium and paint! The department ran up a sizeable debt buying and borrowing these materials from all over the place and struggled through to the next financial year.

A lesson had been learned. The priority from now on was to ensure that enough consumable materials were ordered to satisfy the creative appetites of the students, including some exercise books for those who wanted to use them. The head of department also realised that full sets of textbooks would rarely be needed, but that it was important to have an extensive library of single copies and small sets of books. At the same time the stock of audio visual material would need to be increased and a cassette machine which recorded rather than just played back would also be required. The LEA subject adviser was approached about a special grant for portable video equipment.

Not only had the purchasing policy changed, but also the way departmental resources were used altered significantly. Within the previous traditional style, the resources were controlled by the teacher. He decided on how and when they should be used to enhance the presentation of a lesson. He was the only one with access to the inner sanctum of the stockroom. He organised their distribution and collection, showing, reading, watching or listening. Now the stockroom is always open during lessons and students may go in whenever they need to, and the contents have been re-organised and categorised so that they can find what they want more easily. There is also an extensive library on open shelves in the classroom. Several pencils, rulers and felt pens have gone missing since this open-stockroom policy began, but not more than were taken previously. If theft did become a problem, the teacher would turn it over to the group to solve.

The teacher has other ideas for his room. He wants to establish 'activity islands' within the room so that there is a place for art or craft type activities, a carpeted area for reading, a writing base and a 'free space' resourced with activity cards and games related to the subject to be used in free time. All the furniture is moveable and the organisation will be sufficiently flexible to allow a circle to be created at any time. He is fortunate in having a large enough room. Permission was recently obtained to take the old spirit duplicator from the staffroom and, with a little oil and persuasion from a screwdriver, it works reasonably well.

The departmental library is expanding all the time. The teacher never passes a second-hand bookshop without calling in to see what he can find related to his subject. One shelf is full of paperbacks and there is already a dustbin full of magazines brought in by the students which provide a rich source of illustrations and cuttings. The walls are covered with students' work of all types, which they have put up themselves, and there is an old cabinet from a junk shop fixed to the wall displaying students' models.

Assessment

The common problem

In a traditional framework, students' work would be marked by the teacher, usually by giving a numerical or alphabetical grade, accompanied, perhaps, by a comment. This really could be looked upon as a shortcut to full communication between student, teacher, parent, and school, and as such, is often lazy and inaccurate. There are many factors influencing the mark given, other than the quality of the work done. For example, the teacher's tiredness or boredom, the mood of the moment, a general liking or disliking for the child, or just plain overload. Take the case of the music teacher who teaches all 800 students in a school; even if that teacher practises continuous assessment, he still has to review each student's work and write 800 reports, while still teaching all his classes. How is it possible for him to make a meaningful comment or grade for each person?

The problem does not end here. In order to provide herself with full and accurate records, a teacher has to mark her students' work frequently, perhaps aiming to be fully caught up every week. Headmasters often expect such regularity and college training instills the habit. It is perceived as one of the hallmarks of 'the good teacher'. What does this mean in human terms? It provides a dilemma every day for the secondary teacher, who has to keep

Is there life after marking?

choosing between a private life in the evenings, the weekends, and even during the holidays, *or* marking.

If the choice is a private life, some of the costs are:

a feelings of guilt or inadequacy
b a backlog of marking which will eventually have to be done or thrown away
c insufficient data for reporting
d discontented students who expect their work to be marked punctually
e a damaged reputation amongst colleagues and students, leading, at worst, to criticism from the head, and even weakened career prospects.

If the choice is marking, the results may be even more destructive:

a resentful partner at home
b if there is no partner, lack of opportunities to pursue a social life
c neglected children, friends and relatives
d no time to attend to the routine chores of living, such as answering letters, paying bills, cooking, shopping, decorating.

Faced with this choice, many teachers might ask: 'Is there life after marking?' This may sound dramatic, but our experience has been that many teachers find this conflict one of the most severe disadvantages of their profession.

Underlying issues

What are some of the factors behind this problem of assessment in a traditional setting?

a The physical and social distance between teacher and student, which encourage 'anonymous' marking where some teachers can get away with marking a paper belonging to a name without a face.
b An emphasis on product, rather than process, which generates great piles of work to be marked. Because there is so much to 'get through' during each lesson, there is never time for careful evaluation on the spot.
c Parents, teachers and students collude in creating the need for marks as a symbol of progress and success; these become a substitute for intrinsic satisfaction or personal growth.

The system as it stands is clearly inadequate; there is so much that it does not measure. It is limited, often inappropriate, and unjust. So, what are we offering in its place?

Student-centred assessment

Let's begin with a student's individual day-to-day measuring of his progress. Please notice the change of language here: it is *not* the teacher's assessment of the student; the ownership has been transferred to its rightful place.

1 *Students learn how to assess their own work*

The initial step is learning how to establish criteria for what makes a good piece of work. The following are two possible ways of achieving this; you will be able to develop others.

1 Brainstorm qualities of a good piece of work, discuss each one.
2 Show the class some work which you consider to be good. Ask them to divide into small groups, to notice the good points about the work, and to list them.

It may be a good idea to post the criteria, once selected, on the wall, so that they can always be referred to.

Having established the criteria, a second step is to develop a way for students to evaluate what they have done. We find the following two questions extremely useful:

- What's good about it?
- What needs to be improved?

The questions can be asked in the group circle, or by students sitting alone with their work. The answers may be recorded by each student and attached to the work. Of course, if there is a lot that needs improving, the student may want to do the work again.

2 *Students learn how to assess each other's work*

Having assessed his own work, a student may want to seek a second opinion, or make comparisons. The teacher may want to suggest peer assessment, because it is a process in which a variety of social skills may develop, for example, negotiation, debate, assertiveness, tact. Furthermore, peer assessment helps to develop awareness of personal strengths and weaknesses, and gives a student the benefit of another's perspective on the content. The same two questions could be asked because they are constructive and not derogatory. One way of making the work available for the group is to copy it onto an overhead projector transparency; another way is to make photocopies. It is often helpful to work with the whole group at first, so that the teacher is still supervising the process; later, people could work in pairs.

3 *The teacher's role*

Even when self and peer assessment are established, the teacher has several important roles to maintain:

a making sure the students understand how to evaluate work
b staying neutral – resisting the temptation to override or veto an assessment
c as a group member, the teacher can contribute to group assessment; otherwise he can be invited to join in with an individual or a pair
d making sure that appreciation and acknowledgement, not praise, are given for participation or for completion of a task
e encouraging students to check on inaccuracies (rather than pointing out mistakes).

4 *Recording assessments*

Here are four other ways of recording assessments which we have found effective. They are offered as examples, and the students could really devise their own methods.

a A record card is given to each student, and all cards are kept in an alphabetical file box in the classroom; whenever an assessment is made, the student enters her comments on the card, and dates it. At the end of term the student compiles a summative report based on the card entries. This summative document could be negotiated between student and teacher, and signed by both, and could become the report issued to parents.
b A wall chart can be devised which shows a series of tasks along one axis, and the students' names along the other, with squares big enough for both ticks and comments.
c Graphs could be drawn which indicate levels of mastery of skills, which show personal growth in a certain area, or which describe changing relationships within the group.
d Each student has a diary or logbook and takes time to fill it in. At agreed intervals, or when the student feels it necessary, it could be reviewed with the teacher.

What we are really saying is that the system ought to be overhauled, so that parents come to expect a self-assessment from the student which has been negotiated with the teachers. Obviously this is a long-term change which has to be instituted by the managers of the school. In the meantime, perhaps you can experiment with some of the above suggestions, and include students much more in the report writing process, even if in the end you are the one who puts pen to paper.

5 *Assessment by external examination*

Exam subjects are a special case in that they are externally assessed. How then do the students take ownership?

a The teacher has a strong role to play in providing students with the external criteria and demonstrating to them how examiners mark.
b Students can learn to think like examiners and examine each other's work. For example, they can set and mark their own mock exams and practice questions. They can always go to the teacher to check standards.

There may be many teachers who feel that there is so much to cover within the syllabus that time cannot be given to learning how to do self and peer assessment. However, it is important to realise that while assessing, students are reviewing and consolidating content. A teacher embarking on student-centred methods may have to strike a new balance between product and process. While not reducing the students' chances of exam success, the teacher may have to re-appraise the signficance of the exams in the total development of the students. At the time of writing this, initiatives are springing up which reflect this trend, and which provide accreditation for process, not just content as in traditional examinations. The Oxford Certificate of Educational Achievement (OCEA) is one example.

A case study: overcoming an 'insurmountable obstacle'

Having read all this, you may still feel that your particular situation presents problems which simply cannot be eliminated. In this section we are offering three different approaches to a typical problem.

The situation

Room 19 is the chemistry lab. It is about 40 feet long, narrow, with heavy benches bolted to the floor in rows. At the front, the teacher's bench is on a raised podium. The lab. is Spartan; there is no equipment out. It is all locked away in the technician's room down the corridor. What there is is sparse, incomplete, in poor condition; in short, inadequate. Many of the students in the fourth year examination group have a problem with reading and writing English, since it is their second language. The examination syllabus is couched in technical vocabulary, covers extremely difficult concepts, and requires students to learn a vast amount of abstract information, most of which is irrelevant to their everyday lives. The teacher was taught by lectures and rote memorisation, which are manifested in his own teaching style.

A traditional solution

The problem is traditionally solved by the teacher taking on himself the role of the expert, who interprets the syllabus and takes full responsibility for passing on the information to the kids. In Room 19, this involves the teacher standing on the podium and shouting so that those at the back can hear. Everything echoes, even the slightest whisper from one student to another, or the tiniest scraping of a stool. Thus the teacher has to intersperse the shouting with constant 'Sshhhing'. There has to be strict control to maintain the semblance of attention, which satisfies the teacher, who feels that he

The teacher feels that he has done his job once the information has been broadcast

has done the job once the information has been broadcast. If the students do not receive the transmission, they have faulty equipment: 'I just can't get through to that lad; he's got a screw loose somewhere'.

The broadcast is supported by notes; these come in the form of information sheets, which are read through by the teacher to students who do not understand enough of them even to be able to ask questions, and which are then assumed to be understood and learned. This method produces examination passes, in some cases, only because it is possible to memorise without understanding. Of course, some students have a natural aptitude for the subject, and do arrive at understanding through these techniques.

An extreme student-centred solution

The kids have already learned how to brainstorm and are comfortable using the process to sort out their own problems. The teacher asks them to brainstorm all the problems of learning chemistry in Room 19; the generated problems are then sorted into categories and teams of students begin to work out solutions, using problem-solving methods. These trial solutions are fed back to the whole group for evaluation and selection. After a period in which the chosen solutions are tried out, the group comes back together to re-evaluate, and to choose new ideas if necessary.

It is surprising what can be done. In the Birmingham project, one Biology teacher had the plumbing and electricity supply in the lab. reorganised, and several benches unbolted and sawn in half to give freedom and flexibility.

A middle way

We have just described two extreme positions on the continuum. Now we will explore a way by which a teacher who has been accustomed to traditional methods may begin to make moves in a student-centred direction. The teacher could enlist the help of the students in assessing the problems which face the whole group; she could use brainstorming or open discussion. If one of the problems is the arrangement of the room, students could be encouraged to work in teams and find ways of rearranging the room to suit their own purposes. If another problem is that the syllabus is too big, and contains too much concentrated information, the students could find ways to group topics into categories. They could then divide themselves into self-selected groups to match these sub-divisions of the syllabus.

To enable groups to work at their chosen topics, resources would need to be made available to them. The teacher may trust the students with the equipment, and might need to show them how to use slides, video programmes, or even how to organise their own visits. Having mastered one topic, students could then present what they have learned to other groups, by writing worksheets, giving reports, making presentations or displays, carrying out or devising experiments, quizzing each other or holding a seminar. Meanwhile, the teacher is gradually building up her own supply of resources. As much as possible, the work should be active.

In these days of severely limited resources, teachers can turn to students for help in building up a collection of materials which can later be used by other students. It would be advantageous for a teacher using this style of working to have a well-stocked library, which students can use to research their own topics. But often this is not possible, and it should be remembered that books are not the only source of information. Greater use could be made of visitors and visits, perhaps to local chemical firms, film processing laboratories, metal extrusion industries, and so on. Sometimes these companies have educational materials available. Students could devise questionnaires to send out to firms. The teacher herself can be used in a much more creative way; she could be interviewed, so that the questions are coming from the students. She could be a mine of information, rather than a fountain of knowledge.

This is not to say that the occasional lecture is not appropriate. Sometimes, but only *sometimes*, a lecture is the most effective means of conveying information. However, the purpose of the lecture is not for the students to copy down slavishly every word the teacher says. It is an opportunity to develop certain study skills:

listening	questioning
note-taking	lateral thinking
comprehension	organising, categorising
précis	discussing

These skills, as well as the information contained in the lecture, may need to be reviewed and evaluated by the group.

Summary

Let us re-emphasise that every student-centred classroom is different; this is one of the most exciting features of the process. There are many ways of getting started on a student-centred approach, and all the ways will probably have certain elements in common, most of which have to do with the relationships between all the people in the group:

- sitting together instead of in rows
- speaking openly and honestly to ech other
- listening respectfully
- unconditional positive regard
- joint decision making
- freedom to participate or not.

If all of these conditions are operating, no matter what activities are being used, the environment will now be ready for the students to take their rightful position at the centre of their own learning experience.

3 INNOVATION

Introduction

Even if you are convinced about the validity of student-centred learning and understand certain basic skills and attitudes underlying the methods, you may still be left with the question of how to go about actually changing things in your place of work.

In this chapter we are going to suggest ways in which people and organisations can achieve innovation. The model advocated here is rooted in long experience of implementing change, through counselling individuals and consulting with organisations. If you would like to read in detail about how the model was applied in Birmingham, you can find an account of the Birmingham project in the Appendix on p. 262.

Seven steps to change

It has been a great challenge to attempt to draw out of a complicated process some very simplified steps in the achievement of change. Most of the time, people are so busy with the demands of their daily work that they do not take time to step back and look at what they are doing; they become expert without defining their expertise. However, it can be very useful to stop and examine our practice, so that we can demystify proceedings that otherwise seem magical, and so that our skills are accessible to others. As Schön puts it:

> When a practitioner reflects in and on his practice, the possible objects of his reflection are as varied as the kinds of phenomena before him and the systems of knowing-in-practice which he brings to them . . . Reflection-in-practice is central to the art through which practitioners sometimes cope with the troublesome 'divergent' situations of practice . . . Sometimes he arrives at a new theory of the phenomenon by articulating a feeling he has about it.
>
> (Schön 1983, p. 62)

In this chapter, we will be aiming to clarify seven steps in the process of innovation, a process which we believe would apply to individuals, to classroom groups, or to organisations.

It must be emphasised that these steps do not necessarily occur in any particular order; they are interwoven, and sometimes may seem to happen simultaneously. They are very much dependent upon each other.

1 Motivation

Motivation to change may come from any number of sources. For example, from students, who may say:

"Why can't we do things differently around here?"
"We're always treated like little kids."
"Nobody ever trusts us."

Often these comments are not picked up by the teacher because they seem to be negative 'moaning', and as such they are usually dismissed. In fact, these kinds of statements could be interpreted as signals indicating that students seriously would like things to change.

More commonly, the students themselves do not recognise these feelings or statements as signals. The idea that school *could* be different or that teachers *might* be willing to change does not seem to them to be possible. Thus, it often falls to the teacher to unlock this latent motivation. Our experience has been that the key turns quite easily in the lock, and that once increased responsibility and participation have been offered, they are eagerly accepted.

When we have said to students, 'Would you like to change the way we work together so that you would have more to say about it, and more of the responsibility for planning and making decisions?', the reply has been almost unanimously positive. Not only is the initial response enthusiastic, it tends to gain momentum as new kinds of satisfaction are experienced, along with the maintenance of academic achievement. Sometimes there is cynicism, founded on the mistrust which existed previously. Sometimes there is resistance to change, often from students who are particularly concerned to achieve academically, and who fear that the new methods will reduce their chances of success.

It is not easy to dismantle the stereotype of the teacher as the source of all knowledge, the student as the receiver. Schools often encourage the view that the only way for students to pass exams is to shut up, sit down, and listen to what the teacher says. Once success has been tasted within this system, these notions are reinforced, and it is harder for students to see a reason to change. They have a vested interest in not changing. In this situation, we would hope to ask students if there is *anything else* to learn in school besides *examinable knowldege*.

However motivated *students* may be, it is usually impossible for them to initiate and bring about change within schools on their own. So, we have to ask ourselves, why might *teachers* want to change? We can identify several kinds of reasons.

Emotional reasons

Many teachers express dissatisfaction with their jobs. They may be aware that their relationships with the kids could be better, or that their own emotional needs are not being met, or that they are full of knowledge which they want to give, but which the students do not want to receive. Some teachers simply feel that there must be more to teaching than marking, discipline, and getting students through exams. Also, of course, there are many teachers who have developed an intuition about how school ought to be, and for one reason or another find things are not that way. So, for many there is a distinct dissonance between what they want and what they are actually getting.

> . . . the existence of dissonance, being psychologically uncomfortable, will motivate the person to try to reduce the dissonance and achieve consonance . . . I am proposing that dissonance . . . is a motivating factor in its own right.
>
> (Festinger 1957, p. 3)

Many teachers live with this feeling of dissonance daily, which is very frustrating. It has been our experience that for every teacher who is traditionally based and/or resistant to change, there are many others who would give anything to be able to reshape their jobs.

Intellectual reasons

Ideas for ways of changing may come from outside sources; a teacher may pick up a good book or read an article in an educational journal which stimulates her thinking. A professional course might have the same effect, or a good lecture or in-service presentation. Even the informality of staffroom conversation can generate new ideas or encourage a teacher to try something different. Thus, a teacher might take a lateral step in her thinking about education, and might redefine her objectives.

Ideological reasons

A teacher may have a set of values, grounded in religion, politics, or philosophy, which tells him that kids are human, and therefore precious, autonomous, bursting with potential and inherently to be respected. Within his present teaching situation, this teacher may experience a clash of values, finding himself limited in the way he can operate, either because of the system he is in, or because of the limitations of his training. His conscience may then motivate him to change. One such teacher has said to us:

> 'It was as if it had all built up behind a dam. I knew I wanted the kids to have more space to be human, and I wanted to be released from being so authoritarian and rigid, feeling that I had to control them all the time. When I heard about student-centred learning, it was like opening the floodgates, and my values were able to flow into my teaching.'

Professional pressures

It may be that teachers are put into a position where a change is expected of them. This may be due to a national or local initiative, such as, in our case, TVEI. It may be due to a new White Paper, or to some trend in educational philosophy. More probably, a head of department joins the staff with new ideas, or a new examination syllabus has been adopted, or the policy of the school changes because the headmaster has been on a course. Sometimes an inspector or advisory teacher will offer advice which says, 'It's time you changed your ways'.

Natural reasons

The view of life and human nature which underlies student-centred learning assumes that everyone has a natural, healthy, innate tendency to want to learn and grow and change. This is, perhaps, the strongest motivation of all.

2 Establishing trust

Since what we are trying to establish in the classroom is open communication and the confidence to take risks which will promote growth, the degree of trust which exists may have to be increased.

In order to establish greater trust in the classroom, the teacher may have to begin deliberately behaving in a more trustworthy manner. First of all, people do not usually trust those who tower above them, or shout at them down rows of desks; so the teacher can start by sitting down with the students and actually talking to them. Instead of expounding the 'absolute truth', she can begin sharing with them her perception of the truth as she sees it at that moment.

Time and again we have experienced the phenomenon of telling the truth about what we are feeling and thinking at the moment, and being met with increased openness and evident respect on the part of the student. Children can be acutely sensitive to lies and evasion, and perceptive about identifying the 'ring of truth' when they hear it. If they think they are being lied to they may lose respect for the teacher. This can lead to an attitude of 'Why should I do what he tells me? He's a liar.'

Children can be acutely sensitive to lies and evasion, and perceptive about identifying the ring of truth when they hear it

The teacher needs to be honest about the changes she is planning to introduce, and what she hopes to accomplish by doing so. The teacher will probably be the one to take the first steps. The minute she starts to talk to the students in a different manner, including them in decisions, choices, and plans, the level of trust tends to go up, regardless, perhaps, of some initial suspicion. And if the teacher actually tells the truth, such as: 'I've just been on a course . . .', or 'I've just read a new book . . .' and 'I want to try out some of these new ideas, and I hope you'll like them and enjoy them' (*not*, 'Now today we're going to do something different', without any explanation), then the toe is in the water, and the changes have already begun.

This is the time when the teacher begins to be seen as fallible, even vulnerable; she is beginning to let her halo slip. She is saying, 'This is as new to me as it is to you. I've always been taught the same way as you, in the traditional manner. I don't know if this is going to work, but I'll be asking you all the way along whether you think it works or not.' Everyone in the group is allowed to make mistakes without being criticised or mocked. Each mistake is seen as a learning point; none is ever wasted.

A partnership has now begun; as the teacher changes, so the students respond. As trust grows, motivation and responsibility increase. It is a symbiotic progression. The teacher, through her honesty, creates an increasing tendency on the part of the students to be honest.

As well as honesty, the elements of trust include:

confidentiality
reliability
lack of manipulation
keeping agreements
unconditional positive regard
warmth and love
direct communication

A violation of trust would be to talk about students in a gossipy way in the staffroom, and to tell outside the group confidences that were shared within the group. If a teacher invites confidences and then succumbs to temptation or pressure to disclose information to colleagues, he may not be able to maintain the level of trust within the group.

One of the most common and destructive violations of trust is the use of sarcasm, which we have mentioned earlier. Without labouring the point further, we would emphasise that direct and clear communication is at the heart of a trusting relationship; sarcasm has no place there.

3 Assessment

> Wherever you want to go, you have no choice but to start from where you are. (Popper, Magee 1973, p. 103)

But how to assess where we are, before we go anywhere else?

To start with the teacher: how can he objectively examine his own teaching style? We are suggesting several possible ways:

a Ask a colleague to observe. You can use various instruments for observation which are already available (e.g. Flanders and Amidon, *Interaction Analysis*) or you can devise your own.
b Use the 'do-it-yourself' *Assessment Quiz* on p. 241.
c Make an audio or video recording of yourself while you are teaching.
d Ask the students to assess you; devise a questionnaire together.
e Do the *Alter Ego* games on p. 248 ff.

What about group assessment?

a Do a round of *Resent and Appreciate* (see p. 34).
b Use student assessment forms (p. 243 ff.).
c Devise your own forms.
d With the students, brainstorm negative and positive aspects of the learning environment.

To be effective, assessment must be a continuous process, using a variety of techniques.

It is no use coming into the group and saying to its members, be they teachers or students, or even to yourself, 'We're doing things the wrong way; we should be like *that*'. This is a critical attitude which is threatening to everyone concerned, and usually creates resistance. If the group is invited to take a clear look at the whole picture of the way things are now, the desired changes will make themselves apparent, and will therefore probably be more acceptable. Whatever criteria the group may establish, we have one favourite question we like to ask, and that is: *Does it work?* By this we mean: Is everyone getting what they want, and is the group functioning properly? So, 'Does it work?' is a shorthand way of saying to ourselves, or to the group: Is the strategy we are assessing producing the desired results?

Doing assessment together builds the partnership and generates greater trust. It will probably be obvious by now that the first three steps: motivation, trust and assessment, are clearly interwoven. They depend upon each other, and grow simultaneously.

4 Accepting resistance

Resistance to a student-centred approach will probably arise within the teacher over such issues as:

- I am not the fountain of all knowledge any more.
- I feel like a spare part. I'm not doing my job.

- I'll lose control.
- I don't have the necessary skills.
- Familiarity breeds contempt; they won't respect me any more.
- They won't get their work done, or pass their exams.
- I am responsible for their achievement.

In most cases the teacher will probably not want to dive into the student-centred pool at the deep end. Change may be gradual: the toe is in the water . . . it's not too cold . . . up to the ankles . . . a bit of success . . . over the waist . . . feels good . . . look at me, I'm swimming!

With training, with reassurance and support, with academic accomplishment, the little successes promote confidence. This will only come through experience; we would not expect all resistance to go until the teacher has accumulated considerable evidence that the new methods *work*. Even then, doubts come flooding back; but all teachers experience ups and downs, whatever methods they may use.

Besides, you can always splash back to the safety of the shore, by moving towards the traditional end of the continuum. There is no need to drown!

Dealing with anyone's resistance, including your own, does not have to be a battle. In fact, if you fight, it is inclined to harden. If resistance is met with acceptance, it tends to dissipate. Whatever the resistance is, it needs to be first *expressed* then heard and accepted. There is then no conflict with the source of resistance, be it external or internal.

Beware of saying to yourself 'We shouldn't be feeling this way'; give yourselves permission to feel what you are feeling. Do the same for the rest of the group, or you will increase their resistance. Try acknowledging to yourselves: 'It is OK for us to be feeling this way. We can feel resistance and still go ahead'.

Steven, an RE teacher, told us about the following incident, which serves as a good example. Imagine a fifth year RE group who had to complete projects for external assessment, which they were doing outside class time. Neither the teacher nor the class was feeling enthusiastic about getting them done and a lot of reluctance and negativity was being generated. Steven was beginning to feel very guilty about letting time go by without much being achieved, and he felt that he had failed in motivating the kids. He was, on the one hand, feeling responsible, and on the other hand feeling cross that the students were not taking responsibility themselves.

Finally Steven decided to be honest about how he felt, and to invite the rest of the group to do the same, to get all the resistance out in the open. They sat in a circle and assessed the situation. At the end of the meeting, he felt at peace and the group had agreed to set aside regular time in class to continue the work. After this, the work progressed steadily and the task was finished on time.

There was just one fly in the ointment. One student continued to feel resistant with 'I never wanted to do a project in the first place' and 'I can't do it; it's too hard.' Steven forgot to do Active Listening and tried to placate the lad with empty phrases like 'Oh, don't feel like that. You can do it. It's too late to change now. You'll have to put up with it and make the most of it.' The student struggled with the project to the end and barely fulfilled the requirements.

There may also be resistance from the students, who may well say:

> "We need you to tell us what to do."
> "We won't finish our work or pass our exams."
> "We've never done this before; we don't know how to do it."
> "You're paid to tell us the right answers."

These comments, too, must be heard and accepted.

5 Awareness

In student-centred learning, the route ahead is not mapped out in advance. Preparation consists of internal readiness, willingness to explore and experiment. The ultimate goal, such as an exam, folder, or presentation, may be in sight, but the means of achieving it are open to negotiation. Students and teacher draw the map together.

The very act of planning and negotiating together evokes in the student an awareness that she is now the owner of her learning. If her opinions and ideas are valued, she must be a valuable person. If she is expected to take responsibility, she must be a responsible person. Her awareness of her capabilities is changing. Along with this, there may be an awareness of old habits or ways of perceiving herself which have been getting in her way and which can be revised. So, old scripts like 'I always give up before I finish an assignment' can be updated to 'I *used to* give up before the end; now I tend to complete my work'.

The language change and the behaviour change are interwoven; they cause and enhance each other.

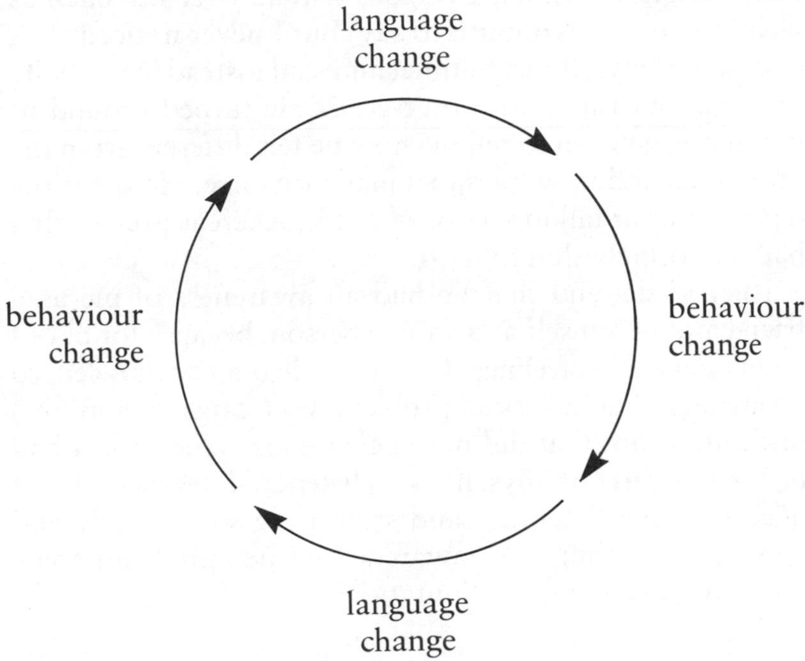

This is where Theory Y comes in again (see p. 24) The more people are given responsibility, the more they accept it and then seek it. Thus, each of our seven steps builds upon the other and interacts to produce change.

Students' awareness of their actual capabilities and potential will not come through half-truths or empty reassurances. It comes back to the teacher's responsibility to tell the truth. A teacher's experience:

> 'In the early days of my teaching, I had a student who became a friend of our family, who used to come to our house, play with our kids and sometimes go swimming with us. On several occasions he mentioned feeling very self-conscious about his spots. He would mention them to me and I would say 'Oh David, I don't even notice your spots', or 'Dave, you are very handsome: I'm sure no-one thinks anything of your spots'. David would invariably stop the conversation at that point: he knew I was lying.
>
> Then I started training as a counsellor and learned how to do Active Listening. I began to realise that people didn't necessarily need reassurance; all they really wanted was to be heard. One day when we were swimming, David said to

me 'I hate these spots; I've got them all over my back as well.' I opened my mouth to say 'But I never noticed . . .', and caught myself just in time, and said instead 'You really worry about this a lot don't you?' He turned around to face me and began to tell me how he felt different from the other kids and how his spots made it worse. He spent the next half hour talking to me about it, whereas previously I had unwittingly shut him off.

I felt at the end that he had an awareness of me as a friend and of himself as a valued person, because for once I hadn't denied his feelings. David also had an acknowledged awareness that his skin problem was causing him real difficulties, but that did not decrease his value. And I had become aware of myself as a listener. I learned that I needed to pay attention and stop being so motherly and comforting. Along with awareness of potential can come an awareness of present limitations.'

6 Problem solving

Building on the other steps, one of the ways in which the teacher turns the responsibility over to the students is to share all problems and the generating of solutions with the group. So, the teacher no longer loses sleep at home over what to do about X and how to handle Y, or what's going to happen if Z . . .? Now, the problem belongs to the whole group, though it may be the teacher who has to provide the opportunity to explore and solve it. As time goes on, especially if regular classroom meetings are held, the problem solving procedure will more and more be initiated by the students.

We have outlined a procedure for effective problem solving on p. 191 ff. Here we want to stress that the important ingredient is the teacher's attitude. The students quickly detect if the teacher is just pretending to share a problem which he has already solved in his own mind. There must be an inner change on the part of the teacher in which he says to himself *and means* 'This is not my problem to solve; I will have to *ask them*'. The teacher must get out of the habit of solitary decision making. When the teacher has a concern and is fairly sure that no-one in the class shares it to start with, and if he suddenly has a bright idea, then he needs to say to the group 'I feel . . .' and consult them about any plan he may have made. If the group do not think it is a good idea, he can ask them what they want instead.

Now, the problem belongs to the whole group, though it may be the teacher who has to provide the opportunity to explore and solve it

If the group makes decisions which the teacher ignores, responsibility and trust could lose momentum. It is not enough for the teacher merely to seek the students' opinions and then go ahcad and make the decision herself, for this turns the process into *consultation* rather than *participation*. Also, if ground rules have been firmly established democratically, there should be no need for the teacher to exercise a right of veto. For instance, if one of the ground rules is that we want to solve problems without punishment and the students propose a solution which involves punishment, the teacher only needs to point to the ground rules as a reminder and would not have to quash the decision by royal decree.

There are many areas of the curriculum in which problem solving methods seem naturally appropriate, such as mathematics, experimental science, and craft, design and technology. In addition, the problem solving approach is extremely useful in solving behaviour problems, in planning for group activities and work, in dealing with emotional issues which may arise, and indeed in working on any problem which may affect the group as a whole. It is, therefore, appropriate in any subject, course or class.

This way of approaching situations does not depend on a certain level of maturity or intellectual ability on the part of the students; in fact, it helps to develop both of these.

7 Contracts

Contracts are a culminating step, because all the other elements must be in operation before they can have any real meaning.

The teacher, as in all the other steps, sets an example by keeping any agreements he makes with the group. If he says 'I will have looked at your ideas and made comments on them and have them ready for Tuesday', he must keep his word. This is what we mean by deliberately behaving in a trustworthy manner, so as to build trust in the group.

The word 'contracts' may smack of Behaviourism and in schools contracts are sometimes used manipulatively, as a means of deliberately changing a student's behaviour towards a predetermined goal. Often such contracts have threats, such as detentions, or suspension or some loss of privilege, built into them if they are broken. We object to contracts being used in this way.

Rather, for us, they are a means of establishing ground rules and firming up agreements. They are negotiated with the students and established voluntarily with no consequences built in if they are broken. This does not mean that no consequences exist. For example, if five students are working together on a project, and they have made an agreement that each person will do a share of the work and have it finished by Tuesday, and one student has not completed his task, it is not the teacher's responsibility to step in and punish him. The student will have to negotiate with the rest of his small group. If a conflict occurs, the teacher may have to mediate in the negotiations. It may then develop into a problem solving session. Perhaps the teacher may suggest a round of resentments followed by a round of 'What do we want to do about this?'

At the close of a lesson, it is useful to have an agreement within the group about what is to be the way forward. Then there will be a feeling of continuity, trust, clarity and agreed purpose. If it is the last meeting of term, or the end of a project, we would want to have a feeling of closure, of completion, and also a contract about the direction in which we are intending to move. The two factors, completion and contracts, can provide a synthesis of satisfaction for now and optimism for the future.

These, then, are what we call the *seven steps to change*.

Everyday stumbling blocks

Of course progress is not always achieved in easy stages; with individuals and with groups, obstacles do appear. In this section we will identify some of the more common everyday sorts of negativity and barriers which block the seven steps to change.

Experience of working with individuals and classroom groups using student-centred methods has shown us that we can usually proceed fairly smoothly through the seven interrelated stages with only minor setbacks; resistance, the major obstacle, is an expected and healthy part of the process. Together the group is a force which can deal with some of the objects in its path. Since resistance is viewed as a necessary step in the process of change, it is not regarded as a deterrent.

However, each of the seven stages has an opposite, or polarity, and it is these negative factors which get in the way of progress. These polarities can belong to the student, to the teacher, or to the relationship between them.

Polarities

Positive Steps	*Possible Aspects of Resistance*
1 *Motivation*	energy loss indifference apathy being stuck hidden rewards for not changing helplessness complacency superficial adaptation dynamic conservatism
2 *Establishing Trust*	cynicism duplicity competition sarcasm manipulation defensiveness secretiveness

3 *Assessment*	predetermined ideas misconceptions about how things are ignoring new factors reaction rather than pro-action indoctrination fear denial
4 *Accepting Resistance*	depression apathy pretence lack of responsibility or blame 'It doesn't really matter'
5 *Awareness*	lack of awareness blindness repression nose-to-the-grindstone looking for short-term solutions habit
6 *Problem Solving*	powerlessness tunnel vision lack of imagination linear (not lateral) thinking builds on errors, to enshrine ineffective practice previous investment in outcomes
7 *Contracts*	unreliability failure to keep agreements hidden agenda unrevealed clauses duplicity

Any of these blocks may appear in a relationship in which the aims involve change of behaviour or attitude. When they appear, they become the short-term focus of the work, and they can be recognised and dealt with; in other words, a mini-process involving the same steps will develop, with the new block as its central issue.

Once again we would like to emphasise that the seven steps do not occur in any particular order, but are overlapping, and are often experienced simultaneously.

But what about the system?

One fundamental problem in introducing participatory methods has not yet been discussed in this chapter: no matter how committed teachers may be, they are working within a system which is highly resistant to change, and in which they usually do not have the power to make decisions in favour of innovation. Even if they did, as Hargreaves says, the system needs changing both from below and from above.

> All the de-schoolers are advocating fundamental changes in Western society's culture and structure as well as in the educational system, and I think they are right when they suggest that there are urgent educational changes needed which cannot wait until other social and economic changes have paved the way. I think they are wrong in implying that massive educational reforms can be effected without at least a few major concomitant social and economic changes. Given the present power structure, we can expect few radical innovations from Parliament, from the Department of Education and Science, from local Chief Education Officers and their Education Committees. Certainly if the reforms are to be made by teachers and are likely to affect them, then changes will be neither sudden nor dramatic. Piecemeal reform and slow, sparse innovation is the more likely development. Educational and social evils do go hand in hand, and we need a growing awareness of this combined with a willingness to attempt radical and speedy solutions. (Hargreaves 1972, p. 423)

John Naisbitt, an American researcher and consultant, in analysing the predominating content of the media, identified several major trends and concerns of the 1980s; similar trends are recognised in Britain. They are the topics which take up the most space in newspaper columns and on television and radio. His book, *Megatrends* (1984, pp. 1–2), outlines ten of these and explores their implications. We have selected a few which seem relevant to this chapter. (Our italics.)

- Although we continue to think we live in an industrial society, we have in fact changed to an economy based on the creation and distribution of *information*.
- We are moving in the dual directions of *high tech/high touch*,

matching each new technology with a compensatory human response.

- In cities and states, in small organisations and sub-divisions, we have rediscovered the ability to act innovatively and to achieve results – *from the bottom up*.
- We are shifting from institutional help to more *self-reliance* in all aspects of our lives.
- We are giving up our dependence on hierarchical structures in favour of *informal networks*.

If we pay attention to these trends, we may notice that they create a climate of innovation. This is the context in which educational change is taking place. Let us look at two of the trends.

Networks

For our purposes, a network is 'an organisation such that any point in it can be the centre' (Lecture by Werner Erhard).

In schools, informal networks may already be in existence. Students who participate in the Duke of Edinburgh's Award Scheme would be one example. Students who meet every week to rehearse a play would be another; those who all play football together every day at lunchtime would be a third. One student could belong to all three networks. These would be self-selected, loosely organised or temporary contacts.

Informal networks may already exist among teachers as well. The teachers who meet for coffee every day in the same corner of the staffroom, or those who run an after-school club, or those who may have a common concern and form a working party, would be other examples.

More formal networks also exist; the Joint Management Team, Faculty Meetings, and many more.

Naisbitt sees networks as a very potent force for change.

> Simply stated, networks are people talking to each other, sharing ideas, information and resources. The point is often made that networking is a verb, not a noun . . . Networks exist to foster self-help, to exchange information, to change society, to improve productivity and work life, and to share resources. They are structured to transmit information in a way that is quicker, more high-touch, and more energy efficient than any other process we know.
>
> (Naisbitt 1984, pp. 192–3)

Using the Birmgingham project as a concrete example, we can see how the networking trend worked to our advantage. There was an existing network of eight TVEI schools, from which a need had arisen and been identified by the teachers on the Staff Development Panel, for training in participatory learning methods; teachers found that they did not have the skills to fulfil the intentions of TVEI.

A consultant was appointed to provide this training, and to act as a catalyst for change in the authority. Her first priority was to organise a new network of interested teachers, again self-selected; this became known as the Core Group. (We would like to remind you that such a catalytic agent is not essential to the formation of an effective network, but in this case it helped to speed up the process.)

The network will continue when the consultant is gone; part of her brief was to make sure that this would happen, and an essential element of the project has been to set up a training network for the future.

In your school, college, or LEA, networks may already exist which provide natural channels of communication, or which may become natural change agents. If not, it would be the priority of those with the motivation to innovate to form a network.

> The vertical to horizontal power shift that networks bring about will be enormously liberating for individuals. Hierarchies promote moving up and getting ahead, producing stress, tension, and anxiety. Networking empowers the individual, and people in networks tend to nurture one another.
> *In the network environment, rewards come by empowering others, not by climbing over them.*
>
> (Naisbitt 1984, p. 204)

High-touch

> The more technology we introduce into society, the more people will aggregate, will want to be with other people.
>
> (Naisbitt 1984, p. 45)

This is Naisbitt's principle of high-tech/high-touch. People do not want to be dehumanised, to relate only to machines; they will compensate for the new micro-electronic world by investing in relationships.

We do not wish to present here yet another argument for student-centred learning, but it does seem that the time is ripe for increased participation because it increases a sense of human worth and value.

This trend creates a climate of acceptance for participatory learning methods. Also, in a high-touch culture, networks can flourish and innovation through relationships of a non-hierarchical nature is more likely.

An example of change in a single school

Schools and colleges are complex organisations, with complicated pyramids built of departments, faculties, and various levels of teaching staff and other workers. Even a small school is not a simple organisation, but let us view it for the moment as a single pyramid.

The small school where I used to teach in California had 300 pupils in 12 classrooms, aged 5–11, and had a pyramid like this contained within its walls:

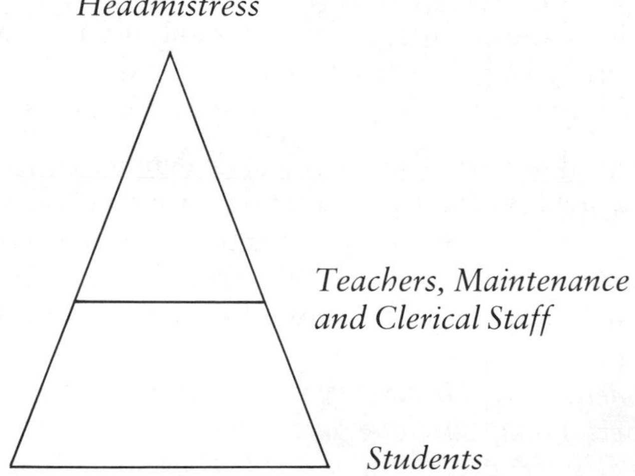

Of course the school did not stand isolated in its own playground; it also fitted into a much larger structure of: LEA, Santa Clara County, the State of California, and Central Government.

I was a classroom teacher when a new headmistress came to our school and began, quite methodically, to change the way it was working. She held a staff meeting and told us that she had some new ideas, and was counting on enlisting our cooperation. She asked us to describe the school, and how it worked, and tell her about the things we liked and did not like (assessment). This was not a school in a state of crisis, and as Nisbet says:

> . . . the school which is well placed to try out a new idea is one in which there are already existing good channels of communication . . . and the capacity to bring problems out into the open. (Nisbet 1974, p. 3)

Our school would have fitted that description, so the headmistress was not faced with as many problems of innovation as she might have been in a less positive climate.

She instituted a new kind of staff meeting, structured along person-centred lines; we took turns chairing it, and the chairperson for the week collected items for the agenda. We kept strictly to time limits. We had a chance to air resentments and share appreciations (establishing trust). The headmistress kept a fairly low profile except when it was her turn to run the meeting; however, she did insist on some changes in policy. For instance, corporal punishment was abolished completely, and all punishment avoided as much as possible; she persistently explained her reasons for this policy (explaining ground rules).

A student council was formed, and students participated, with the help of a staff consultant, in developing responsibilities and rights of students (problem solving at all levels).

The atmosphere in the school began to change for the better. Discipline problems decreased; academic improvement was not formally measured, but was reported by teachers; teachers expressed loyalty to the headmistress and to colleagues; meetings were interesting and for the most part free of conflict. We learned to listen to each other. Problem solving structures were used in staff meetings and in classrooms, and even the appearance of the school improved; less vandalism, less litter; kids were planting vegetable gardens and growing flowers. These changes happened over a three-year period before I moved to a high school.

Change in a wider context

This was an example of change in a single pyramid organisation, initiated by a single person, but where participation was encouraged at all levels. We have simplified a complex process. In an organisation consisting of *many* hierarchies we would go about implementing change using the same methods, but would be initiating movements on a much larger scale.

In the figure below, the Xs signify organisations where one person can have considerable impact on initiating change. In the more complex systems, one person can still act, but they would either have to have enormous power, or would have to be enlisting support and creating a team effort.

Indivividuals	Loose network of colleagues	Tight single organisation (a school)	Unstructured organisation (a consortium of schools, geographical grouping, TVEI)	LEA	Government or Political Party
X	X	X			

Top-down or bottom-up?

Top-down innovation does not always work well, because there may be resistance to ideas imposed from above, and because the people at the top are often not well enough informed about the conditions at ground level.

In the case of the Californian school which we described, the innovation began with one person, but her first step was to involve everyone concerned, *at every level.* She broke down the traditional hierarchy to create a combined effort.

A bottom-up scheme for introducing change is exciting, because ordinary people are demonstrating that they care about an issue, that they are not apathetic. But there is always the danger of the big hammer of power crashing down from above, stopping the action and leaving people feeling defeated, crushed and powerless. There was an incident in a different school in California, where 200 students, in a supposedly democratically-run school, staged a sit-in, protesting over a small issue: they wanted some vending machines installed for drinks and snacks, using Student Council funds. They sat down on the grass after lunch, and refused to come in to class. The Principal raged around through the crowd for a bit, ordering them to move and, when they didn't, he set up a public address system and threatened them all with suspension if they weren't in class in three minutes. Looking ashamed, and probably imagining what their parents would do if they were suspended, they stood up and straggled back to class, joining their less courageous friends who had not attempted the sit-in. The big hammer strikes again!

In a paper on in-service training, David Settle, Director of Professional Support Services for Birmingham, wrote:

> Past evidence indicates that where change is introduced without the support of the classroom teacher it may flourish momentarily, based on the personal credibility of the initiators, but there will be no sustained integration into normal practice . . . The message for me is clear. As long as learners, whether they be teachers within INSET or pupils in classrooms, remain as mere receivers of someone else's view of what they need to know, to become, to be, then the outcomes will be limited to that which is visible today: teachers with a dwindling commitment to their work and pupils who cannot wait to rid themselves of school, taking with them the bare remnants of 11 years' learning which for them had no explained purpose and in which they had no say, either in what was to be learned or how the learning would take place.

We would take David Settle's theme one step further; we agree that the support of the teachers is needed if innovation is to succeed, but it will have an even better chance to flourish if support comes from *all levels* of the system, including managers, and especially from the students or clients of the system.

We asked a group of fifth year students how they saw the hierarchy of their school, not necessarily in terms of power, but in terms of whose needs were being met, *whose convenience* was being considered. This is the model they produced:

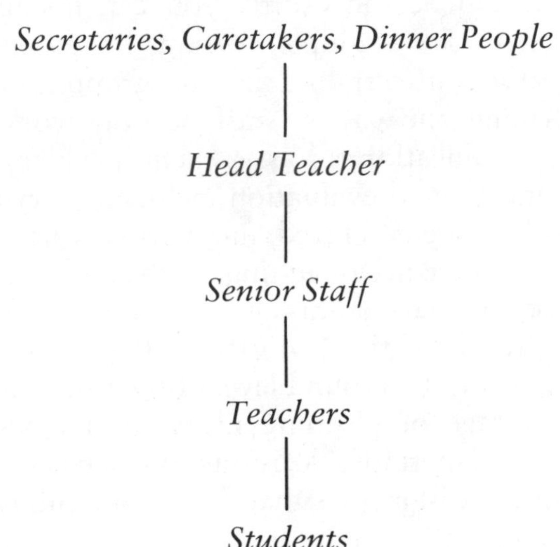

If the needs of the students were being given primary consideration, the model would have to look like this:

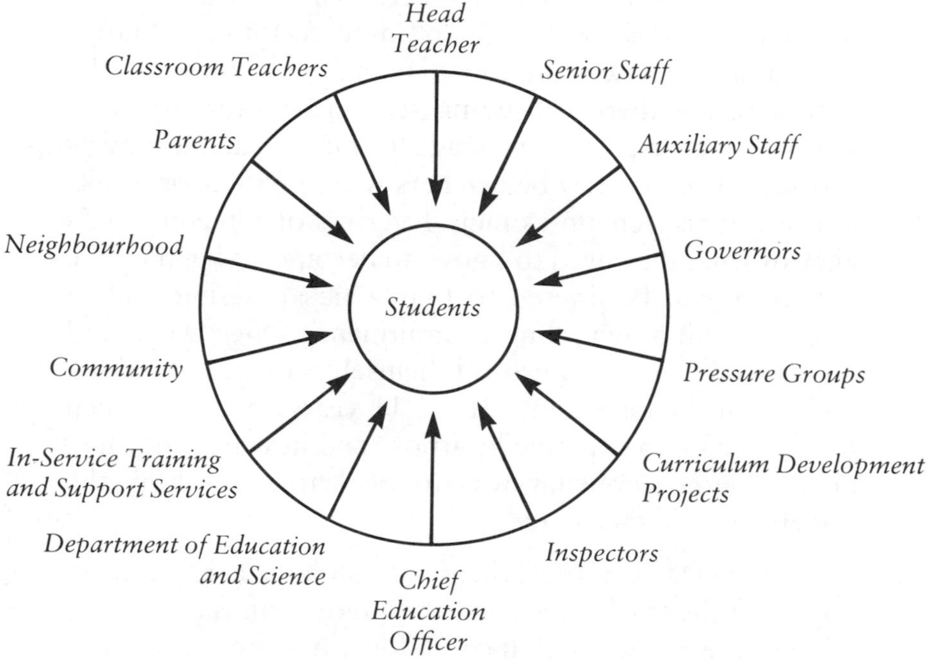

To be really accurate, the above diagram would have to have arrows flowing in many more directions; but we want to emphasise the radical nature of a student-centred model where all the energies of everyone concerned are focused on the needs of the students themselves. If you visualise the above model as a network, so that any point on it can be the centre, you can imagine innovation starting everywhere. For example, perhaps the parents might want separate education for certain religious groups, or the teachers might want to change the way the staff meetings work.

If lines of communication for assessment, problem solving, planning, implementation and evaluation included everyone, and if the system were truly student-centred, innovation, whatever its source, would stand a better chance of getting off the ground.

To summarise the main points: a bottom-up model of change is sensitive to the needs of the majority of the people involved, the clients, or workers on the ground level of the usual sort of pyramid. It has the advantage of gleaning ideas from a wide variety of different angles, and therefore decisions can be based on much more informed thinking. Naisbitt says that there is a trend in this direction in America:

> The failure of centralized, top-down solutions has been accompanied by a huge upsurge in grassroots political activity everywhere in the United States. Some 20 million Americans are now organized around issues of local concern. (Naisbitt 1984, p. 113)

However, the two major weaknesses of a bottom-up model are the lack of resources and the lack of power; power to prevent intervention from above, and power to carry out executive decisions, to make things happen, and to overcome resistance. Zimbardo et al. put it this way:

> Resistance to change in a social, political or economic system is the analogue of resistance to persuasion in the individual – multiplied by a hard-head factor of 10^{10} . . . (Zimbardo et al. 1977, p. 195)

A strictly top-down model has the advantage of executive power and greater resources behind it, and this ought not to be underestimated no matter how enthusiastic or optimistic we innovators might be. Later in the chapter we will explore some of the major obstacles which can arise in the process of mobilising initiative in the face of that power at the top. But the top-down model does have major weaknesses too, in that it is insensitive to the needs, demands, and ideas of the people who will be most affected by the change. In fact, Naisbitt claims that initiatives which are taken

> by the state or neighbourhood in the absence of an effective top-down solution . . . have staying power . . . are resistant to top-down intervention and become models for others still grappling with the problems. (Naisbitt 1984, p. 112)

There are many other arguments in both directions in the literature. *We are arguing in favour of a combined model with involvement at all levels.*

The seven steps applied

The seven steps described earlier in the chapter can also be applied to larger systems. The change agent mentioned below could be anyone in the network who is setting out to innovate.

Motivation — Someone in an organisation decides that change is necessary, that the systems being employed do not *work*, i.e. do not work to the organisation's net advantage, in terms of cost effectiveness, morale, good health, productivity, working conditions, positive energy or spirit.

Establishing trust — The person wanting to institute change can work to establish trust, open communication, partnership, at all levels of the organisation. Networks in which responsibility is shared can be established to replace rigid hierarchies; people can be valued and consulted at every level, as a start. Not everyone will *want* to be consulted, especially at first; this has to be acceptable as well; people can opt out *or* in.

Assessment — Change agent can get feedback from all parts of an organisation, can ask members to take stock of what is happening now, what is not working, what solutions have been tried in the past.

Change agent is not critical, and is looking for the most divergent feedback.

Resistance — Change agent helps the organisation see what it is getting from the status quo, from *not* changing. Blame, criticism and praise are avoided, resistance is used as part of the process. People are less likely to stay stuck when they see others participating in movement.

Awareness — Focusing on areas of the organisation where problems are noticed, figures emerge from the background, people learn, notice and discover, become more conscious of their environment, and of their own behaviour within it.

Problem solving — People in networks throughout the organisation can use their pooled ideas and extended imaginations to come up with new solutions, new ways of behaving. Worker participation promotes change at all levels. Lateral thinking is exponentially increased.

Contracts — Agreement is reached as to which new solutions will be tried. Everyone participates in re-focusing and revision. Change occurs in small, manageable steps which are open to continual evaluation by all concerned.

Our experience leads us to take a risk and suggest that our seven steps can work on a scale larger than the single classroom, that is, in a whole school, college, an LEA, or any other large organisation.

> Looking at larger social systems, we find as common problems impasses, escalations, and grand programs that are structurally identical to those encountered in the more personal areas of human life . . .
>
> On the other hand, it should not be assumed beforehand that our approach will be impossibly difficult to apply to large systems just because they have posed great difficulties to other approaches – especially if these approaches were of the same problem-engendering nature as the ones we have studied. The only reliable basis for judging the value of a method remains the result achieved by its application.
> (Watzlawyck 1974, pp. 158–9)

How our system would work in a school

Imagine:

1 The Head of Science in a large comprehensive school goes on a course in which student-centred learning methods are demonstrated and discussed. He is fired with motivation to change his own teaching style, and to pass the word on to his colleagues in his department. *(Motivation)*
2 Some of his colleagues are mildly interested, but see that they would need support and in-service training. Others are very cynical about it; their views are listened to and they are told that they are not being required to change. The headmaster is approached, and gives his approval to take it further. He may or may not be convinced himself. *(Assessment, Motivation, Resistance)*
3 An expert within the authority is consulted; this could be anyone with the appropriate skills, e.g. another classroom teacher, or someone specifically appointed to promote these kinds of methods in the authority. A contract and goals are negotiated. *(Problem solving, Contracts)*
4 The consultant comes into the school, and facilitates a careful assessment of the present situation. *(Assessment)*
5 A network is established by publicising the availability of training

within the school, or even beyond it. Participation is encouraged from all levels of the system. There is an initial in-service meeting. The head attends and finds himself very interested. *(Motivation, Establishing trust)*

6 The assessment made earlier is brought out into the open and discussed. The outside consultant leads a series of exercises designed to promote good communication and to build trust within this training group. *(Assessment, Awareness, Trust)*

7 An agenda for future training is generated within the group and ways of implementing the new methods at different levels of the school structure are created and tried, e.g. Governors' meetings, staff meetings, senior management meetings, student council meetings, tutorial times. *(Problem solving)*

8 Everyone who is interested is encouraged to participate at all stages of this exercise. The trainer bases all exercises upon the stated needs of the group, and gradually begins to render herself obsolete, so that the new system is self-perpetuating. The trainees become increasingly responsible for their own development, and for the future dissemination of these methods. *(Awareness, Problem solving)*

Plans have to be made to form new networks and to share publicly what has been happening in this school.

The Head of Science is the internal change agent and the consultant or trainer is the external one.

Finding allies, creating new networks

The model we have outlined above is meant to demonstrate that the seven steps process designed for individual change can be adapted for use in complex organisations, and that when the organisation is very large it will take time and many innovators to make it work. Our experience has shown us that within almost any system we can find people who think as we do, and who only need some agreement, encouragement and support, as they are already motivated to make changes.

Dealing with the right/wrong trap

Why are people so doubtful about the widespread effectiveness of student-centred methods? The answer to this question, to our way of thinking, is that people want to be *right*. If we come along with a new method and demonstrate that it works, then in order to accept that, your mind has to reject some old ideas, and thus to admit that you have been doing something 'wrong' all these years. Or so many people think.

> What the mind does to survive is to try to keep itself intact, replay the same tapes, prove itself right. That becomes now the purpose of the mind: to survive by again and again proving itself right . . . the mind begins to do all it can to avoid dealing with the new material. It runs away from the training data the way you and I run from a burning building, and for the same reason: SURVIVAL.
>
> (Rhinehart 1976, p. 172)

Wanting to be right is another form of resistance. One way to deal with this resistance is to use it, to turn it to good advantage by exploring its payoffs and comparing it to other possible ways of behaving. Another way is to avoid the whole concept of right/wrong, success/failure. Our approach when working with teachers, for instance, is: 'There are many different ways of encouraging learning. Perhaps you haven't heard of the one that we're offering, and you might like to explore it. It belongs on a continuum of:

traditional didactic ◄————————————► student-centred participatory

methods of teaching, and you can place yourself anywhere on that continuum once you determine what is comfortable for you, and once you are familiar with the whole range of methods. While it is true that we belong on the far right edge of that particular continuum, we know that not everyone is comfortable there. But until you are familiar with the whole range, you cannot make an informed choice.' When we take this stance, instead of telling teachers they have been doing it wrong, we usually get a positive response.

Fitting the culture

The new system or innovation should be designed to fit the culture of the existing institution.

> Anyone who has spent time with any variety of organisations, or worked in more than two or three, will have been struck by the differing atmospheres, the differing ways of doing things, the differing levels of energy, of individual freedom, of kinds of personality. For organisations are as different and varied as the nations and societies

> of the world. They have differing cultures – sets of values and norms and beliefs – reflected in different structures and systems. And the cultures are affected by the events of the past and by the climate of the present, by the technology of the type of work, by their aims and the kind of people that work in them . . . modern theories of organisation are increasingly persuaded of *the wisdom of the appropriate*, of the match of people to systems, to task and environment, of inter-relations between all four, of what has come to be called the *systems* approach to management theory. This is a word sufficiently vague to cover all manner of specific approaches but it tends to connote inter-relationships, feedback mechanisms, and appropriateness of fit.
>
> (Handy 1976, p. 177)

'The wisdom of the appropriate' is a very appealing phrase to us; it embodies, once again, the principle of the client-centred approach: the way to find out what is appropriate in the way of innovation is to ask the people who will use it. Every school has its own culture, its own way of doing things, its own blend of social and racial mixtures. It has its own ethos, an atmosphere that you can pick up almost as soon as you walk through the door. So, you would not set out to innovate in the same way in any two schools.

Major obstacles

Overshadowing issues

What we have said so far may have sounded very positive and optimistic, which is how we prefer to be: for change agents to indulge in cynicism is self-defeating. This does not mean that we are naïve, or unaware of the tides of apathy, fear and doubt that are prevalent in society. We believe that there are many people working for positive change in the world, but the task of innovation is made all the more difficult by the serious and enormous negative forces that exist. Many people feel burdened by such overshadowing issues as:

- nuclear war, nuclear energy
- terrorism and war
- social inequalities
- unemployment
- industrial action

- presently incurable diseases, such as cancer and Aids
- inadequate provision for education and other services.

Most people would not put educational methods in the same sort of category of concern as the major social problems mentioned above; it is a small issue compared to those.

Because of the enormity of such problems, some people develop attitudes which say:

Why should I care; everything's in a mess anyway?

or I'm helpless against all those overwhelming pressures

or No one up there cares about me, so why should I bother about anyone else?

or Eat, drink and be merry, because there won't be a tomorrow anyway.

Power v. change

As Zimbardo et al. have said:

> Every change in one part of a system creates a reaction in another section. Even when you know how to produce a desired effect . . . there is one more obstacle to overcome before principles of change become policy-*power*. When new ideas are transplanted into policy, they invariably are opposed because change is threatening.
>
> (Zimbardo et al. 1977, p. 193)

Thus political controversy and resistance can cause paralysis of movement. Even when an innovation is initially encouraged from above, a change of power or control can cause the hammer to fall. As Naisbitt says:

> Power that is bestowed from the top down can be withdrawn if the donor's priorities change.
>
> (Naisbitt 1984, p. 112)

The force of tradition and dynamic conservatism

Tradition can be heartwarming and can bring people closer together. But it can also mean inertia. The deep-rooted traditions of didactic teaching and of punishment, for instance, can be of such specific use to people that they would be extremely difficult to change.

People sometimes fight to keep things the same because it costs less financially, involves less risk, and often entails less work. Often it seems that young people are keener on change than the old, who have more to lose and are more entrenched. Each generation sees the younger people wanting change 'for its own sake' partly just to be different from their elders, but also to sort out the injustices that they see in the old system. The optimal condition would be a synthesis of the best of the old ways and the best of the new ideas, but this is extremely difficult to achieve, partly because of the force of dynamic conservatism.

Determined optimism

These and many more forces are ever-present in our society. So, what stops us from turning into lemmings or sloths and just giving up the fight?

We are not intending to dismiss these serious problems when we assert that each person has his own way of dealing with the nightmare issues. Among many other ways, people choose:

- religion
- optimism
- despair
- escape
- joining causes and pressure groups
- fatalism and hedonism
- working very hard at innovation.

We choose what we call determined optimism; we do not want to live in an emotional state of cynicism or despair, so we work very hard to achieve what we consider to be worthwhile innovations, which address, on some small level, the major issues listed above. In fact, the more we are told, 'It can't be done', the more we want to work at doing whatever 'it' is at the moment. For us, and for many of our professional friends, the feeling is: *there is nothing else to do but keep working.*

It does not seem likely that there could be an easy way to counteract the hammer effect, that is, the use of power to squash an innovation which might threaten a precious status quo, either by legislating against it or by withholding resources. Certainly, by ourselves we do not have a ready strategy. What we do have is a growing conviction, based on experience of innovation and on increased familiarity with research regarding the initiation of change, that a multi-level team could find ways of warding off the hammer blows, or even enlisting the powerful forces onto its side.

A word of caution

In this opening section of the book we have been laying a theoretical foundation for the ideas and activities which follow. We want to end on a note of caution, lest the system we are advocating should emerge as a structure just as rigid, predetermined, and closed to innovation as the ones we are hoping to replace:

> In drawing our journey together to a close we must be cautious about urging you to go out and change the world. Idealists, freedom-fighters, self-actualizers, liberationists and revolutionaries are, under other attributional perspectives, mad dissidents, troublemakers, opportunists, and usurpers. To all would-be agents of social control, we say, do not demand that we give you our children to live in a world of *your* design even if you can *guarantee* they will emerge as saints not sinners, specialists and not nobodies. The world should be of *their* design, too, their world even if created by their follies, fantasies, and foibles. They must choose rationally to follow life's paths, not be chosen randomly to play out someone else's script. Most crucial is our realization that what you now ask to be *given*, you would *take* if and when you had enough power to do so. Our actions as agents of change must then be informed with knowledge, tempered with wisdom, and always infused with compassion. (Zimbardo et al. 1977, p. 195)

Section 2

REFLECTION

INTRODUCTION

Throughout the project, since we began writing and compiling, we have wanted to share the ownership of this book with the educators and students with whom we have been working. They took on the responsibility to varying degrees, depending upon how they each felt about the book, and whether they were personally excited by it, saw it as a tool which they would be able to use in the future, or in other words, felt they had a stake in it.

Section 2 is a compendium of their personal experiences, thoughts, poetry and essays which reflect the struggle and the tensions as well as the exhilaration of moving along new paths. The first part of the section is about the Core Group and what they experienced in coming together to become a force for learning in Birmingham. Some of the articles look back on lessons taught and lessons learned in school, making points which we hope can be useful to other teachers and students.

In this section we also present feedback from students who were asked what they thought of the ways in which we were now working with them; in many cases the students were very enthusiastic about the book itself, and about having their own opinions in print, as well as being very positive about student-centred learning.

We hope that this collection of thoughts and feelings will bring the book to life, because they are from, by and about real people who are deeply concerned with education and how to make it work better.

THE CORE GROUP

At the beginning of the Birmingham project, teachers with the motivation to explore student-centred learning methods were invited to join an intensive programme of training. This self-selected group bravely committed itself to a three-hour session each week for six months; it became known as the Core Group, for no particular reason, except that these teachers were at the heart of the venture. It was a title that was never intended to stick, but which was impossible to shake off. From the start, the group operated in a student-centred way, with Donna, the consultant to the LEA, acting as facilitator. A diet of group work, problem solving, discussion, rounds, games, role play, training inputs was devoured; apathy was rarely a problem.

Of the initial 30, a few dropped out, others joined, and in the end 26 reached the finishing post, an unusually large percentage for in-service training. On the way, members grew to love and trust each other, and developed together in a shared learning experience. Although the group consisted of classroom teachers, inspectors, advisory teachers, the Director of TVEI, and headmasters, hierarchical barriers tended to break down as we went along; they no longer mattered.

The Core Group did not end when the consultant left; a momentum and energy had been created, arising out of a passionate conviction that student-centred learning works. Some of the Group's members went on to be trainers, and so it became the seedbed out of which the innovation would grow.

Each week in the Core Group we asked someone to write their 'Reflections' on what had happened and how they felt about it. Sometimes, after the call for a volunteer, the silence was lengthy. Each week, the acknowledging applause was enthusiastic.

A dilemma experienced frequently by the group facilitator was how to achieve a balance between providing rigorous training and allowing awareness to arise that the group really was responsible for its own development. For example, on more than one occasion, the sessions seemed to meander, and one or two members announced that they were bored, as if it were the leader's fault, and her job to do something about it. The leader too was bored, and had chosen not to rescue the group from the quagmire. The responsibility was left where it belonged, with the group members.

The agenda for the Core Group

After some basic principles of student-centred learning had been introduced, the group brainstormed the kinds of skills they wanted to master during the course. At that moment, the group leader came up against what is a very typical problem in the classroom; the agenda which had been generated had, from her point of view, several glaring omissions, such as listening skills, enhancement of self-esteem, and others. So the leader added these to the agenda determined by the group, and then asked the group for their approval of the new list. There was no resistance; people actually seemed delighted.

Another dilemma was created by those in the group who repeatedly demanded to see 'where we were going', wanting an outline of what lay ahead, which is a practice at variance with the aims of student-centred learning, but which often occurs in school in the shape of syllabuses and exams. The fundamental principle is that if a demand is repeatedly made by members of the group the leader is obliged to take it seriously. So, an overall plan was produced and delivered, on the understanding that it could be changed if the group wished. Both the plan and the agenda are included here, as they were used in the Core Group.

Brainstorming the agenda

I, your friendly facilitator, have taken the liberty of dividing the list we generated into three categories:

1 The topics which received the most votes;
2 Other topics listed on the board;
3 Topics not chosen but which I consider absolutely essential as skills for student-centred learning.

1 aims
assessing our resources, human and physical
assessing our existing teaching skills
practical subjects, e.g. science ground rules
getting started on a student-centred approach
listening skills

2 counselling skills
parental awareness
expectations of pupils, parents, teachers
self-discipline
presentation of work
learning processes
work records
passing exams
feedback
self-awareness
evaluation
strategies across the school
social interaction
deeper introduction to the principles
transfer of learning
preparing for jobs

3 active listening skills
direct communication v. sarcasm
telling the truth
problem solving
assertiveness training
self-enhancement
self-esteem
value clarification methods
games and approaches, e.g. rounds, continua, small groups, feedback

The plan

One of the wonderful things about student-centred learning is that the agenda is very flexible: without a fixed agenda we can allow what happens to happen, and respond to immediate needs and wishes. (Unless, *of course*, there is an exam and a syllabus, which we have so far managed to avoid!)

However, there are some overall directions in which this course is headed, including developing skills in student-centred learning, becoming a cohesive group, and preparing to train other educators in these methods. The following is less an agenda, more of a long-term plan. Anything more specific we can develop together.

January to mid-February half-term:

- Getting-to-know-you, building trust and safety in the group.
- Increasing self-awareness and self-esteem.
- Working towards an understanding of student-centred learning.
- Active listening.
- Assertiveness.
- Problem solving.

Mid-February to Easter:

- Classroom management and discipline.
- Individualised instruction.

- Attitudinal change.
- Theory X and Theory Y.

Members of the group, singly or in pairs, begin inventing and leading parts of the sessions (and receiving feedback).

Easter to May half-term:

Every member of the group has a chance to lead the group and plan portions of the sessions, and receive feedback.

Mid-May to end June:

- Plan and organise training activities for next year.

Accepting responsibility in a student-centred group

One of the rare times when the facilitator took a very firm stand with the group occurred about half way through the series of meetings. The group had been consulted about whether or not they were willing to receive a visitor the following week, and had consented because they wanted to hear what he had to say: they had also been rehearsing, and reading about, guidelines for receiving visitors. But when he actually came everyone sat back waiting for someone else to welcome him, to offer him the now famous egg sandwiches and tea, and to introduce him to others. The group did not take the trouble to find out about him; once the session had started, they passively sat back and waited for him to deliver. We're not sure how he felt about this lack of welcome, but that is beside the point . . .

After he had gone, the facilitator asked the group how they felt they had received the visitor, and considerable controversy arose over the issue of whether or not they had avoided responsibility. This incident is reflected in the tirade which follows: it is included here because it embodies another typical classroom problem, the question of who in the group is responsible for how things go. The answer is *everybody*!

A student-centred tirade from a friendly facilitator

Every one of us is 100% responsible for how this group goes. We are not here to take responsibility for anyone else. If you managed to dominate this group, whoever you might be, I for one, would be very surprised . . . you can trust the people in this group to tell you now if you are getting in the way. All the rest is excuses:

- I am holding back so I don't say too much . . .
- I am holding back because I'm shy . . .
- I am holding back because I'm too old/too young/too thin/too fat/too clever/too stupid . . .
- Everyone else in the group is: cleverer/more experienced . . . funnier/prettier/more likeable/more important/less important/a better teacher . . . whiter/blacker/browner/bluer . . . more masculine/ more feminine . . . than I am!

You and I are here to be ourselves, fully, creatively, caringly, contributing to the group, each in our own way.

If you find the mathematics of 'Each of us is 100% responsible' too hard to grasp, then put it this way:

'I am 100% responsible for *me*.'

As facilitator I want to tell you that I believe there is *no* excuse for holding back in this group, not political, not hierarchical, not sexist, racist, or any other -ist. We are all here to be as fully ourselves as we can be, and to give of our best to each other.

A visit from Her Majesty's

On 29th April we received two HMIs as visitors. Having learned our lesson with the last visitor, we welcomed them properly, and then got on with the group activities. The HMIs were obviously sincerely interested, and non-judgmental, so when one of them asked 'How have you all changed as a result of being in the Core Group?', Carol-Anne suggested that we do a round of 'How I've changed', and we embarked upon it. It took a long time; people had a lot to tell; we include just a few of the comments here:

> 'I was previously very didactic in style. Being student-centred has made much more work for myself and the technicians (Physics). The way we work now is for students to brainstorm ways to tackle topics, rather than me making all the decisions. We usually finish a piece of work by evaluating how well it worked and how it could be improved.' (Eric)

'For years I've not been sure what teaching and learning is about. I've felt for a long time that I cannot teach anyone anything, but have not been sure where to go from this point. Although Information Technology and Science, my subjects, allow kids to do active learning, there was still something missing in my classes . . . students were not working together as a group. So we've worked on listening, getting rid of put downs and so on, and now the kids feel cheated if they've not had the chance to do an activity in each lesson which enhances self-concept and group identity.' (Dave)

'I was Drama-trained, and so much of this course has confirmed what I already knew or did. It has been a rejuvenation course. I now face the challenge of applying its principles to school management.' (Rhoma)

'There is a big difference between a subject lesson with a set syllabus, and working with volunteers on what they want to do. I like feeling that I *can* slide up and down the continuum, and that I do not *have to* be at one end or the other.' (Kay)

'I'm here because I'm interested in helping people to give their best. I want to learn new skills for myself and to pass on to others.' (Keith D)

'I came into TVEI because I wanted a new, dynamic, approach in my teaching. I didn't get it until this course. I had tried on my own to implement new strategies, e.g. group work, but without success. I can now see why and how that happened. Being in the Core Group has helped me to put everything into perspective. I want versatility, and I don't mind saying that I still use traditional methods at times, when I feel they are appropriate.' (Ali)

'I am finding student-centred methods very useful in dealing with teachers; for instance, active listening, assertiveness, and getting teachers to assess themselves on a continuum.' (Keith H)

'This Core Group course has given me a complete philosophy, and a means of support.' (Marian)

'My thoughts about education have been crystallised. I had always felt that what we did in school was inappropriate and that the best way to learn was by being involved. The Core Group has helped me solve some of my dilemmas.' (Tony)

Benefits of the Core Group

Towards the end of the course, members brainstormed what were the benefits of the Core Group.

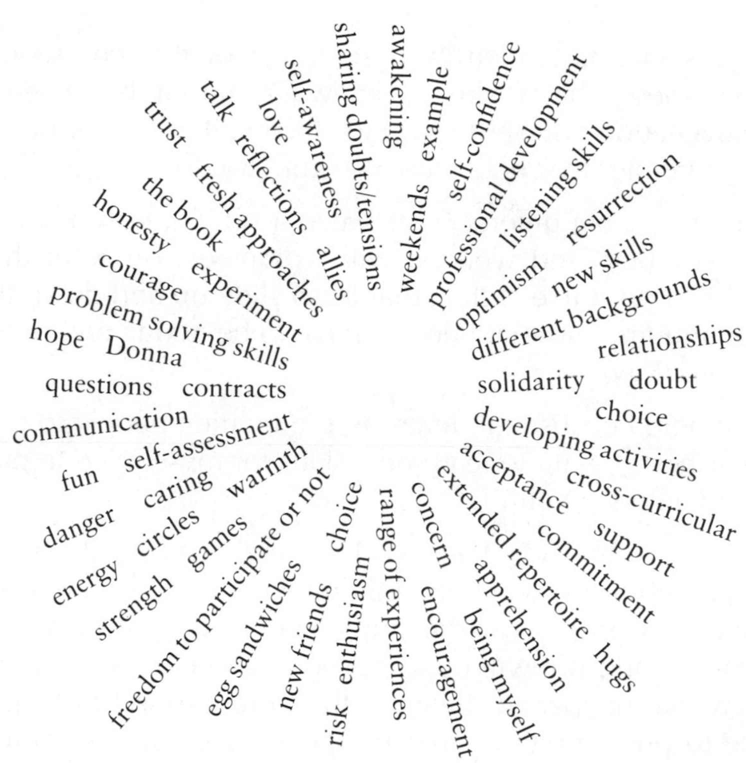

Island of ye CORIANS (as it appeared at the end of the Core Group course)

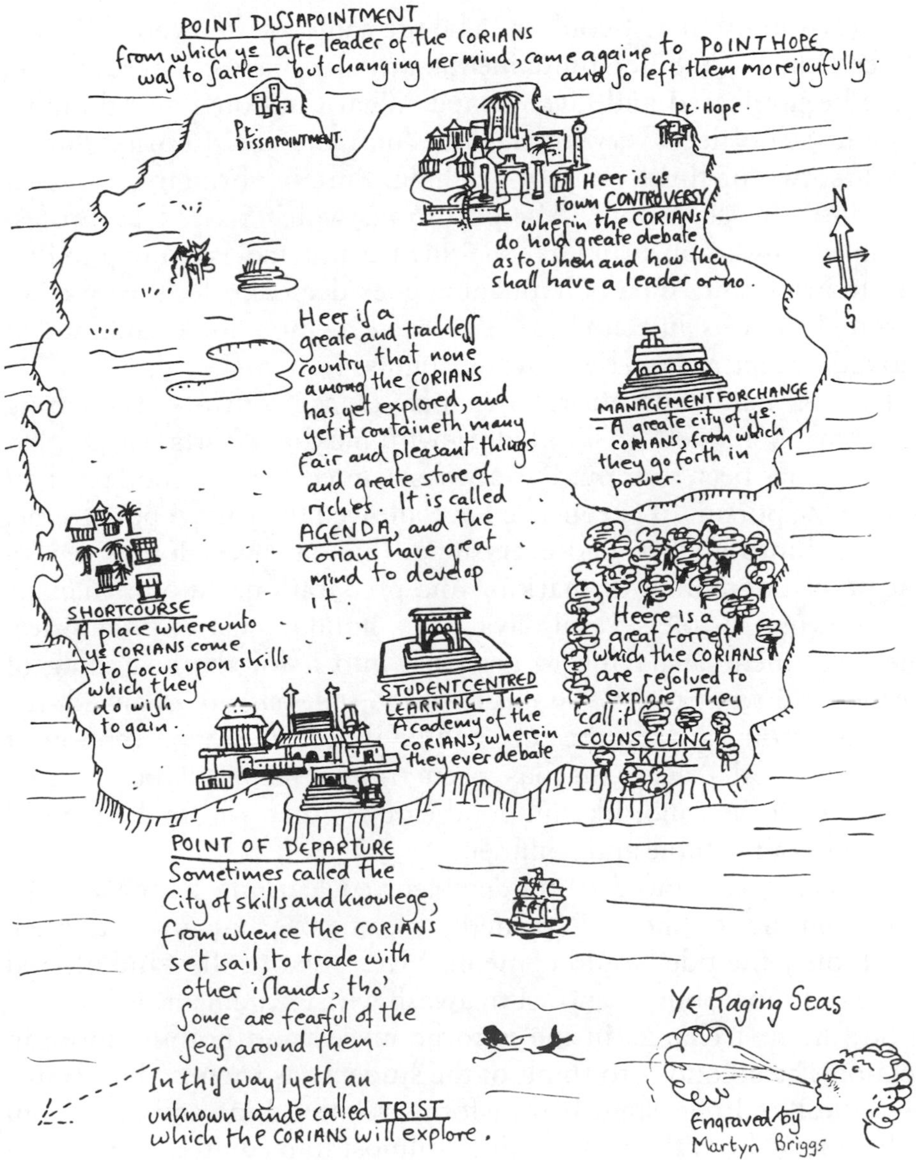
POINT DISSAPOINTMENT
from which ye laste leader of the CORIANS was to saile – but changing her mind, came againe to POINT HOPE and so left them more joyfully.
Pt. DISSAPOINTMENT.
Pt. Hope.
Heer is ye town CONTROVERSY wherin the CORIANS do hold greate debate as to when and how they shall have a leader or no.
N
S
Heer is a greate and trackless country that none among the CORIANS has yet explored, and yet it containeth many fair and pleasant things and greate store of riches. It is called AGENDA, and the Corians have great mind to develop it.
MANAGEMENT FORCHANGE – A greate city of ye CORIANS, from which they go forth in power.
SHORTCOURSE
A place whereunto ye CORIANS come to focus upon skills which they do wish to gain.
Heere is a great forrest which the CORIANS are resolved to explore. They call it COUNSELLING SKILLS
STUDENTCENTRED LEARNING – The Academy of the CORIANS, wherein they ever debate
POINT OF DEPARTURE
Sometimes called the City of skills and knowlege, from whence the CORIANS set sail, to trade with other islands, tho' some are fearful of the seas around them.
In this way lyeth an unknown lande called TRIST which the CORIANS will explore.
Ye Raging Seas
Engraved by Martyn Briggs

HERE I AM

Already I know that I could not be the same again, even if Donna never came back. Some fundamental attitudes have changed, others have been released and given shape. What I'm doing and thinking now in school feels very much to be 'me', the 'me' I buried during the first two or three years of teaching. I'm now bringing 'me-as-I-am' into the classroom. My posturing, which passed as professionalism, is disappearing like melting ice and 'me' is coming to life; I'm thawing out. What's happening goes deep and feels very comfortable. It feels like home – I've been away a long time and it looked strange at first, but now I recognise it.

I'm not making an effort to change; on the contrary, I'm letting go of making an effort. I'm fed up with making efforts. Up to now teaching has been a strain. I've always wanted to be a 'good teacher' and in the pursuit of excellence have allowed the role to possess me. It spilled into and spoiled everything. Life has been dominated by the perpetual motion of marking and preparation. I'd only manage to come out of role several days into a holiday, just in time to feel the resentment of having to get back into it for the beginning of term. I still want to be a 'good teacher'; that has not changed. It's just that from now on the role will be different. My perception of what a 'good teacher' is has been transformed. I'll be wearing different clothes and, like all good clothes, they will make me feel relaxed, comfortable and confident.

Becoming convinced of student-centred learning happened like waves on the sea shore. Repeatedly it came over me and retreated, but I knew the tide would come in. My castle of solid sand offered some resistance, but . . . now I'm awash with excitement.

So, the first change in me is to be myself and nothing more in school. The second is to think of the students as friends. This is just as radical and releasing. It transforms relationships and classroom behaviour – both theirs and mine – almost immediately. These two amount to a change of heart. From them, student-centred learning flows.

A TEACHER RE-BORN

I used to be a disciplinarian with soft spots, who demanded attention and would shout several times a week. Sarcasm was my stock-in-trade. I would use factual questions as my technique of teaching and have the desks regimented, and often direct my questions to individuals. I now feel that I am a 'teacher re-born' – resurrected might be more accurate. Everything I have been doing in eighteen years of teaching (Mathematics for the most part), has been brought into question.

My personal approach to the pupils changed first and only of late have my teaching methods begun to alter.

I use the Waiting Game with some degree of success, but it can still take two or three minutes with a lower set. Sarcasm has disappeared (almost), speaking instead in a pleasant manner, calling pupils by their first names. I even apologise to pupils I may have upset. One girl in particular made me lose my self-control and I smacked her wrist. I didn't see her for three lessons. I enquired as to her whereabouts and was politely told that my action was not called for by a small group of her friends. We discussed the matter, the girl returned and I apologised to her in front of her friends. I was genuine and it was accepted.

I encourage more, help more, talk to the pupils more about how they feel about the work, and I am prepared to talk about other topics on occasions. I am prepared to answer their questions as honestly as I can, treating them as individual human beings.

Transferring the ownership of behaviour is proving more of a problem. However, I do not remonstrate any more, but pose questions:

> "Do you think your behaviour is acceptable?"
> "How could you deal with it?"
> "You are responsible for your own actions – how is it affecting others – and your own work? Is your reply honest?!"

The response is difficult to quantify, but I do feel there has been a general improvement in behaviour, apart from a couple of individuals.

For one particular group I teach, I have been a little more 'directive':

> 'We must listen to each other and not interrupt.'

"We must not be rude to each other."
"We must not put each other down."
"We must not drop each other into trouble."

In general, it is working, but again individuals need frequent reminders; however it is early days yet.

Questions by me when teaching have increased; I accept all answers, hearing each contributor out.

With some groups, discussion of approach to a topic can take half or more of the time available – some get bored and ask to start – permission is granted.

I still set the topics and the work, but the pupils pick which questions to do in the selected exercises. They realised that this was a problem for marking and now mark their own work on the majority of occasions.

More recently, I have shared a problem with a group. I have asked 'What do I do with people who refuse to work?' and a group discussion follows (with guidance) as to what should happen – solutions such as 'give more homework' have been met with stony silence.

I am a person who would use a mild swear word, and innuendo and often used to put people down with sarcasm. I have stopped such practices (almost) – as I found that the pupils would reciprocate in the same manner and before long the lesson could deteriorate into a slanging match. I thought that my personality would pull me through.

In school I acknowledge pupils' presence, have time to talk, open doors, pick up litter, help children pick up dropped articles. Doors open for me; I am acknowledged. I have stopped shouting – although I still want to at times, and do on rare occasions. I listen more carefully for two reasons. Quite often if a pupil can be heard out, I find that he *has* understood the problem in hand, and can answer the question, but cannot articulate very well. The other is that if someone has something to say, it is important to that person; after all, I think what I have to say is important.

I have a long way to go, but I am happier and I believe the pupils are as well. For the first time in many a year some pupils have said they enjoy the lessons. I am excited as to where we shall go, sharing the responsibilities. I can now look forward to a few more years of teaching.

Much of what I have said may be obvious to many, but it has been a conscious effort for me to change. I would like to relate a few lessons that I have tried recently, with what I believe to be a great deal of success:

Lesson 1 – Maths: Similarity (Fourth year, top set – perhaps five may do 'O' Level)

A desk was covered in paper and much equipment.

Problem: We have a pair of triangles identical in every way except length of sides – some discussion followed as to what this means.

Instruction: Divide into groups of your own choice. Take any equipment you like and draw such a pair of triangles, and discover what you can.

Results: Many of the girls needed help – right angled triangles predominated. A triangle was drawn and another with sides of double the length – at least a principle was understood.

Discussion followed as to the relevance of their own proof and as to an alternative approach – in other words, ignore length of sides and construct identical angles. Calculators were available.

One group of boys discovered that if sides are doubled, area is quadrupled; if sides are trebled, area is nine times bigger. This idea was developed later when all were asked to confirm it – discussion followed as to the approach.

All pupils understood the relationships and some were able to transfer immediately to finding missing sides in a pair of similar triangles.

This was the first lesson in which I had changed my approach – the value that came out of it convinced me to try others and perhaps put more onto the pupils.

Lesson 2 – Maths: Vectors (Second year, top set – wide range of ability)

The room was cleared of desks and chairs (to the perimeter); the pupils sat on the desks. The floor is tiled. We established rules of communication – one at a time. I threw something on the floor and asked how we could describe its position.

Coordinates soon appeared.

I moved the article to another place and asked how one could describe the movement.

Many different ideas came forward, all of which were relevant. Someone said, 'We have to have a standard that everyone understands, anywhere in the world.' An international standard was arrived at, with a few inputs from me.

Negatives came up – from the pupils.

Ten minutes before the end, I said 'What usually happens now is that I ask you to open your books and copy down these notes'. Everyone groaned.

I asked for an alternative, the reply being (from several) 'Why don't we write down what we think we have discovered?' This met with general agreement and produced good results.

This method can be developed to multipliers – dividers and resultants – the pupils can be used as the corners of squares.

This developed in a later lesson by the pupils deciding to get into groups and write exercises for each other – very successfully. They thought they learnt a great deal.

Early days, but exciting. I'm still feeling my way, but I do see that there is much power in the pupils' thoughts that can be tapped. One aspect is that several pupils are speaking for the first time and having their ideas accepted. There is a new rapport building up and a new impetus to work. I love it.

Peter Beckhelling

In old lessons you have to sit and listen all the time, and then you're set the work and have a limited amount of time. However the new lessons are more enjoyable and exciting. Everyone can put their mind into what work or discuss the points of work. It's very interesting because you're learning things for yourself.

I hope that this kind of organisation will continue, as far as I am concerned, because it would help us to get along with each other and not feel as if we are not included in the work we were to produce.

The kids have been much more interested in their work and the teacher has just been a 'helper' not a 'dictator'.

I liked working with other kids and sharing my work.

ASK THEM

No more gnashing of the teeth,
No more wondering what to do,
No Us above and Them beneath,
No This is Me and That is You;

Ask Them.

Without a doubt, the school is theirs;
The way it feels, the way it looks,
The battered desks, the squeaking chairs,
The marks, the syllabus, the books;

Ask Them.

When things go wrong, no sleepless nights,
No uptight head, no fear of noise.
The questions, problems, choices, fights,
Belong by right to the girls and boys;

Ask Them.

No more confrontation now.
No futile clashing of the wills.
They'll solve it all, give them a chance –
Don't underestimate their skills;

Ask Them.

Don't take a new dilemma home,
Or search the Times Ed in Despair;
Just talk about it to the kids.
They will support you, if you dare;

Ask Them.

THE B-BOYS

5-B was one of the two groups at Queensbridge which we had agreed to work with over a period of six months. We chose them for several reasons: first, because they were reputed to be an 'impossible' class and we wanted to see how the methods would work with such a group. Paul had been teaching them for two years, and was frustrated; he simply did not know where to go with them. They were certainly not interested in RE, but Paul felt he had no alternative to offer. Secondly, since it was a non-examination group, there was no required syllabus, so we were free to work on social and personal development. Our strongest motivation was the challenge; if our methods could work with 5-B, they could work with anyone!

The class knew themselves as 'the B-Boys', which was significant in itself, as there were actually three girls in the group, but they seemed to make little impact. The B-Boys had an image to maintain of being the toughest lads in the school, and they looked the part. Out of the 20 students, there were about six strong leaders, who had a dominant influence over everyone else. This was reflected in the amount of talking they did; it was generally recognised that they were the spokesmen. Few people questioned their authority, but they were not blindly followed. It was more like the course of least resistance, as if the others had long ago given up, and no longer wished to show any initiative. One of the leaders was so garrulous, so wrapped up in himself, that rarely did anyone else even have a chance to get a word in. In fact it was unusual, in December, for anyone, ever, to complete a sentence without interruption. The communication that was going on ranged from good-humoured sarcasm to outright cruelty.

Donna, after 26 years of teaching experience, felt daunted when she saw them; the were straight out of 'The Blackboard Jungle'.

Most of these students had been labelled 'remedial' for most of their school careers, but it was generally felt in the staff room that the term was inaccurate, and that really many of the problems were to do with language difficulties. With just a few exceptions, none of them were taking any exams. Each staff member seemed to have their own way of dealing, or not succeeding in dealing, with 5-B, but their antics were notorious to say the least. For example: throwing a banger into a maths lesson; carrying flick knives, rice-flails, and other interesting weapons; eggs thrown at the hall windows during end-of-term assembly. One of them played truant for a month, coming in only for his free school lunch each day, another was temporarily suspended for almost strangling a first year lad . . . These were the B-Boys.

Here is a comment from an established and experienced teacher who, after covering a lesson with 5-B, was moved to write a note to the Headmaster. It indicates the relationship which existed between the class and a number of its teachers.

"The following comments were made in the spirit of a reaction of dismay after the cover lesson described, because the behaviour and atmosphere in the classroom were completely untypical of my relationship with the classes that I teach. I like a relaxed working atmosphere in which there is mutual respect and courtesy, and feel that it is very important to be able to trust a class to behave sensibly.

In a good working situation, I feel that I should be able to go into a stockroom to get something, be able to go round the room without having to watch everyone, and even, if the occasion arises, to leave the classroom for a short period, and not find that any problem has arisen when I return.

I found the conduct of this class most unsatisfactory during the lesson for the following reasons:

a Certain members of the group would not remain quiet whilst their work was explained to them.

b Quite a number of them lacked the equipment necessary to do any written work.

c One boy was sent out for scribbling on another boy's work. When I went to check on him I found that he was not sitting outside the staffroom. He claimed that he had gone to the toilet.

d Throughout the lesson a group of boys kept up a barrage of chatter, some of which was deliberately obscene and offensive. I do not usually have to tell pupils off for swearing in lessons.

e As they had not troubled to listen at the start, some of them found the work difficult, but when I left the teacher's desk to help individuals, others took advantage of this to move around the room without permission and open windows.

f One of the leaders was eventually moved from his cronies. At first he sounded off about teachers ordering him about, mouthing words to the effect that he didn't see why he shouldn't sit where he liked. He seemed to think better of it when I insisted that he sat where I had told him to, but I felt that a confrontation situation had been narrowly avoided. Even so, he had to be told to sit where he had been directed to a second time when he decided to 'consult' his friends.

g Some of the boys showed a distinct lack of respect for each other. Twice other pupils tried to take a pencil from a boy because they didn't have pencils and he did, despite the fact that he was actually using his pencil at the time.

Not all members of the class were misbehaving, but enough of them to make the atmosphere very unpleasant. I would not be very willing to cover this class again if I had a choice in the matter."

After we had agreed to work together with 5-B, Donna observed Paul teaching them, so that together we could make an assessment of the situation. Paul used all of the three techniques he had seen Donna use and afterwards wrote:

> 'I felt exposed, vulnerable, threatened, lonely and lost. It would have been better had Donna not been there, but she was and it had to be that way. How else will I learn? I will overcome my nervousness – soon, perhaps. While I'm so self-conscious, though, things cannot flow. It's even worse than usual. Donna must be very disappointed.'

The prospect looked grim, but in the next lesson the idea of the circle and rounds was established, Rule of the Game was played and the value of the new way of working discussed. Changes were already beginning:

> "It is the first time I ever remember smiling at them, and is certainly the first time they have smiled at me. What a great sense of unity in the class; the atmosphere is so relaxed, yet purposeful and positive."

After just four lessons, conditions had improved to the point where people were listening to each other, put-downs were rare, and there was a much greater feeling of purpose and cohesion. Students were arriving at the lessons on time, wanting to get started, and there was never a time when anything stronger than a reminder to listen was required. Donna, returning after Christmas, could hardly believe it was the same class, the difference was so remarkable. And the most impressive thing of all was that this transformation had been accomplished by the group through making just two agreements: to listen to each other, and to stop putting each other down.

From then until school-leaving time, we were able to work smoothly with the group, mostly doing exercises in personal and social education, aiming to build their self-esteem before they left the school. One of the factors in this was the class recognising that Paul had changed too; his positive regard for them had grown enormously; they knew they had changed together, and were able to talk openly about it.

One of the early lessons was observed by Jacky West, a teacher on secondment from a Suspension Centre. Her report of that lesson follows.

In these days of cut-backs, increased teacher stress, ever-increasing work loads and the mounting disaffection of pupils, aware that their destination after school is quite likely to be the dole queue, a new approach to learning which promises less work and fewer discipline problems for the teacher, more success for the pupils and greater satisfaction all round might seem to be pie in the sky. If the same approach also claims to offer increased opportunities for personal growth at the same time, the sceptic might reasonably be excused for dismissing such ideas as preposterous and certainly not realisable in the hurly burly of everyday school life.

I visited a school where several of the teachers are attending an in-service course to learn just such an approach and where one of them, Paul, with the support of the course tutor, is testing the method with a 'difficult' class of fifth year non-examination pupils.

When I visited them, they came into the classroom quietly and sat down; no-one had to be told. When the teacher took his place behind his desk, they were immediately quiet. 'That was very good', he said, 'Last week that took seven seconds; this week only six'. He went on to say that, for the benefit of the people who had not been there the previous week, he wanted to explain again the agreement that he and they had come to about the way their lessons together were going to be from then on. He said he was not going to shout at them any more, nor they at him, or at each other. He was not going to get angry with them any more. That was going to be hard sometimes but if he did forget and get angry they were to tell him. He was going to play the Waiting Game if he wanted to say anything and this meant waiting quietly until everyone was quiet before he spoke. He asked if anyone could remember the other thing they had agreed. A boy put up his hand.

'We've got to look at the person who's talking.' 'Great!' said Paul. 'So you have two important things to remember.' Then he reminded them that the previous week they had talked about listening; that looking at the person who is speaking shows that you are listening and that the person who is speaking is important.

'Now', he said, 'would you put your chairs in a circle?' The class did this in less than a minute and with no fuss or noise. They all sat down. 'Before we start what we are going to do next', the teacher said, 'you might like to ask our visitor some questions. You can take it in turns round the circle but if you don't want to say anything, just say "pass". Who would like to start?' The boy next to me put up his hand. 'Pass', he said, but no-one laughed. The teacher thanked him for starting and continued round the circle. Two people asked questions. They all seemed relaxed and unembarrassed.

The lesson I was observing continued. Paul asked the class to go into pairs. 'One of you will be A', he said, 'and the other B. A is to tell B what he has been doing this weekend. B is to listen carefully, not to speak or ask questions but to show interest by smiling, nodding or anything like that.'

The class started right away. I moved round the classroom. Everyone in the room was talking about their weekend. Then Paul stopped them. 'Right,' he said. 'Now I want the Bs to tell the rest of us what the As have been telling them.' There was some laughter. Several hands went up. Paul had to wait briefly because two of the boys were still talking. This was the only interruption in the whole hour and ten minutes of the lesson. Paul chose someone to tell what he had just heard, which he did well. Several more boys had a turn.

At this moment, Donna arrived. The class were obviously pleased to see her. Many of them smiled. She started to talk about the work she had been doing with other classes in the school. She told them that one of the things she had noticed about this school was how good, expert in fact, everyone was at putting people down. 'What does it feel like' she asked 'if someone puts you down?' Someone said it made him feel small. The boy who seemed to be a leader said that you got used to it. Everybody did it. You took no notice.

Donna said they were going to play a game in which they were going to say nice things about each other. Someone had to go out and while he was out the rest of them had to think of three positive things to say about him. When he came back he would have to guess who said them. The boy who was a leader volunteered to go out first. The class played the game with enthusiasm until the end of the lesson. One boy was asked by a teacher in the corridor why he had been sent out. He was very amused. The class wanted Paul and Donna to go out too. They went together. No-one took advantage of their absence. They continued to play the game and could hardly wait to tell Paul and Donna what had been said. One boy said you could relate to Donna. Another said Paul had changed a lot. Someone else said this was a lot better than being put down. Before they left, Donna asked the class if they would call her by her first name. 'I really hate being called Miss,' she said. The boy next to me winked. 'We'll try Miss,' he said.

After they had gone, both Donna and Paul said how pleased and surprised they were to see how much the class had changed in the four weeks they had been working with them. Their behaviour was quite remarkable compared with the way they had been four weeks earlier and, unfortunately, the way they still were in other lessons with other teachers.

Our good feelings about what happened with 5-B in the classroom were tempered by one major problem. Their behaviour in the rest of the school stayed the same, and on some occasions got worse. There was a suspicion emanating from staff members, that our work with 5-B was becoming counterproductive. In other words, that when students have become accustomed to taking responsibility in one class, it may become more difficult for them to accept the traditional structures elsewhere. Some of those staff members who didn't feel that we were directly to blame for the deterioration in 5-B's behaviour, still felt that our methods ought to have more carry-over effect. While we would agree that, given more time, the positive learning ought to transfer over to other situations, we also feel that we cannot take responsibility for how other teachers interact with their students. Anyway, our task was clear: it was time to talk to 5-B about their reputation.

This became a major event. They were fascinated by the subject, and loved talking about it. They recognised that there was a problem of severe inconsistency in their behaviour, but they never *owned* it in our sense of being willing to do something about it. The most important reason for this was that they enjoyed their reputation as the B-Boys; it gave them status with the rest of the students. This was the main stumbling block. The other important issue was that they thought if their other teachers would change first, they would be willing to change too. They felt it was the teachers' responsibility to initiate the changes; they were not prepared to make the first move.

Here is an extract from one of the discussions we had:

Donna: *Our problem is that other teachers are still saying that you are a difficult class. But when you are with us you are not difficult.*

Class: *Other teachers don't treat us the same way that you do.*
When other teachers come in they shout and say things like shut up, sit down, get on with your work.
Mr. X, superman with the muscles, said he was told in the staffroom we were the hardest class to teach, so he was really hard with us, and after a couple of weeks, we were all right with him. We'd be frightened to move; he's so big.

Donna: *You have chosen though to be this way with us. We haven't made you this way. You've decided for yourselves. How would you feel about being this way in all your lessons?*

Class: *We have this reputation in the school. The small boys look up to us because we are hard.*

Donna: *Would you look soft if you changed in all your lessons?*

Class: *Yes.*

Donna: *And yet you don't mind being like this in these lessons with us.*

Class: *But we enjoy these lessons. What are we going to do if the lesson is boring?*

Donna: *Well, that's a good question and it's something you have to decide.*

At this point the class divided into groups of four or five to generate solutions to the problem. All the suggestions were about how the *teachers* could make things better. They said they would only change if teachers changed first.

So we had arrived at an impasse and, frankly, we were getting tired of talking about it. We had said that what we wanted was for them to leave the school with people remembering them in a positive light. We felt that we were not willing to force them, put more pressure on them, or bribe them to change, and we said as much to them. In the end, we all chose to go on with some work.

One of the keys to success in the remaining time was through Drama. A big turning point came when we did an improvisation about a bank robbery. For the first time they worked solidly together for three lessons, with high levels of participation from everyone, including those who had previously been uninvolved. In the last few weeks of school, when about half the class had already left and demoralisation was setting in, the group chose to produce a video film. The last thing that they did in their school careers was to complete this film, and they stayed behind on the day that they officially left school for ever, so that they could get it done. So they departed on a high note, each clutching his or her Farewell Mug (our leaving presents to them), with mingled feelings of pride, self-esteem, and sadness. Certainly we were sorry to see them go . . .

The new lessons have been much better than the lessons we had before, there has been a completely different atmosphere. I think it's like this because people are enjoying what they're doing.

I think the class has changed because it now interlinks and pupils willingly contribute their feelings to the class.

I think the lesson went very well because we all communicated with each other.

I liked it because we had to do it ourselves, we had to trust ourselves. When we were writing on the blackboard . . . one was writing, the other was holding a dictionary for words that he/she could not spell.

TECH 1: DOING IT THE HARD WAY

Introduction

The second of our two groups at Queensbridge presented quite a different picture to 5-B; it was a fourth year TVEI General Studies group, with only ten boys 'of mixed ability'. For the first term, Paul had begun teaching the course in a very didactic manner, with lots of structured assignments and tight deadlines. Work was getting done, but there was some resistance to the strict requirements.

When Donna came, and we chose Tech 1 as our other class, we had some disagreement as to how we should proceed. Donna felt we should take some time out to introduce the student-centred methods and do a considerable amount of trust-building, with the aim of forming a very cohesive group. In four double sessions, a good start could have been made. Paul felt that the most important priority had to be the General Studies work, as they would be having a CSE assessment of their folders, and the students must not get behind with their course. Since Paul was their teacher, we chose the second option. We *did* institute such changes as sitting in a circle, talking in rounds, making joint decisions about the assignments, self-assessment, working in self-selected groups; in other words, many of the *techniques* of student-centred learning were in operation. But what we didn't do was take the time to build relationships and improve communication; therefore, it took much longer for them to begin to take ownership; the key element was missing.

Getting started

What we did on the very first day was to sit in a circle together and talk about what Donna was doing there. We discussed what 'student-centred learning' meant, and how it might change the way they worked together.

We all watched a video about Tanzania, to introduce that as a new topic, under the general subject of 'Less Developed Countries'. When they had seen the film, we did a round of 'What I noticed', and they had noticed a lot of interesting things. Donna asked them to talk to each other before the next lesson, and to decide how they were going to approach the work. Three spontaneous responses were:

> "We're not very good at making decisions."
> "We never get the chance", and
> "Leave it to Mr. Ginnis."

Donna's closing comment was 'I think learning is supposed to be fun', which was met with general laughter and exclamations.

In the next lesson we brainstormed some ideas, and the boys divided themselves into two groups, and began their planning. A group of seven boys decided to make a board game which would incorporate ideas about less developed countries. A group of three said that they would do a radio play.

New wine, old wineskins

The problems generated by not preparing the group for a student-centred approach were apparent after only a few weeks, when Paul wrote:

'I was more than a little worried about this lesson, with "the trio" not producing very much and Donna away in London. Tech 1 were disappointing both of us. We had had such high hopes and an encouraging start, but the expected openness and closeness had not developed. It was all so painfully slow and circular. What had changed since Donna came on the scene? What had we achieved? What had the kids produced? Nothing. This was to have been our show class which would prove for ever that student-centred methods get people through exams. Now it was backfiring. Cynics were beginning to ask awkward questions and I was secretly scheming about becoming didactic again as soon as Donna left.

With these cheerful thoughts in mind, I arrived at the lesson laden with materials for the 'game group' who would carry on on their own as usual while I concentrated on Amjid, Arshed and Imran. Like it or not, I went in 'honest', not prepared to pull any punches because I'd had enough of soft-pedalling encouragement and understanding! I explained my frustration: nothing added to the folders since the beginning of December, a trail of empty promises and a litter of broken agreements. I told them what I thought of them. It was a pretty adult conversation – I didn't get aggressive and they didn't get uptight, which didn't surprise me at the time but has since.

They were honest in reply. Imran had never really been interested in the play idea, Amjid still was keen, especially on doing the sound effects, and Arshed didn't know.

We then discussed how the decision to do a play had been made and why it had not been carried through. It had all happened casually. "The trio" had not realised the independence of their decisions or the consequences of their actions. They had been expecting, perhaps unconsciously, some sort of "divine intervention" – rescue by the teacher had always been available before. The whole tedious situation showed how conditioned they were to having the teacher make all the decisions and impose his or her will on them. It seemed impossible for these lads to work without the usual pressures and structures. They were passive learners par excellence. Yet how could I blame them for not getting this play off the ground? After all, I had spent the last two years getting them to do as *I* said, when I said, how I said.

I had adjusted to the new methods quicker than they. We should really have taken four or five weeks out to develop the foundation skills and feelings necessary for student-centred learning to take place effectively. We didn't because of time and the pressure to get work into the Mode 3 folders, but we regret it now. Time spent in this way would be regained several times over by the end of the course. We were trying to operate a new system while old attitudes persisted. We were pouring new wine into old wineskins. "The new wine will burst the skins, and be spilled, and the skins shall perish."'

At the end of the day . . .

In an attempt to patch up our mistake, we took an afternoon out and went to Donna's house for lunch and group work. We had an enormous amount of fun, and they were so very different in that setting. They laughed, talked, took risks in communicating with us; they even played a practical joke on Paul, which seemed like a great luxury.

It turned out to be a crazy afternoon of trust-building. The blind walk, for example, had resulted in a scattered dustbin and an enquiry from a passing police patrol. Still, 'Guess who said it' *(Gamesters' Handbook S9)* put things right and converted the nervous sense of fun into a feeling of togetherness and mutual appreciation.

Just before leaving, we had a chat about the afternoon. It was clear that the lads had enjoyed it enormously.

'How did you manage to get time off school for us to do this?', someone asked.

''Cos we've been learning,' was my reply, met by murmurs of disbelief.

'What *have* we learned this afternoon?' I continued.

The group cast about for answers.

'We know what it's like being blind.'

'We've learned how to make ice cream sundaes.'

Neither reply carried conviction.

So, we discussed what we had learned about each other and our relationships, about the group and about trust. You could almost see the light dawn and hear the pennies drop. Then someone remembered Donna had said when she first met Tech 1 that learning should be fun. She was laughed at then. This afternoon it had come true. There were broad smiles.

At the end of the day, what is student-centred learning all about? At the end of *this* day, it was not about a set of techniques and strategies – it was not even about process. It was about relationships measured in terms of closeness and trust. In essence this is what it's about in the classroom too: teacher–student and student–student relationships. These relationships provide the climate for the teaching–learning process. They determine the style of teaching and the quality of learning. Student-centred teaching techniques and activities could be used in a different climate but, like fish out of water, would fail to survive.

Sadly, the afternoon and its effects were over too quickly; by the next lesson, we were almost back to the former dryness. And we still had to press on . . .

New territory

Gradually, the relationships between us did begin to change, and there were some high points. Donna was able to write:

> 'Today was a great lesson with Tech 1. I felt for the first time that they saw me as a human being, looked me in the eye, smiled, chatted, no long embarrassing silences. But they *still* call me Miss! This was, I am sure, a result of their visit to my house the other Thursday.
>
> I thought that since we were in the hall for our lesson,

we should take advantage of the space, and use it to its fullest. I asked them if they'd like to play a game, and save the questionnaires for Thursday. They seemed quite eager.

We played "Territories" *(Gamesters' Handbook S22)* – they each went off and built themselves a "country" with their chairs, and then sat down and made up their "laws". It was very interesting watching the characteristic ways in which they chose and built their territories:

Mark: *in a far corner, with chairs upturned for a very prickly barbed wire fence . . .*

Stephen: *sized up the situation, took over the surrounding territories, including Jasvinder's and Kurshid's . . .*

Jasvinder: *first, thought ahead and blocked off the doors as part of his territory, so people could not go in or out without his permission. Then let Steven take him over without even finding out what the rules were.*

Paul: *no speech problem at all, shouting, giving orders, very much in charge of his territory, which was 'hilly' to warn of enemies approaching.*

The others all ended up following either Steven or Paul . . . we tried various ways of making it work as a play. At the end I asked them what they had learned about themselves, and they made very perceptive comments, incorporating a lot of what I had noticed.'

Student's assessment sheet

Here is the assessment sheet we gave to Tech 1 after they completed the unit on Tanzania, along with a few of their responses, both negative and positive. Introducing it, we said:

> 'We want to know how you feel about the way we've been working in General Studies since January. We feel that the way of working has changed very much, and we want to know what changes you have noticed. We want very honest and private answers to these questions, please. You can see by the way that the questions are written that you are requested to ask *yourself* each question, and then answer it.'

Questionnaire

(There are no right or wrong answers: we want your real opinions.)

Me

Q.1 *How have I changed while doing things the new way?*

I think I have enjoyed the lesson more than I used to.
I can trust people a lot more now in Tech 1 than before.
I think that now I know everyone in my Tech group, as if I had known them very well.

Q.2 *How hard have I worked?*

I think I have not worked to the best of my ability.
I have worked very well, but I cannot show it on paper.

Q.3 *How much have I learned about Tanzania or LDCs this way, compared to what I would have done with the old methods?*

I think I have learnt the same about Tanzania as I would have in the old method.
I think I have learned a lot more because when the old way we just wrote everything down then I never revised it – this way you get a lot more fun and you can easily recall this.

Q.4 *How carefully did I choose the group I have been working with? Would I choose the same way next time?*

I did not choose the right group because I only chose it to be with the friends. During our work project I realised we were not getting very far with our work. I think the next time I would choose a group in which I would know I can work.
Yes, because in a way I feel as if we carried some people through a little but we got a good result.

Q.5 *How carefully did I choose the kind of project I did on Tanzania? What did I learn about choosing, for next time?*

I chose a project before thinking if I could do the job or knew what to do. I chose without thinking of how I could get on with the task and if it would be easy.
I think that we had plenty of time to do the project and didn't organise it properly. This meant coming back after school to

finish it. Next time I think we should organise a time for every different section of the project.

Q.6 *How well have I worked with others?*

Not very well because I didn't like the idea of the play. I sometimes like other people telling me what to do because I find it easier.
I think I work very well with some people but with some people I didn't work so well. I think that the General Studies lesson has improved the amount of self control in us because I have been in trouble for assault, and now being in the same corner again with another teacher I resisted the assault.
I have worked well and we have discussed many of the problems as a group which bound us closer together.

The lesson

Q.1 *What is Donna doing here?*

I think that Donna's purpose is to prove her theory that teaching can be fun, and I think that her theory is true.
Donna is teaching teachers other ways to teach pupils, not just copy from the blackboards.

Q.2 *How has Mr. Ginnis changed?*

Mr. Ginnis has let us alone making all the decisions while he helped us if we needed. He has not nagged at us for work.
Mr. Ginnis has changed from being as if he has a grudge and now he seems to enjoy lessons.

Q.3 *Would I prefer going back to the old, traditional way of working?*

I would rather carry on the way we are though I would choose a different group.
No, because that way was boring and I found that it dragged on and on but now it is a good lesson.

Q.4 *How do I feel about the amount of work, and the quality of work, going into the folder?*

I feel bad.
I think the amount of work is great for the folder and the quality of work is improving.

There isn't a lot of work but it is of a higher quality than before.

Q.5 *How does General Studies compare to your best class?*

I think general studies is one of my best classes because as well as work it is fun.

Q.6 *What did I get out of the trip out on Thursday?*

I think I learnt that work could be fun. Also teachers change a lot on an outing.
A meal, a laugh, and the knowledge of knowing when you've offended someone and who to trust, what type of person to trust.
I learnt about trust and honesty and got a good dinner.
I learn that teachers are not serious all the time and can be a lot of fun and think good things about other people.
I found a lot about trust and how to join up together for the best result.

Q.7 *Did I get enough help from Mr. Ginnis and Donna? (On my project.)*

Really we didn't need that much help in our project but if we did they were always ready to help.

Responsibility and trust

Q.1 *How well did I keep my agreements about the project?*

At first I kept far from my agreement, now I'm OK.
I kept my agreements to what I agreed on doing, and I felt my trust in others was let down a bit.

Q.2 *Did I do my share of the work?*

No, because I had no interest in it.
Yes, I did more than my share of the work.
Yes, I can truthfully say that I have done my share of the work.

Q.3 *Do I feel that I had some good ideas?*

Yes, I think I put in a few good ideas.
Yes I did because I developed the game and helped with the rules.

Q.4 *Did the others in my group do their share?*

Yes I think everybody did their share.

Some did but others made promises and then broke them. I felt that people who made promises and then broke them made me feel mad at them, which made me feel not like working.

Likes and dislikes about General Studies

Dislikes

When lessons start to become boring. When Mr. Ginnis starts to tell us off or nags us and doesn't let us do any work. When I'm told to stop work when I'm half way through something.

There are too many rounds. Not enough in folder.

Likes

It's fun in the lesson. The work is good because we get a chance to do what we want. Improved relations.

The way we now work. Everybody gets on with others. Not many boring lessons only the odd one or two.

I think people have started to trust each other more. I like the hospitality in the group, it's good. I like the games, I also think I learn from them. I think this way has improved relations with another person. I think we can speak out more about a lot of things.

The amount of trust. New style of lesson. The games we've played. The group as a whole. The way we have improved relations.

Starting a new topic in General Studies using a student-centred approach

After completing and assessing the Tanzania work, this is how the group began the next section of the syllabus.

1 *Reaching completion on the last topic.* We used the student assessment sheets which were 'purpose-built' for the Tanzania project; Paul made it clear to the students that we did not want anything except very honest answers; that there was no right or wrong about it.

2 *Introducing the new topic.* We brainstormed ideas for the next topic in the syllabus; when we asked them what it was, they said 'Home and Family', which they remembered from some weeks ago. They reviewed the rules for brainstorming which they also remembered since January.

3 *Preparing for making choices.* We gave them a piece of mental homework, which was to look at their own families and consider what they would like to find out about them, what they would like to know about other families, what areas might be private and what kinds of ideas they could feel free to share.

4 *Preparing to work out how to do the projects.* They made a very strong point, without prompting from us, that they wanted to spend the class sessions working on things for their folders, which they were now taking more seriously, and do the other activities, games, drama, etc. outside of class time, after school, lunchtimes . . .

We felt extremely gratified with this session, because they were taking responsibility for themselves, and produced a large quantity of good ideas.

Brainstorm of ideas related to home and family

jobs
divorce
marriage
unemployment
food
education
parents making decisions
neighbours
friends
visitors
hospitality
extended family
nuclear family
no kids in family
family tree
birth
relations
relationships
comparisons with other families
differences
health

background
communication
separation
letting go
old people
addiction
alcohol
getting your own way
sex
freedom
abuse
cruelty
housing
clothing
communes
cultures
different ways of living
problems
family structure
who is in charge
money

The students then read over the list and ticked five or six topics which interested them. Their choices were listed on the board. Each student wrote a short description of a project they wanted to do for their folder and linked with others interested in the same or similar things. So groups were formed and work began.

A major breakthrough came when Paul realised that he had yet to give up ownership of the learning; he still felt responsible for the work which, as he saw it, he was 'letting the kids do badly'. Logically, there were two ways out of this dilemma: one was to retain responsibility and make the kids do better, and the other was to *really* transfer the ownership over to them. In the end, it was not a rational decision. In an unexpected moment of enlightenment, Paul suddenly realised that he need worry no longer; in fact that the worry was impeding progress. The exam, the syllabus, and the folders, all belonged to them. At the beginning of the next lesson, Paul told the truth and explained how he felt about all this; and the effect was that, immediately, people began to take their responsibility more seriously.

Some indications of this were that when they had a supply teacher, unfamiliar with student-centred work, they took the initiative in explaining the way the group functioned and how to get on with the work. Another time, when the Director of TVEI was taking the lesson for us, two boys were ready to lead the group in an exercise on family life. Instead, as a group, they chose to postpone this and take the opportunity to receive Chris and his Australian cousin properly, to find out about them. By the end of the lesson, the boys had suggested a twinning arrangement with an Australian school, and had agreed to prepare for that by the next time they met. What's more, their CSE folders are becoming fatter!

So Tech One is getting there . . . the hard way.

I have learned that there is an amount of trust that we must not break.

I want to be involved every bit in making my own decisions. I feel it's a duty for me to go about doing my work my way. It's like practice because I'll have to make decisions when I'm older. I like running my own lessons. It makes me feel like a teacher.

I think I have changed because we do something with our own thoughts.

I want to take a part as though I am like a teacher who has to plan my work, read it through, set my homework, when to hand it in, etc. . . .

GARDENERS' QUESTION TIME

The Deputy Headmistress is already at breaking point with the pay dispute, and today has thrown up even more chaos and confusion; her mood is not good.

While going about her duties, she passes some students working in a courtyard area of the school.

> *What are you doing?,* she asks.
> *Gardening, miss,* replies one
> *Whose group are you?*
> *Mr. Hamer's, miss.*
> *But Mr. Hamer is not here today!!* cries the deputy.
> *We know, miss,* replies the group.
> *Then who's taking you?* enquires the deputy.
> *Nobody, miss.*
> *Who told you to do this?* asks the deputy.
> *Nobody, miss,* replies the group.
> *Where are the rest of the group?* pleads the deputy.
> *Some are cleaning the fishpond, some the waterfall, some watering . . .*

Enough, enough; make sure you pack away at the end of the lesson, growls the deputy, disappearing into the school building.

The group in question was a CSE Horticulture class of 16 mixed pupils. Student-centred learning techniques had been used from day one of the course.

Marian McFall

FRENCH WITHOUT TEARS

Lesson 1

Class: 3KNR (bottom set).
Topic: *Le déménagement* – moving house.
Tour de France, Book 2 Unit I.
Objectives: Revising/consolidating vocabulary for furniture/rooms.
Seats: Circle, including teacher (teacher not in 'teacher's seat').

1 Wait for quiet.
2 Explain what the lesson objective is.
3 Brainstorm for appropriate French words, e.g. *le frigo*, *le fauteuil*, *la salle de séjour*, etc.
4 Round for meanings (volunteer to start). Each student picks a word from the board, gives meaning, crosses it out.
5 Pupil leader in middle of circle asking (in a round) for French for certain words. Anybody not managing can pass or, if he/she wants, take 'teacher' role in the middle (idea to help poorer ones learn by listening to others – most opted to be leader).
6 Pairs work. One questioner asking in French 'Ou est-ce que je mets . . .?' 'Where shall I put . . .?' Partner answering with

dans (in)
sur (on)
sous (under) } + a noun.
devant (in front of)
derrière (behind)

7 Group activity in fives or sixes. One volunteer leader for each group asking questions. First with hand up and correct answer scores a point. Leader keeps score. Winners from each group to have a 'final' next period. Commendations for group winners. (Each commendation goes towards school certificate programme, e.g. ten commendations = certificate from headmaster.)

Evaluation

Pupils already used to a lot of teacher-directed paired work. Rounds/brainstorming/pupil instigated questions were new ideas.

Each activity was very successful in terms of participation. Interesting that leaders unconsciously did not ask the very poorest children (remedial maths/English students) the most difficult questions. (Teacher was – unfairly I think – asked the most difficult questions!) Overall impression – rowdily enthusiastic.

Lesson 2

Class: 3KNR (bottom set).
Topic: *Le déménagement.*
Objectives: Preparation for speaking test, introduction of idea of a visitor.
Seats: Circle.

1 Once pupils had all arrived, no waiting involved. Introduced idea of deputy head coming to class next week. Did they mind? 'Yes!' 'Why?' 'He'll see how bad we are!' 'But Mr. Watson doesn't understand any French!' 'Oh well then! – How bad is he? Worse than us?' Flattery from teacher. 'You will have to help him; you will have to work with him, give him tests!'
2 Round – Do you mind if he comes? Decision: No.
3 How do we let him know he can come? Decision: letter. Volunteers to write a letter – 90%. Volunteers to fetch him at beginning of period – 100%.
4 Letter duly written in French – pupil ideas/teacher help. Translation in English underneath to help him. Letter duly delivered.
5 Practice for speaking test. Look at lay-out. What would you say here? Teacher directed to get ideas – help with hard ones and pronunciation.
6 Rounds to practise it – one part each (of own choice).
7 Pairs work on test (oral).
8 Group contest like last week (last week's finalists as leaders).
9 Round likes/dislikes – main complaints 'I wanted to write the letter.' 'Group leader didn't ask me enough.' Likes – 'Good fun, I like being in charge.'

Evaluation

Very rowdy, but nobody was time-wasting in the group work. Very surprised that a deputy couldn't speak French – appeared to improve their self-confidence a little. There is much less aggravation between pupils than a few weeks back.

Receiving a visiteur

Following a break-time discussion with the school deputy head about Core Group activities, I decided to take the opportunity to invite him to 3KNR's French lesson. Being interested in the work, he agreed to come. I asked the class if they would be prepared to accept and help him, and Jackie volunteered to write a letter asking him to come, which she duly delivered personally. The class then arranged for John to go and meet him and bring him to class at the start of the period.

When the day arrived, Nicola explained to him what he was expected to learn in the period and that the class would help him.

Objectives: to be able to describe self in terms of eye colour, hair style, height, shape.

1 Brainstorm – for vocabulary.
2 Round – for meanings (pupils choose a word, cross it out, give meanings).
3 Pairs practice of sentences – Martin helping deputy.
4 Round for two sentences, each describing self.
5 Volunteers to be described – Mr. Watson second volunteer.
6 Volunteers to describe someone else.
7 Group competition – team leader winners from last week. Twenty five points, leaders making up questions, e.g. how to say 'I have green eyes'.
8 Circle – to find out what Mr. Watson learnt.
9 Applause, congratulations, thanks for coming.

Afterwards, some wrote evaluations of the lesson. Their comments included:

> *When Mr. Watson came he seemed to be very nervous. It seemed that he enjoyed it and managed to learn it very quickly, and managed to say five things.* (Andrew)

> *We would like Mr. Watson to come again because it was interesting to see what we are doing, and see if an adult can learn about it. Mr. Watson was very good for his first attempt. I enjoyed the lesson very much except I don't like going round saying things about yourself, because if you get a word wrong you feel embarrassed. I think we taught Mr. Watson something because before the end of the lesson we asked him about himself and he was very good so we gave him a clap.* (Annette)

> *The lesson was good because we were able to teach him instead of him teaching us. We taught Mr. Watson quite a lot. I think we were nice to Mr. Watson and I think we*

did help him in his French. We would like to ask him back. (Karen)

I'll be pleased if he would come back and learn some more because he's a good student to listen too. (Nicholas)

Carol-Ann Heeks

I can work in a group with other people. And I can work out answers and if I don't understand the question I can ask a friend.

It wasn't that easy really about making decisions about our work. I found that you had a good idea and someone else had something to say about it. It was the same for the rest of the group. We talked, sort of argued about it and came to something we all decided on.

I think we learn more if we do things the way we want to because we enjoy them more.

When all the work is put together it feels good because it's a group effort.

BLACK THURSDAY

Pupils arrive thoroughly disturbed – rowdy, loud, uncontrolled. Press on none-the-less I think.

1 Round: 'How do I feel?' 60–70% pass, rest bored, fed up.
2 Teacher talks about listening skills. Why is listening important? What happens if people don't listen?
3 Introduce idea of sabotaging, round on meaning, how do pupils/ teachers sabotage class? Foolish move, judging by reaction: no listening, discussions of other things in little pockets round ring – just gives them more ideas.
4 Waiting Game – teacher – how our lesson is being sabotaged right now! Introduce my problem – I cannot teach you at present. Can you help me solve it?
5 Brainstorm solutions. Interesting that this caused a lot of interest, for a short period. Ask them to think about these for next period.
6 Change of focus here.
Problem for them, taken from learning unit *le déménagement*, house removal. Problem – removal company needs more work, has to expand into Europe, needs to devise a phrasebook for its work force to help them compete.
7 Groups of four-five formed. Each given a teacher-prepared phrase-book, choose company name, make decisions on relevant vocab/ phrases. Works well for three-quarters of class. One group totally ruining proceedings. I'm afraid I eventually lose patience and put one girl out – immediate recovery of rest of group. (Unfortunate; I must try and organise better to prevent this again.)
8 Round – what were problems of today? (Hooray! Group shouts at one individual for sabotaging round! This makes up for all the rest today!)
9 Long discussion after class with excluded girl. Do not feel any progress is made. 3.30 – she returns and apologises profusely without any prompting – I can hardly believe it! Make sure I give due appreciation of apology, discuss what will happen next time!

Evaluate
Disaster in some respects, but on reflection cannot expect instant 100% improvement.

Carol-Ann Heeks

WHAT'S NEW?

For a 70-minute lesson per week, for eight weeks, student-centred methods were introduced with a third year class. The first two weeks were spent on trust-building, communication and listening exercises, on evaluating the present state of things, and on deciding what work to do.

Four weeks were then spent on topics and projects ranging from written folders to models, tape-recordings, posters and a play. It was what the students wanted to do, and they worked either individually or in self-selected groups as they wished.

Two further weeks were spent sharing and assessing the work, after which the group evaluated the process by completing the Assessment Questionnaire on p. 242. These are some of the points which emerged.

1 *Changes*

'. . . if anyone didn't do any work, we couldn't blame anyone but ourselves.' Students had perceived and appreciated the shift of responsibility from the teacher to themselves – 'I've noticed that (the teacher) doesn't tell us what to do', but also (the teacher is) 'more helpful than he used to be', a reflection of the teacher's own changed attitudes.

2 *Achievement*

'I forgot to eat and play and concentrated hard on my work.' It was evident from the answers given that there had been great gains in confidence and satisfaction and that other things had been learned of which students were not always immediately aware. So the complaint that 'depending on each other causes more of the pupils to argue with each other' encompassed the valuable experience of working and communicating with other people and the lesson that this could be productive – 'When all the work is put together, it feels good because it's a group effort'. In reply to the question 'Did you get more work done?', one student said 'No, but I understood more and found it easier to concentrate'.

3 *The work*

About half the students found the projects they had chosen themselves easy and the other half found the work difficult. A big difficulty for them had been that of reaching agreement as a group, although they had all got on well together. There was considerable evidence that groups had enabled group members to work harder than was their normal practice – 'At first Farooq never (worked), but gradually he became one of us' – and that there had been considerable peer group pressure on each group member to do his share. 'If there's one thing we done right, it was our share of the work.'

They had had problems with supplies of materials, lack of time, coping with mistakes, but all these were overcome, indicating resources of ingenuity and imagination and often straight-forward generosity – 'We used my house', 'I went out and bought it', 'my Dad helped us' – not previously called on by schoolwork. All but two had found the teacher helpful, particularly in supplying the materials they needed, while frequent mention was made of not needing help because we helped each other. Of the two who claimed not to have been helped, one said this was because 'he (the teacher) didn't tell me how to do my work', and the other, who was in the dance drama group, had had to wait until the stage could be used.

4 *Assessment*

All but one were keen to continue working in the new way, several remarking that any other work would be dull by comparison. The dissenter seemed to have found the group discussion and disagreement rather tiresome and was glad when it was all over.

Many of them had ideas about what they would do next and were keen to start. They enjoyed the experience of personal responsibility. 'I feel it's a duty to go about doing my work in my own way', said one, although another took fright and maintained 'We need someone to make sure we work'. They saw that the experience they had gained would enable them to do better work. Some had discovered how easy it was to over-reach themselves and had had to back-track.

All saw that they had 'taught ourselves things' and that although it took a lot of practice, it 'turned out good'.

Parents were more involved, one mother remarking that her daughter had for the first time talked about work and 'proclaimed her enjoyment'.

Jacky West

CONFESSIONS OF A BIOLOGY TEACHER

Since becoming a member of the Core Group on student-centred learning, I have found that I have looked carefully at my former teaching methods and have not always been satisfied with what I have seen. I have always hoped that I may eventually achieve a situation in my lessons where each child was involved, interested and motivated to learn. I don't think my former teaching methods would permit that to happen and therefore I welcomed the new approach offered within the Core Group.

I have tried out a few ideas already and have been pleased with the results. I have had, on the whole, favourable feedback from the children, so that can only be encouraging.

I should like to relate details of three lessons, and some practical difficulties I had with my lab.

Fifth year Biology

This relatively small group (20 – rarely all present) has low achievement in this subject. They are a lively group and quite pleasant and likeable, but tend to lack concentration.

In this lesson they had dissected an eye. I had asked them to be as observant as possible and answered any questions when asked, while they did the practical.

After clearing up, they brainstormed the parts of the eye. They then worked in discussion groups in an attempt to work out the function of each part observed. They did this *very* well!

They wanted to record this information and sorted out how they wished to do it. Then a member of each group used the blackboard to record what they had found out.

Although this was not an ambitious lesson, I was amazed at how well they had got on, with relatively little 'interference' from me!

On leaving the room, one girl said 'I enjoyed that lesson, miss!' – no-one had ever said that to me before! I also had enjoyed the lesson.

Fifth year TVEI Biology

We had a visitor from another school who wanted to talk to some TVEI pupils about their experiences on the course and their hopes for sixth and seventh year in school or elsewhere.

I was fascinated and impressed by what they had to say – they sounded so mature! When asked about the way they had been taught in their small groups, they said they had enjoyed being in small groups. One girl said *she* couldn't understand why teachers *hadn't* changed in some cases. Why did they stand up at the front at the blackboard doing *all* the talking and telling – surely they must realise that they, the students, were perfectly capable of finding things out for *themselves*! I later explained about our group and how a number of teachers were searching for new ideas to encourage pupil-centred learning.

Fourth year Biology, 16+

They don't like sitting in rows facing the front of the class because they can't see each other; they can't hear each other; and they have to keep turning around.

They don't like me telling them things; they want to find things out for themselves.

My lab.

Benches are fixed to the floor with a low voltage supply to them.
How am I going to rearrange them?
Where can I remove benches to?
What about other teachers who teach in my room?

A few weeks later I was able to write . . .

Lab. benches

If you are a Science teacher, as I am (Biology), you may say to yourself '*How* can I make a circle in here?' With five eight foot long benches nailed to the floor because a mains electricity supply is connected to them, the answer is not easy to find!

To start with, I thought I would try without moving the benches, but gradually I realised that it just would not do . . . Somehow they *had* to be moved.

My head of Science was not so sure – maybe student-centred learning would not catch on and then where would we be? In any case other staff might not like it. I argued that at least if they were moveable, there would be a choice and, as head of the Biology department, I wanted that flexibility. He gave in and agreed to contact the Science Inspector.

Fortunately our labs. were due to be rewired. The Science Inspector was summoned. Would it *now* be possible for the electricians to dismantle the electricity supply and render the benches moveable?

Why did I have to be on a field course when the Inspector arrived? I returned to school with bated breath! Had the Science Dept. Head acted in my best interests?

Two of the benches would be moveable (Hurray!). What is more they could also be sawn in half (by my Head of Science) and made into easy-to-move four foot benches.

It worked out even better than I thought.

The electricians move into my lab. next week and my Head of Science is bringing his saw; I will be there to check!

Yvonne Hanson

THE VALUE OF ARGUMENT

One day last March I visited an English Literature class in a Birmingham school. I had been working alongside various teachers in the school to introduce student-centred learning, but this was an observation of a particular teacher. I did not know her at the time, nor did I have any idea what to expect.

When I came in and saw the kids, I felt that they looked as if they could be a handful, if they were confronted. I thought they would rebel. They were very big fifth years and looked *tough*.

Ruth, the teacher, passed out to everyone a poem called *The Battery Hen* and asked them to read it through, which they did without a murmur. She then asked them what they thought were some of the key points to be noticed, which they told her with considerable clarity.

Ruth then asked them to form into groups of four or five, and to discuss the poem in depth, looking for the poet's meaning, insights and feelings. They proceeded to do that, and they continued with it for 40 minutes, listening to each other intently. At times the arguments grew very heated, but each time the question was resolved within the small group; at no time did they need the teacher's help, although they did consult her or draw her into the discussion.

A lad I knew from another lesson came in to see me. They ignored him completely and got on with their debates. They had greeted me as a visitor, but did not feel the need to prove or display anything to me. They were totally absorbed in what they were doing. I was astounded! They stayed on the task for the full 40 minutes, without a break, without any further motivation from Ruth.

I felt it was the most impressive lesson I had yet observed; I raved about it to the Core Group and others. Finally I asked Ruth to describe how she worked with the students to achieve this unusual expertise in what I think is an undervalued skill, the ability to argue. I believe her response speaks for itself, on the following pages, but lest anyone still questions the aims of such a lesson, I'll oblige by listing them:

Aims of argument

1 To develop confidence in verbal skills and expressing personal opinions.

2 To be able to listen to another's point of view.
3 To appreciate and understand an author's concepts (or a problem, or a historical or political event).
4 To take responsibility for one's own learning about a topic.

So often, teachers are looking for consensus, for agreement. Everyone has to view an idea from the same standpoint; it is our moral duty to inculcate the *right* values, so they say. On the contrary, I think it is our duty to encourage freedom of opinion, questioning of values, challenging of moral standpoints, and the students have an inalienable right to their own ideas.

Before we turn to Ruth's description, I'll set my enthusiasm in context by saying that the day before, I had been working in a school where the kids were completely subdued and repressed; in each of six lessons that I visited, they were afraid to ask a question, express an opinion, or in any way to challenge the teacher or each other. I found that depressing; I delighted in the contrast of Ruth's argumentative class.

Ruth's account

I took over this group in their fourth year at school, after the first term of a CSE/'O' Level English Literature course. The majority of the group were pupils from Asian backgrounds, with a smaller number of pupils from Afro-Caribbean and indigenous backgrounds. There were similar numbers of boys and girls.

If I had to summarise my approach to any group of pupils, it would be 'to create the conditions in which learning can take place'. This sounds rather clichéd and also rather glib, but it is based on the theory which emphasises the centrality of talk in the learning process. To create conditions in which pupils can feel confident to explore a new idea, especially when they are likely to feel insecure and hesitant, can require a great deal of patience and perseverance.

Within the English Department, talk is valued as a means of exploring new ideas, as a means of sharing ideas and as an essential part of the writing process, but with this particular group it quickly became clear that such objectives were not being achieved. Three loud boys dominated the group, each being over-confident, fiercely competitive and intolerant of others. They were the focus of attention in the group and, despite a tendency to make rash generalisations, they were rarely questioned by other members of it. The rest were reluctant to take part even in small group discussions. Hardly surprising when the 'terrible trio' as they called themselves, listened carefully to see if others could be 'spotted' for making mistakes! When this did occur, the 'culprit' was pounced upon with a degree of cynicism uncommon in 14 year olds.

At this point, I decided that there was a great deal which had to be done in order to improve the self-esteem and confidence of the quieter members of the group, in particular some of the girls, and to make the group more cohesive. Taking them out of the school environment seemed a good idea, and with only a little prompting from me, some of the more reserved pupils took on the responsibility of organising the visits. This involved making phone calls and giving the rest of the class information and instructions. Interesting to note was the reaction of the 'terrible trio' to a strange environment, during a visit to another school which was hosting a book fair. In their attempts to avoid contact with pupils from the other school, they made new friends in the class. After a visit to the theatre to see one of the 'set' plays, the subsequent discussion was extremely positive. The main reason for this was that the reviews in the press had been so varied that everyone felt confident to speak his or her mind.

A variety of approaches was then used. Having listened carefully to the few who spoke during lessons, including the three boys, it was evident that a further problem was the difficulty of the materials which they were expected to discuss. Even those who talked regularly were missing the point and failing to see relationships, implications or symbolism, and I was having to do a great deal of laborious explanation. Working with younger pupils, I had regularly used the diagrammatic approach. I decided to try it with these pupils. The class was given a series of tasks in which they had to represent aspects of the text diagrammatically. They were divided into fairly large groups, which changed regularly, and were asked to devise posters and charts depicting characters, symbols, themes etc. Initial ideas were brainstormed and the group had to organise them for a wall chart. Pupils then went around the room to collect the relevant information for a piece of writing. The next stage was for each group, having constructed a chart, to explain it to the rest of the class or another group.

After these activities I was approached by a few pupils from the group who asked if they could use the kind of diagrams which they had been using in IT. It was agreed that those who had studied this subject should be divided amongst the rest to help them devise flow charts. Complicated, but carefully-constructed and colour-coded charts emerged, which displayed the relationships between the characters in the book which we were reading. Reasons for joining characters had to be explained very carefully and justified to the group, and comparisons were made between the various charts. The following written work was, not surprisingly, of better quality and greater depth than earlier pieces and I took the opportunity to discuss why this was so. We revised the stages undertaken to arrive at the finished product and the benefits of sharing ideas through talk were clearly evident, as was the purpose of representing them diagrammatically and comparing charts.

There was still a tendency to look for 'right' answers and with it the associated reluctance to risk being wrong, but I was concerned to build on the tolerance and respect for different viewpoints which was beginning to appear. I decided on a subject with two clear viewpoints – nuclear weapons – and we watched two television films and a debate which clearly outlined the differing arguments. Three poems on this subject, each with a different viewpoint, were read and divided amongst the class. Then groups gathered to discuss them. A few questions suggested where they might start, but for some these were unnecessary. The discussions were long and heated and concerned not only the subject itself, but the way it had been presented in each poem. Thus we discussed not only the subject but the way a point of view can be presented to form a convincing argument, and the power of language in general.

Subsequent sessions have involved pupils discussing an ambiguous poem and justifying their interpretation to the group. During these sessions I noticed that their vocabulary had begun to change. This has become clearly evident in the written work which has followed. They are actually using words like 'imply' and 'suggest', which to me indicates that they have finally got onto the 'wavelength' of literature.

The final stage in the whole process has been for the pupils to prepare and present seminars to the rest of the group. Having to cover a collection of short stories in a fairly short space of time, we read and discussed them very briefly as a group. Pupils elected to be responsible for further work on one story and membership of a group was based on which story they liked best. All groups performed equally well when conducting the session and it was notable that they presented the session as a group rather than one person doing all the talking.

Looking back over the five terms which I have spent with the class, there is no magical activity which caused the 'breakthrough' in the pupils' attitudes to their work and each other. The subject, English Literature, probably lends itself more than some others to an approach which focuses on the pupils themselves. For me, of crucial importance was the need to develop the skills which pupils needed in order to learn. Continually looking for approaches to achieve this aim, I was very grateful when the pupils suggested new ones!

The name 'the terrible trio' has somehow disappeared. It is perhaps ironic that one of the three decided to talk on the subject of teaching in his recent English Language Oral examination. He made it clear that group work was the way he learned and that he would like to see all teachers move out from 'behind the barrier' of the desk.

Ruth Harker

The class is much more united. The atmosphere is more relaxed but we do more work and learn more ourselves.

I knew what I was doing and I wasn't afraid. In the old lessons I used to be afraid if I did anything wrong.

TALES OF THE UNEXPECTED

In this second student-centred lesson, 2R and I sat in a circle, did some work on sabotage and then discussed the previous week's homework, which had not been done very well. The whole principle and value of homework was questioned and then discussed in threes and afterwards in a round. The class was fairly well divided on the question of whether or not RE homework should continue being set.

At the end we did a round of 'I thought the lesson was . . .' Comments included:

> *I enjoyed it because we didn't do any writing.*
>
> *This is the only lesson in which we can really say what we think.*
>
> *It's great to be able to give your honest opinion without feeling under pressure.*
>
> *I think you are a very brave teacher letting us make these kinds of decisions.*

Those who wanted to were invited to write 'What I/the class got out of this lesson'. Among those who did this at home were two who had spoken out strongly against homework! Here are one or two extracts:

> *It's good that 2R as a whole class can express their feelings to one another and solve a problem which concerns us all together. We should be able to go up to someone in our class and talk to them easily, not only girls but boys too.*
>
> *I think the lesson was a great success. For the first time we were given the opportunity to discuss the issue of homework. Also the teacher did not affect the debate and we could voice our feelings.*
>
> *I was impressed with the way the class spoke out and learned that 2R as a whole realised they had to stick together. People in the class were prepared to share their views with the rest of the class. The most prominent thing which the class showed was, quite simply, their feelings. After this session I felt I knew a lot more about the class.*

I think that this way of teaching is very impressive.

Well, yesterday's lesson was ultra-different. I enjoyed it in a way because I'm always surprised by how honest the kids in my class can be. I like being honest about my views and this lesson gave me a chance to say things I wouldn't normally. RE lessons sometimes even make me think about things I've never considered before, like 'is there any point in doing RE homework?' I was very pleased to see how seriously the class took the question. However, since the lesson I have felt a little sad that this question was ever raised, because the class is divided now, and soon we will have to come to a decision that affects us all. Whichever half 'wins' will make the other half feel bitter and I think it would have been better just to have kept having homework and not to have thought of this. I slightly suspect Mr. Ginnis of posing the question to gain the respect and attention of the class, trying to show at the same time his respect for us.

I didn't see the relevance of how people sabotaged lessons to the homework question. I think to try and be subtle in telling us why it's 'naughty' to talk in class is a bit silly. Perhaps Mr. Ginnis doesn't realise how deeply the talking, dossing about syndrome is cut in us.

Reflection

What came out in this lesson surprised me. I *had* thought things were going well with 2R. After all, there were few problems. Work was being done in class, homework was usually handed in and the atmosphere of the lessons seemed fairly pleasant. Things certainly *were* going well – judged by my old standards which emphasised quietness, quantity, writing and passivity. This class knew how to play by those rules. They accepted my decisions and, with one or two exceptions, followed my instructions. They had been conditioned by this old system, had tasted some success by it and so were content to operate within it. I interpreted this as 'things going well'.

So, I entered the student-centred scene with 2R convinced that they would choose to carry on in much the same way. I would have the satisfaction of knowing how much they liked RE, and me, and how they found it all very interesting. What a shock! There was dissatisfaction, reluctance, rebellion and, worst of all, apathy. How the class had been suffering in silence, since speaking out was against the rules! Now they could say what they thought. The lid had been taken off and for the first time I saw inside the class.

Two things came out of this experience for me. First, it highlighted the enormous gulf which can exist between teacher-perspective and pupil-perspective. As the professionals, we usually assume that our judgments and evaluations are correct. We tend to accept unquestioningly the teacher-perspective and are often reluctant to listen to anyone else's point of view – least of all the students'. 'In my professional opinion . . .' we say to raise ourselves above reproach. How many educational crimes have been committed against children because of 'professional opinion'? But why *not* ask them what they think? What other organisation, system or service would deliberately ignore customer opinion? How myopic and insecure we teachers can be. We say we want to meet our children's needs, yet *we* often decide what those needs are. Then we blame the students for not always responding to our provision. I have discovered that I can trust kids to say something for and about themselves. It is essential to have the pupil-perspective if the approach is to be truly student-centred.

Secondly, I learned that an 'honesty session', such as happened in this lesson, cannot be predetermined or prejudged. Be prepared to have your expectations dashed. Things may be exposed which will hurt and shock, but in so doing, layers of pretence and falsehood will be pared away and a bedrock of trust and honesty will remain. From this foundation, genuine motivation and genuine learning can arise. Student-centred teaching cannot be manipulative, calculating or political, or nothing will increase except suspicion.

ESTABLISHING GROUND RULES IN PRACTICAL SUBJECTS

In order to initiate student-centred methods in any subject, preparatory sessions to accustom pupils to the new ways of working are important. Without this preparation, it may be difficult to implement a student-centred approach. In practical subjects, such as science, CDT and PE, safety considerations make this vital.

Students and teachers together will need to negotiate the ground rules which can lead to safe work in the laboratory, workshop or gym. The dangers of learning by experience are obvious, and so strategies must be devised to allow pupils to develop both an awareness of the need for certain rules, and ways of keeping to them.

Some ways in which this could be done are by role-playing dangerous situations, playing simulation games or by using films or cartoons which portray dangerous practices. These could be followed up by group or individual formulation of rules, culminating in an agreed set of ground rules for the group and the situation.

Students could monitor the keeping of these rules by the encouragement of individual or group responsibility for safe working and/or by the use of external reminders. These could be, for example, a 'yellow card' warning system (as used by the Football Association) operated by students, or a notional points system where points may be lost for unsafe working. (Of course it may sometimes happen that the teacher would be given a yellow card by an observant pupil.)

The use of student-centred methods in practical subjects cannot mean an abdication by teachers of their ultimate responsibility for the safety of the students in their charge. The aim should be to encourage and help pupils to become aware of, and take responsibility for, their own and others' safety.

David Greer
Kay Chaffer

WORK CONTRACTS

When I was eleven, in a suburb near Chicago, my Sixth Grade teacher was a blue-eyed lively woman of about 30. I loved her with all my heart; she was so much fun, so alive and so much *with* us. At the time I took for granted all that we did; now, as an educator, I know that her methods were unique and very progressive.

At the beginning of each half-term, we were given a contract consisting of six weeks worth of work in every subject. So, for example, in Maths, there would be three tracks of work, difficult, average and easy, to do with long division. There were also games and activities. We could choose the track we wanted, and tick the work we intended to do. The work was divided into small achievable units. We then could work at our own pace to complete it, at any time of the school day. There would be times when Mrs. Brogan would work with us as a group, to present a new topic, or to correct a general problem. She was always there to support us if we got stuck.

There were three similar tracks of work and activities for each subject in the curriculum, and these were frequently changed and new activities added so that the contracts were fresh and new.

When we had completed our own contracts, we could do what we liked. The room was richly resourced (I now suspect, mostly from Mrs. B's pocket!) with all sorts of books, art materials, tools, costumes, scrap wood, toys and lots more.

My friends and I used to race through our contracts, but aiming for them to be perfect. We worked at each other's homes after school, and checked each other's products. No-one ever had to tell us to do our homework; we couldn't wait! When we triumphantly brought our completed contracts to Mrs. Brogan, usually after about three weeks, she would check them over in our presence, and we would correct them if necessary. Then we were free to do what we liked. We put on grandiose plays of our own devising; we did the lights, the costumes, and lots of gushy make-up. We were able to go by ourselves to some corner of the school to rehearse, and we never caused any trouble that I can remember. Our class and other kids would come to see our plays, and we enlisted cast members from all over the school, who were encouraged to join in.

This was in an ordinary state school, and the year was 1944 . . .

Is it any wonder that I chose to become a Sixth Grade teacher myself? Now I am aware of the extra effort Mrs. B. had to put into her planning and preparation; I know, because I've done it this way myself. Yes, it took hours and hours to devise the contracts; and to resource the room cost me both time and money. But it paid off over and over again, in terms of enthusiasm and motivation on the part of the kids, and the lack of discipline problems.

If I were using the contract system now, with the further training and experience I've had, I'd work with the students themselves to devise the contracts, thus moving further along the continuum of teaching styles, as well as saving the time that I might have spent in preparing parts of the contracts which students would not choose to pursue.

CLASSROOM CONTROL

To my way of thinking, classroom control demands only one quality: inner strength on the part of the teacher. This is manifested in a feeling of confidence which says 'I know *I can* handle whatever happens in this class'. It is not the same as saying 'I *have to* handle whatever happens in this class'. There was a time when I did a survey among teachers, asking them what they dreamed about. Of the 200 teachers I spoke to, both inexperienced and seasoned educators, almost everyone admitted that they had nightmares about losing control of the class, about the kids running wild, someone getting hurt. Why *should* 30 kids do what I tell them, anyway?

Levels of personal power

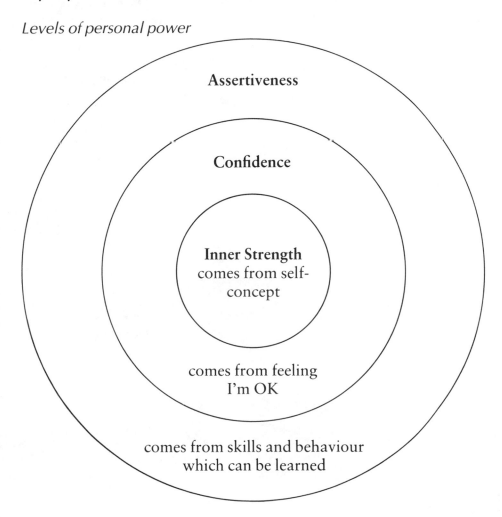

Assertiveness

Confidence

Inner Strength
comes from self-concept

comes from feeling I'm OK

comes from skills and behaviour which can be learned

Shouting and ssshhing

(or, how to learn to hate the sound of your own voice)

A phenomenon I never experienced as a pupil or student, but which is very common in the schools I'm now visiting, I call Shouting and Ssshhing. It goes:

Teacher *(at top of voice)*: *As I was saying yesterday . . . Ssshhhshstst* (I'm having difficulty conveying the exact sound; it is a sort of short, sharp, loud, explosive hiss)

Teacher: *So as I was Sshhtsshtssh saying, I was talking to you yesterday about Sshhsh Henry the VIII who was a very Sshhhhtttsh Abdul! Rashida! You're not listening. If you listened you might learn something . . . Good. Now as it was Ssshhhthhhst*

I ask myself: how do I feel listening to this? Sad, embarrassed, nervous, my head aches.

Does it work? Does the teacher have their attention? What are the signs that they are involved or disenchanted?

CLASSROOM POWER

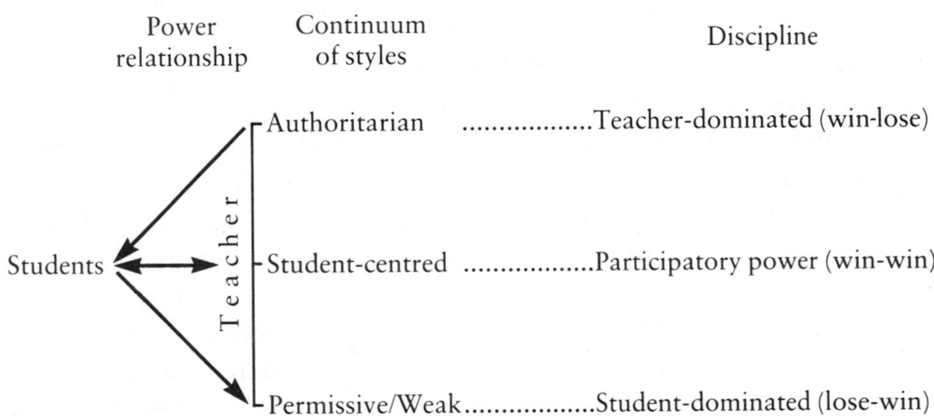

I have described only three positions on the continuum. In reality, teachers can, and do, occupy any position.

Most classroom power structures are of the 'win-lose' type. At one end of the continuum is the authoritarian, *teacher-dominated*, model, in which the will of the teacher is imposed, often without explanation, either by force of personality or threat of sanctions. It is a system largely maintained by negative reinforcement. A high level of conflict, or at least underlying tension, in the teacher-pupil relationship is accepted or even expected. One way or another the teacher must win and, because of the structure of the relationship, the kids must lose. This model is part of a general educational philosophy in which the teacher is the expert whose job it is to impart knowledge and skills to the pupils. Learning is passive. As you move away from the authoritarian towards the student-centred position, the need for a system of rewards and punishments decreases.

At the other extreme is the *student-dominated* model. Sometimes, but not often, this situation is deliberately created as part of a permissive, laissez-faire policy. More often, the kids do as they please and have their own way, not because the teacher wishes it, but because he can do nothing about it. This weak-teacher problem usually arises within the same authoritarian structure as the teacher-dominated model, with its inherent conflict and tension. There have to be winners and losers and in this case, for some reason or other, the teacher is unable to win. No matter what other qualities and skills this person possesses, because of this one *in*ability, he is labelled 'a bad teacher'. So much energy and effort goes into trying to win the power game, that real teaching potential is not released. The teacher remains unfulfilled, frustrated and feels threatened by the pressure to 'succeed' in the conventional way. If the authoritarian model produces head-down pupils, the permissive/weak model produces head-down teachers. Both positions fail to bring out the best in teachers or students.

There is another way – the way of *participatory power*. It is based on a sense of partnership between teacher and students, a sharing of responsibility for decisions and discipline. Neither teacher nor students are dominant – indeed, the idea of dominance is itself removed and with it goes the idea of losing. There is no struggle for power, no underlying tension. Discipline is not imposed, rather it is achieved naturally. Everyone owns the classroom and has a stake in its atmosphere, relationships and congeniality. Class behaviour is no longer just the teacher's problem, but is owned by the whole group, of which the teacher is but a member. This takes the pressure off the teacher to win, and off the kids to plot, subvert and resist. All this energy can now be channelled into more creative pursuits.

Such a situation of 'natural discipline' is achieved through relationships of trust within the group. The teacher will need to trust the students with full and genuine participation in the decision making process. The students will not only *feel* responsible, but actually *be* responsible for the situation, being allowed to enjoy or suffer the consequences of their own decisions and actions. This strategy may seem radical, but is, in fact, only human. While various techniques described in this book, such as the round, problem solving and ground rules, may be helpful in establishing and maintaining natural discipline, the teacher who is used to traditional structures and methods will *first of all* need to reorientate enough to accept himself and his students as human beings – nothing more and nothing less. This acceptance, which generates a sense of equality, unity and common purpose, is the starting point for participatory classroom power.

FROM DIDACTIC TO STUDENT-CENTRED TEACHING

The movement from established well-known ground to explore new teaching strategies is a tough challenge for any of us. It requires more and more courage as we get older because we have more to lose in terms of personal status, dignity, self-esteem – especially if we make mistakes on the way.

Professor Ted Wragg of Exeter University pointed out to a TVEI Co-ordinators' Conference in July 1984 that the average classroom teacher experiences something like 300 student contacts a day which adds up to 1500 per week, or 60000 a year!

After 20 years of active teaching we are likely to have adopted and internalised a particular style or mode of relating to our students which it is very difficult to change – habits die hard. The older we are the more likely we are to have encountered progressive young teachers with their bright ideas – not to say ideals – and seen some of them struggle and even capitulate to the control norms of the school, buttressed by expectations of traditionally orientated parents.

If we have clambered a few more rungs up the ladder we may have joined the ranks of heads and deputies with management styles based on maintenance of order, stability and deterministic control systems. The whole of this progression will have been based on a teacher-centred classroom control mechanism, which could be referred to as the didactic, heads down, absorb it and reproduce mode of teaching and learning.

Unfortunately, some other modes of classroom operation with the brand name 'student-centred' wrapped around them have done little justice to the real product, and this article is designed to distinguish between the real product and the false one by looking at three models.

Process A: the didactic

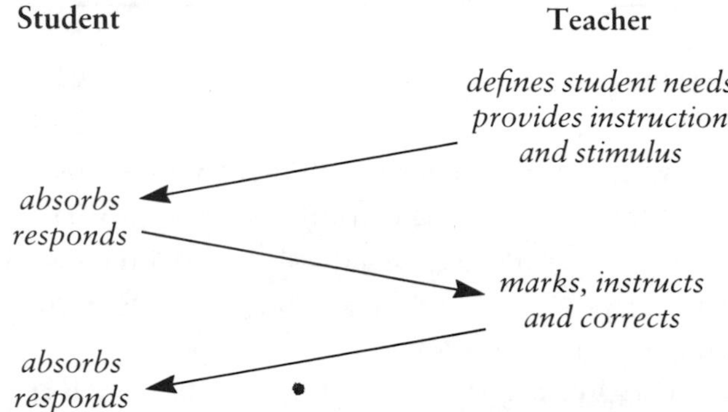

Using this approach, the teacher takes on the impossible task of interpreting the needs of every individual student in the group. The teacher instructs, instils pre-digested skills and knowlede and keeps the student busy. The teacher is the hub or generator of all activity and is the controller of events. Students are totally dependent on the teacher to learn – remove the teacher for a while and students 'mess about'. The problem of such an approach is that it does not educate students to take responsibility for their own learning, to be self-evaluating and self-determining. They are being expected to learn by example, not by discovery.

Process B: the loose-ended approach

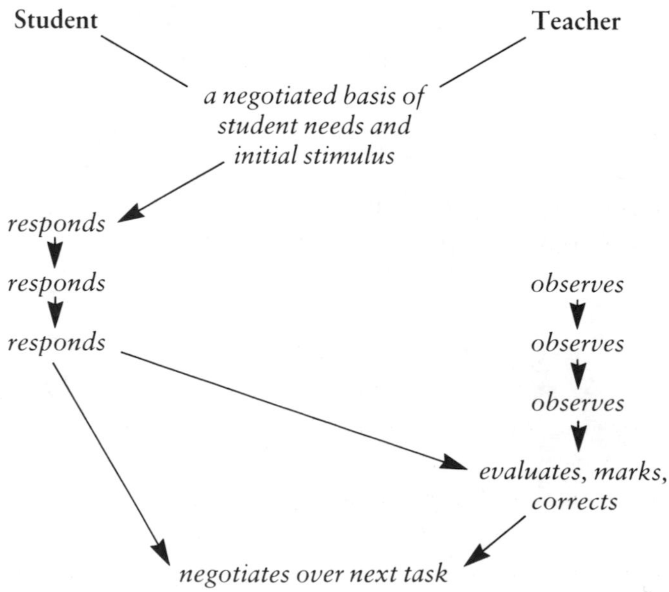

In this model we see a more active student with the teacher taking a back seat. Learners determine their own way ahead and this model may be used, for example, for post examination projects in the summer term.

The failure of this model is one of a very low level of interaction between student and teacher – in fact the teacher is losing responsibility for the process and the learner has little direct guidance – although students can learn from each other better than under a didactic regime. The growth of student capabilities is a hit-or-miss affair.

Process C: the interactive process

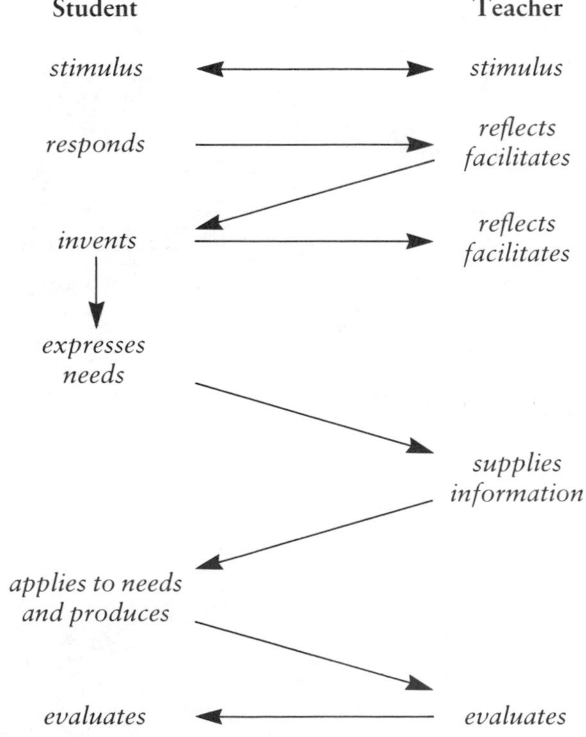

This process is truly student-centred with his/her motivation propelling the process and the teacher acting as the sensitive facilitator. The teacher and learner operate in an interactive two-way process, with the teacher exercising temporary periods of control, but with the student retaining overall ownership of the process. Also students can more readily learn from each other and learn to work in a team or group. There is easy transition of the roles of teacher and learner and there is scope for real growth for both. Learners are learning how to learn as well as producing results – they are self-determining, gathering motivation and learning for life beyond the classroom. There is no loss of contact – on the contrary, there is growth of shared control of learning. The problem is that the teacher needs to have the wider range of skills and trust which the learner wants to learn. The management of a school must also share the same philosophy or the teacher can be undermined – not least by didactic, directive teachers who feel threatened by this alternative approach in their midst.

Chris Lea

STUDENT-CENTRED RELIGIOUS EDUCATION

Within a liberal state education, in this multiethnic, increasingly secular society, it is easier to teach *about* religions, to impart information about the varieties of religious experience, belief and practice than it is to cut through the tangle of educational and philosophical problems and do what for me is more genuine RE. Religious education, as I see it, is to take a child on in his religious development, to *explore and expand his awareness of life's spiritual dimension.* It involves improving the child's perception and appreciation of his *own* spirituality and that of others. It also involves assisting the child in an interpretation of this awareness.

A parallel could be drawn with PE. The physical dimension of a child's existence is developed through a programme of exercise and play. In this way, a general physical education takes place. Physical abilities and capacities are improved, which may then be turned to a particular sport. Training and coaching in the chosen sport will now be effective because of the general level of agility, co-ordination and fitness. The *spiritual* dimension of a child's existence is no less real, though it is usually given far less attention because it is less obvious. The job of the RE teacher is to improve spiritual abilities and capacities, just as the PE teacher improves physical ones. This improved spirituality, this spiritual fitness, forms the foundation for, and enhances the 'training' and 'coaching' in a specific faith of the child's, parents' or community's choice.

How is this kind of RE done? These goals are not likely to be achieved simply by the objective study of the phenomena of religion. There seems to be little use in a child just collecting religious information. What does it profit a man if he gains the whole body of knowledge about religion and loses his own soul? Can a person become physically fit by learning about sport or even visiting sports grounds and watching matches? By the same token, much that is done in modern RE is not the real thing. It is often second hand, dealing in other people's experiences and beliefs, with a vague hope that the student will make the connection and find it of some benefit. Often the point of the activity is missed and the work becomes dull and irrelevant. Effective RE will, I believe, have to be less cognitive than this.

So, what is the way forward? If spiritual development is to take place within a child, the teaching and learning will need to be first-hand and personal. The work will need to establish a dialogue with the student. It will need to make contact. It may challenge or confirm something held to be true, it may settle or disturb the emotions, it may raise questions or suggest answers. If it does none of these things, it cannot, for me, be genuine religious education. *The focus of RE can be the student and not religion.* Material from various religious traditions may be used, but in order to provide a mirror in which students see their own spiritual reflections.

Relevance

Even so, who can say that the RE teacher, with all his expertise and professionalism, always knows which religious material will work best and be most relevant and stimulating? How can the RE teacher guarantee that essential 'contact' and 'dialogue' between the material and the student? Furthermore, how can he be aware of, and cater for, the needs of each individual in his class, in each class he teaches? Surely it is essential for the students to be able to say what work they wish to do and/or how they wish to do it. Who knows better than they what their interests and needs are, even if they cannot always articulate them? In my experience students can be trusted to make this choice.

Confluence

Such participation means that the work is tailor-made to meet individual or group needs, which we have argued is essential if effective religious education is to take place. It is no longer second-hand. Nor is it merely cognitive. Naturally, there will be a cognitive element, but in the process of doing the work a whole range of skills, such as organisational, decision-making and research skills, will be exercised. More significant than the development of skills, there will be a personal involvement in the work by the student, through which attitudes and values will be affected. A student-centred, participatory approach leads not only to active learning, but to involved learning. Such an educational experience is *confluent*, with development taking place in three domains at once: cognitive; skills; affective.

If we value religious freedom and are aiming to promote attitudes of tolerance and sensitive appreciation of those who believe differently, then these values must be reflected in our methodology. Values may be communicated more through method than content. How can such religious values be transmitted within an authoritarian, teacher-dominated system, where everyone has to do what the teacher says, when she says it, how she says it – or else! Where is the tolerance, freedom and sensitive appreciation? Such a system wars against the values we are trying to teach; there is incongruence. Students receive conflicting messages – our actions and our words speak differently. It is a form of hypocrisy. In order to teach tolerance, acceptance and appreciation of others, these values must abound in the classroom. They must be the teacher's attitudes towards the students and the students' attitudes towards each other. They must ooze from the methodology.

Motivation

Work approached in this student-centred way seems to generate greater enthusiasm. RE often suffers low status in schools and rarely features high in the popularity polls, with few people opting for it as an examination subject. Students' motivation can, however, be transformed. I have found that adopting a student-centred philosophy, making and keeping group decisions, produces excitement, creativity, productivity and a warmth that I had never known in my lessons before. Students will not choose work that bores them. There is a commitment to the job in hand, a pride in the work, because it is theirs and not mine. The problem of unwanted work being imposed by the teacher and resisted by the kids just does not apply any more. There is a natural motivation, not one created by carrot and stick. Motivation grows from within and is not manipulated from without.

Safe self-disclosure

Apart from increased relevance, confluence and motivation, I feel there is an even more important reason for, and benefit of, participatory teaching in RE. If, as I have argued, RE is about spiritual development – about aspirations, wonder, questions, doubts, the formation and rejection of beliefs – then it is intensely personal and potentially private. In order to 'get at' these inner things, and allow spiritual development to take place, students will benefit from being open and honest. Superficiality will not do; there may need to be a willingness to share experiences, emotions and beliefs. Unless this happens, a student's spiritual awareness, capacity and understanding may not be enlarged. This kind of depth and honesty is not easy, perhaps impossible, to achieve within traditional teaching structures; it depends on trust. No-one is going to bare her heart if she is laughed at, criticised or ignored. Verbal cruelty is rife in most classrooms. It destroys trust, and with trust goes the possibility of open communication. So, there is a lot of repairing and rebuilding to do. Participatory, student-centred teaching is essentially about trusting, open relationships and so provides the right climate for safe self-disclosure. The 'feelings' side of religion, sometimes suppressed or observed only in the experience of others in RE, is now given expression. As members of the group share their experiences, they may help each other to find their ways to individual stances for living.

The group would benefit from the teacher being open and honest too. RE teachers who have a strong conviction about a particular faith have sometimes been expected to keep it quiet or play it down, lest it put unfair pressure on vulnerable minds. This can be a very frustrating and limiting experience for the teacher, and can impoverish her teaching by depriving it of a valuable and rich resource. It is true that within a didactic framework, where the teacher is dominant and surrounded by the myth of infallibility, an expression of her personal faith would be very influential and therefore inappropriate. If her relationship with the students were more open and trusting, however, and her status within the group that of facilitator, there would be far less risk of indoctrination. If the teacher became used to speaking the truth as she sees it at the moment, then expressions of personal faith could not be avoided. They would not only be appropriate, but also necessary – a refusal to declare 'the-truth-as-I-see-it' may undermine the trust which is being built up.

For all the reasons above, Religious Education would, I believe, benefit from the use of student-centred approaches. I believe that, in dealing with the problems of indoctrination and the conflicting truth claims and values of religions, RE should not travel further down the path of objectivity. Nor should it turn down the side roads of sectarianism and have each faith community teaching its own dogmas. Nor does the way forward lie in the development of more authentic resources which recreate and 'bring to life' in the classroom the experience of others. Too often, to me, the stage of RE seems to be occupied by the various phenomena and paraphernalia of religion. The students become the audience, while the teacher combines the roles of director, producer and compère. I am not suggesting that we make changes to the way the play is presented, but that we may scrap the set play altogether, let the students take over the stage and decide on their own productions. The teacher, with his experience in this 'theatre', can help them make the things they want to do happen.

> *The lessons enable you to create your own opinion of religious work and your beliefs in that certain area. The lessons provide a large amount of freedom for everyone involved, for you are not actually condemned to one subject . . . I believe that the lessons are more active, more educational and exceedingly fascinating!*

PAC MAN

In Transactional Analysis (TA), communication between people is analysed in terms of:

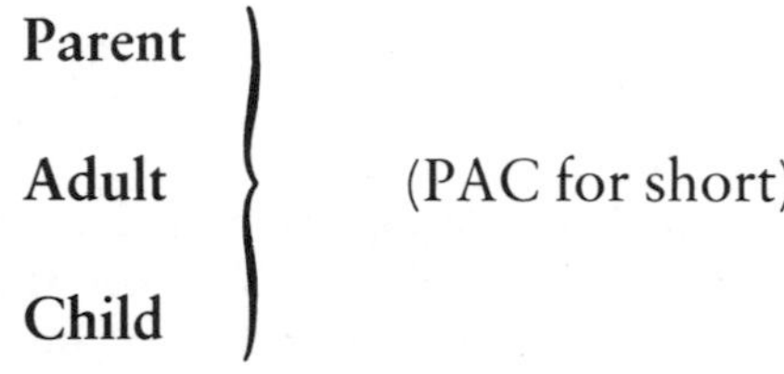

Everyone is capable of operating in these three frames of mind at different times. In TA they are referred to as 'ego states', and each has a distinctive set of attitudes and behaviours. The ego state I am operating in at any moment is given away by the things I say, my tone of voice and choice of words. My body postures, gestures and facial expressions also act as non-verbal indicators. We all change ego states frequently, even within the same conversation. They may be described as follows:

The *Parent* ego state is characterised by setting standards, making and enforcing rules, pronouncing value judgments, exercising control of others, looking after others, and taking responsibility for others.

The *Child* ego state may be divided into two: the *Free Child* characterised by the spontaneous expression of feelings and wants, emotional reactions, impulse, no inhibition, curiosity, creativity, intuition; and the *Adapted Child* (who has learned a degree of self-control), characterised by compliance, politeness, submission, servility.

The *Adult* ego state is characterised by rational assessment, estimation, realism, logic, decision making, negotiation, discussion, questioning, consultation, reflection.

Conversations can be seen as chains of transactions, a transaction being a basic unit of communication consisting of a stimulus (usually spoken) and a response to it. In the classroom, many transactions take place between teacher and students, for example in a question and answer session, in giving instructions, in helping individuals with their work. Many also occur between students and students, for example in a class discussion, in an 'illicit' conversation, or during group work. One of our main concerns in student-centred learning is with the content and nature of these transactions, as they influence the quality of relationships in the room and thereby determine the learning environment. The PAC analysis is a useful one in enhancing awareness of what is going on in the classroom and how interactions between people in the group can be improved.

Using the PAC analysis, transactions may be grouped into two categories: *complementary* and *crossed*. An example of a complementary transaction would be:

> "Ashurst, your homework was rubbish."
> Yes Sir. I'm sorry Sir. I'll try to do better in future!"

This transaction could be represented in diagrammatic form, like this:

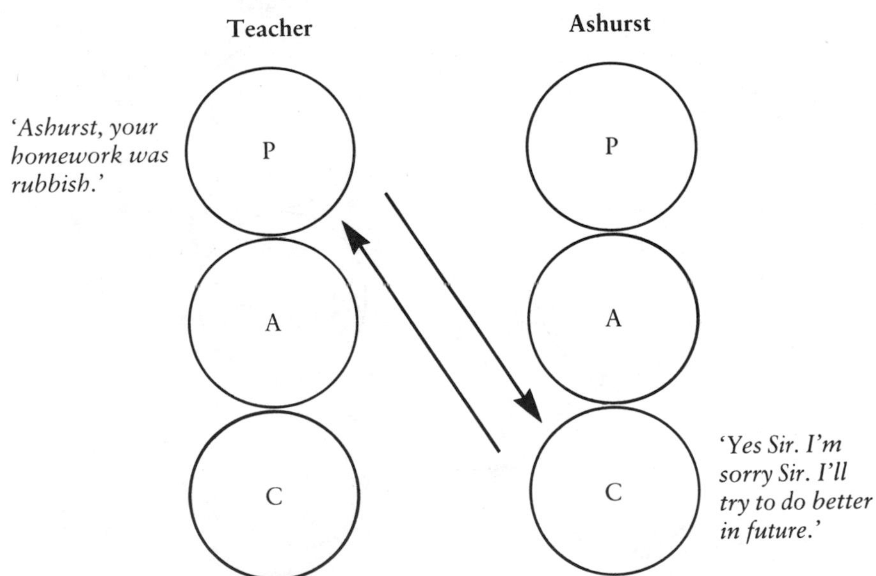

The initial remark was made to the student's child, and the student replied appropriately. So, a complementary transaction is one in which the reply comes from the ego state to which the statement was directed. In other words, you get the sort of reply you expect. It is worth reflecting on how often teachers operate in the *Parent* mode, expecting *Adapted Child* responses from their pupils. For example, in controlling movement around the building, giving instructions, explaining new material, and especially in 'laying down the law', complaining about work and dealing with trouble-makers. It is sometimes the case that teachers operate in this *Parent → Child* mode in all formal situations, letting it drop only during the informality of an extra-curricular club or sports match. If the teacher's expectation to be replied to from the student's *Adapted Child* is met, then things go well. If, however, replies are made in the *Free Child*, with Ashurst saying for example, *'I don't care. I thought the homework was a waste of time anyway'*, there's likely to be serious trouble. This trouble may come from the teacher's *Parent* or, more likely, from the teacher's own *Free Child* ('He's taken it personally' we say).

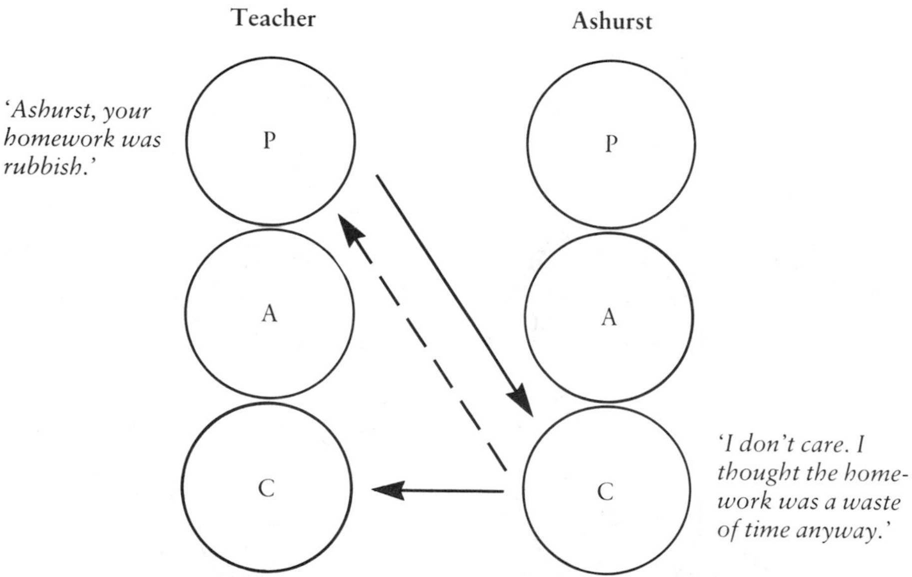
Teacher
Ashurst
'Ashurst, your homework was rubbish.'
P
A
C
P
A
C
'I don't care. I thought the home-work was a waste of time anyway.'

These *Parent–Child* transactions which seem to dominate many classrooms and which, when used frequently, could form into a *Parent–Child* relationship, inhibit students' development and can generate a good deal of tension. The teacher is taking responsibility for right and wrong in the classroom, for standards of behaviour and work, and is insisting on compliance and acceptance rather than questioning and discovery. In short, she is blocking off the potential for personal growth and is denying personal autonomy. Such a *Parent–Child* relationship retards educational development and cannot be the basis of a student-centred classroom. Moreover, it contains an inherent tension as maturing students find it less and less acceptable to be treated like children whilst being denied the right to say openly how they feel.

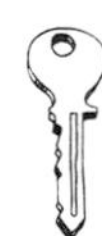

To avoid these problems, teachers and students may find it helpful to move towards *Adult–Adult* transactions. Some *crossed* transactions may take place while this change is being made. For example, the students could be the first to move to the adult ego state and so Ashurst could have replied about the homework: *'What is it exactly that you feel is poor?'* This appeals to the teacher's adult and, unless he is a particularly hardened case or is in an unusually bad mood, is likely to draw an adult response from him, affecting not only the tone of *this* conversation, but it may well influence the future relationship between the two parties. It may even be the beginning of a general change within the class.

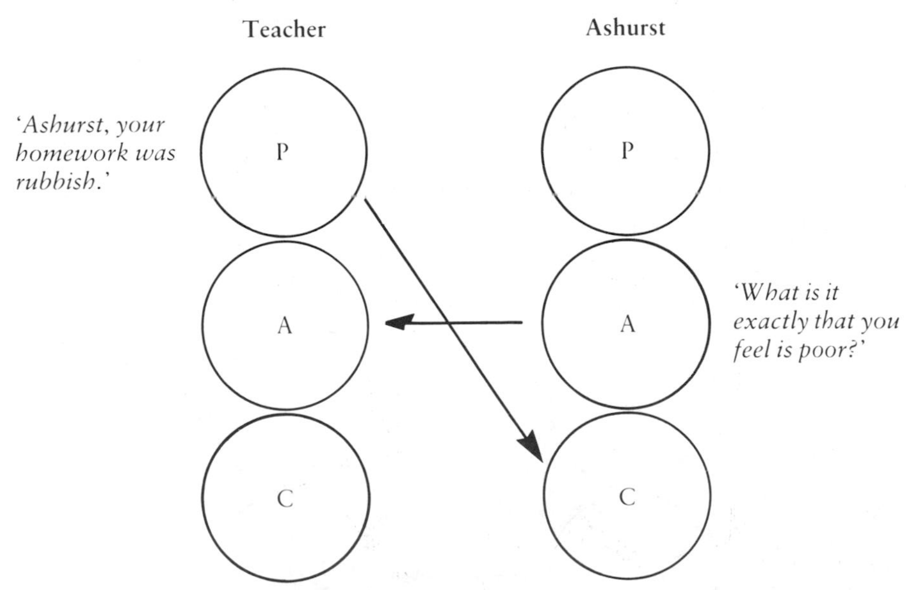

More frequently, though, it is the teacher who will initiate a change in classroom transactions. He may, for example, reply to the question, *'Sir, will you do this for me?'* with *'Now, where do you think the problem lies?'* or to the sudden outburst *'This lesson's boring'* with *'What would it take for you not to feel so bored?'* or, when he is told *'You make me sick'*, he could reply *'What is it I do which makes you feel this way?'*

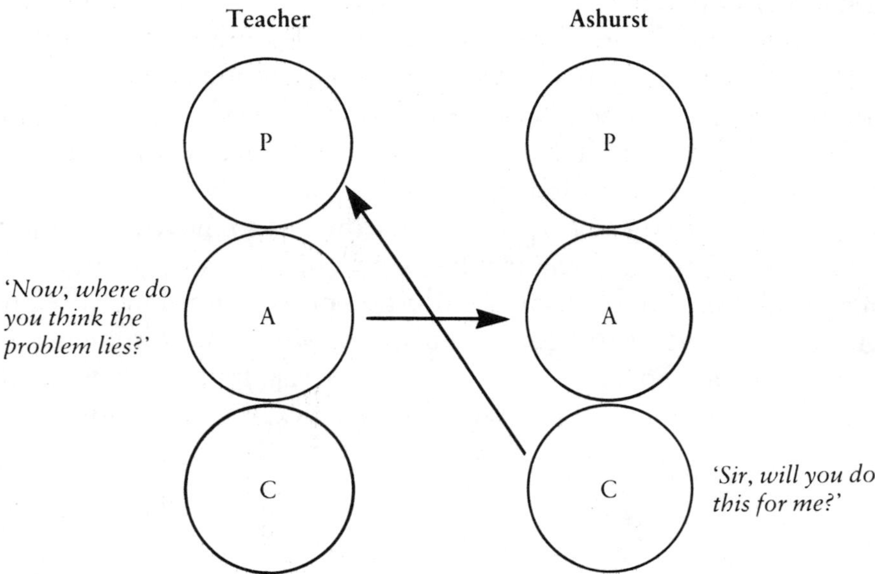
Teacher
Ashurst
P
P
'Now, where do you think the problem lies?'
A
A
C
C
'Sir, will you do this for me?'

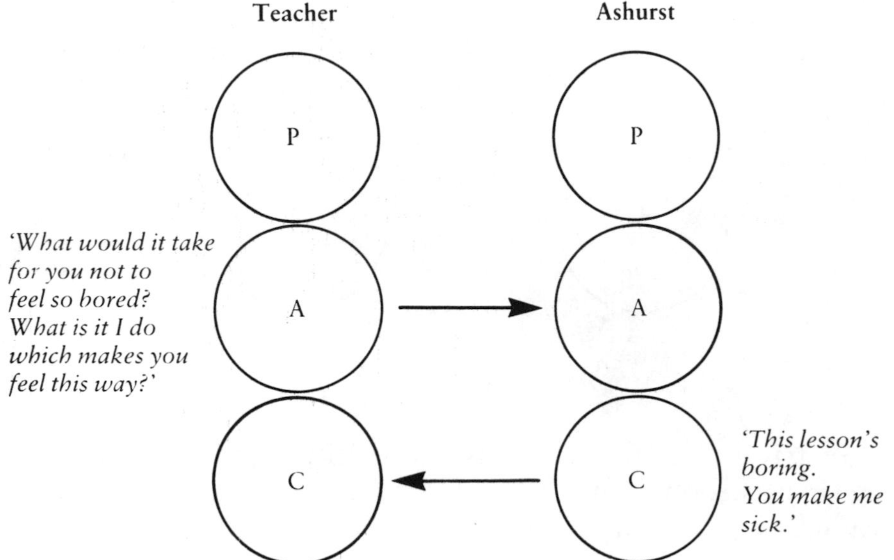
Teacher
Ashurst
P
P
'What would it take for you not to feel so bored? What is it I do which makes you feel this way?'
A
A
C
C
'This lesson's boring. You make me sick.'

The value of these replies does not lie in their element of surprise, but in the way they put a transaction, and potentially a relationship, on a new footing. They value and take seriously what has been said and the person who said it. This is the beginning of open, effective and constructive communication. It also opens the door to negotiation, problem solving and joint decision making.

Section 3

ACTIVITY

Values in school

There is a debate in the literature about values in education. Some educationists believe that morality must be taught in school, that it is our duty as teachers to instil firm principles of right and wrong in our students. Others believe that we have no right to impose our values on young people, and that we could better serve them by allowing time and opportunity for the exploration of moral issues and personal values.

We do not intend to explore the debate here; this book speaks for itself as to which side we are on. It contains many activities specifically designed for personal and social development, and it propounds a view in which students take responsibility for their own learning.

Many activities which encourage students to explore their own values, and compare them with other people's, appear in books by Sidney Simon, Leslie Button, and others, as well as in the *Gamesters' Handbook*. The use of a continuum for illustrating a spread of values in a group has already been described in some of the books mentioned above (see *Gamesters' Handbook*, P88). Such value clarification exercises can also be used as assessment activities or can be used to define a problem more clearly at the beginning of a problem-solving exercise. We offer here two variations.

2-D value continuum

Aims: [illegible], self-disclosure, self-awareness.

Materials: None

Procedure 1 Choose a topic which has several aspects to it, such as student-centred learning.

2 Choose one aspect which has two extremes, e.g. *knowledge about student-centred learning*. Outline the two extremes by placing a chair at one end of the room and describing that extreme, and another at the other end, e.g.

I know everything there is to know about student-centred learning | I have not one shred of information about student-centred learning

3 Each student places him/herself along the line, and says why that position [illegible].

Martyn Briggs

INTRODUCTION

One of the most rewarding outcomes of this project has been the high quality and increasing numbers of activities generated for use in the classroom. In this section we have included several kinds of activities:

- guidelines for important skills;
- exercises for teachers;
- exercises applicable to different school subjects, e.g. maths, biology, physics, and others;
- activities specifically designed for assessment or evaluation;
- games for fun or for enriching work.

We have also included some 'lesson plans', which are not meant to be taught, but which serve to illustrate the way in which a student-centred teacher *talks*, and to exemplify the attitudes underlying this approach.

These ideas (except the lesson plans) are meant to be useful as they stand, but most of all we hope that they will serve as inspiration. They are intended to be used as paradigms, or springboards for the invention of many more. Just as these were created by ordinary teachers and students, the activities that you yourself may need can be purpose-built for your own lessons, once you realise how much fun it is to design just the right enrichment exercise for any subject or occasion.

GUIDELINES

Values in school

There is a debate in the literature on values in education. Some educators believe that morals should and must be taught in school, that it is our duty as teachers to instil firm principles of right and wrong in our students. Others believe that we have no right to impose our values on young people, and that we could better serve them by allowing time and opportunity for the *exploration* of moral issues and personal values.

We do not intend to explore the debate here; this book speaks for itself as to which side we are on. It contains many activities specifically designed for personal and social development, and it propounds a view in which students take responsibility for their own learning.

Many activities which encourage students to explore their own values, and compare them with other people's, appear in books by Sidney Simon, Leslie Button, and others, as well as in the *Gamesters' Handbook*. The use of continua for illustrating a spread of values in a group has already been described in some of the books mentioned above (see *Gamesters' Handbook* P58). Such value clarification exercises can also be used as assessment activities, or can be used to define a problem more clearly at the beginning of a problem-solving exercise. We offer here two variations.

2-D value continuum

Aims: Exploring values, trust-building, self-disclosure, self-awareness

Materials: None

Procedure:

1 Choose a topic which has several aspects to it, such as student-centred learning.

2 Choose one aspect, which has two extremes, e.g. *knowledge about* student-centred learning. Outline the two extremes by placing a chair at one end of the room and describing that extreme, and another at the other end, e.g.

I know everything there is to know about student-centred learning	________________	I have not one shred of information about student-centred learning

3 Each person puts a chair along the line, and says what that position means for him or her.

4 When the whole group (except those who are passing, of course) is spread out along the line, the leader introduces another dimension by outlining two extremes along a perpendicular line, e.g.

I want to be the very best
student-centred learning
teacher ever in the world

I couldn't care less about
student-centred learning, I
don't want to know, it's no
use to me

5 The group members then move themselves forward or back from where they are sitting, to make a pattern in two dimensions.

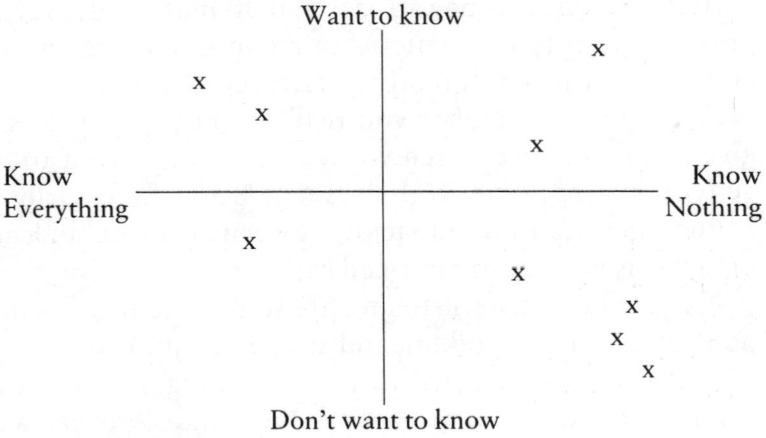

6 Again, people discuss their positions.

Variations: 1 Apply the 2-D model to any school subject or topic, or any general moral issue, or any 'live' question in the group.

2 A discussion could take place between the four quarters. Afterwards, see if anyone wishes to change places.

Concentric circles

(This is very similar to the preceding activity, except that it has a different shape, and therefore, perhaps, a different 'feel' to it. It can also be applied to any topic or school subject.)

Aims: Exploring values, trust-building, self-awareness, group awareness

Materials: None

Procedure: 1 People who feel very good about a topic, e.g. student-centred learning, bring their chairs into the centre of a circle.

2 People who feel neutral or mild about the topic make a circle around them.
3 People who feel angry, or bad, or ignorant, about the topic make an outer circle.
4 Discuss how it feels to be sitting where you're sitting.
5 See if anyone wants to change where they're sitting, or where someone else is sitting.

Variations: Reverse it, and have the negative feelings in the centre. See how that feels to people.

Active listening

Teachers who want to work with students on their listening skills probably want to become quite proficient themselves before they start, so a good deal of practice will be required.

Active listening is not an easy skill to master; it goes against many of our conversational patterns of rejoinders, questions, interruptions, and two-way input. It requires strict self-discipline.

When you decide that you really want to listen to someone, and give them a chance to tell you whatever they want to tell you, then active listening is appropriate; it will not necessarily always be a counselling situation; in fact it is extremely useful in leading a group or class, as we have mentioned earlier.

The aims of active listening are to put the listener into a neutral, non-directive, non-judgmental frame of mind, so that she can give full attention to the person who is speaking, and allow him to make his own way through his story without interference. We often think of it as a gift, because the luxury of talking through an issue without interruption or blocking of any kind is very rare indeed.

There are several parts to the process. The listener:

a sits quietly facing, and looking at, the talker;
b relaxes, and makes any non-verbal responses that come *naturally*, like nodding, or smiling, or making eye contact, but only if it is comfortable;
c as much as possible, in her mind,does nothing *but* listen, suspending all judgments and questions;
d makes verbal responses which consist only of reflecting, or paraphrasing, the key points in what the talker has just said, or making open-ended comments such as 'Yes, I understand', 'What else would you like to tell me about it?'

A script for active listening would go something like this:

Talker: *'We are having problems deciding about where to go for our holidays. I want to go to Devon to a cottage and just relax, and my husband wants to go to visit his family in London.'*
Listener: *'You haven't come to an agreement about it.'*
Talker: *'That's right, and because we are disagreeing about that, we seem to be arguing about everything.'*
Listener: *'It's getting in the way of other things.'*

From this small sample, you can see that there could be many other choices of responses. The listener, in ordinary circumstances, might ask *'Do you own a cottage in Devon, then?'* or *'Does your husband have a big family, then?'*, and might perhaps be wondering if the talker doesn't like her husband's family, and where the cottage is, and many other wonderings about the missing information.

Questions from the listener have the effect of blocking the flow of what the talker wants to say, and *directing* the conversation in the direction of what the listener wants to know.

We have found that, even after a great deal of experience, we cannot manage to do active listening and *anything* else at the same time; that is what we mean when we say it requires strict self-discipline. If you are to pay close enough attention to be able to reflect back the essence of what the talker has just said, then 100% concentration is demanded.

Perhaps it will not be necessary for the students to learn this advanced form of active listening, but if the teacher knows how to do it properly, it can offer many rewards. You can listen to your own family and friends more effectively, and give them space to be heard without interference. You can take a stand in class that neither praises nor blames, nor finds answers right or wrong, but which just reflects the students' ideas and opinions, so that they feel valued by you.

This is not a skill which can be easily learned from a few instructions in a book. Training is desirable, but if that is not available, a good idea would be to find someone else who is interested in learning how to listen actively, and practise with them, taking turns being talker and listener, and giving each other feedback about your progress. It is not always a good idea in the early stages to practise on your unsuspecting family, because they tend to say things like, 'What's happened? You sound like a tape recorder.' or 'How come you're listening to me all of a sudden?', which isn't particularly beneficial to your own self-esteem!

Once you are feeling fairly confident about your own skills, you could, if you wanted, try with your students some of the simple exercises on the following pages. Usually the kids find them enjoyable and interesting, and, in the end, rewarding, as they almost always have the effect of improving communication and building trust.

How we don't listen

1 Start the lesson by talking about something for a few minutes, then tell the students that you are all going to consider how people don't usually listen to each other very well, and ask them what they were doing in their minds while you were talking, besides just listening. Brainstorm the answers. They will probably include such ideas as:

- daydreaming
- thinking about something else
- worrying
- arguing
- preparing what I was going to say next.

Whatever they say, write it up on a blackboard or flip chart.

2 Discuss how they feel when they are talking, and whoever is listening is obviously busy doing something else. Ask them if they can remember the last time they felt someone was not listening, and ask for examples.

3 Divide the group into pairs, and ask A to start talking, and B *not* to listen. Switch over so that each one has a turn in each role. Then discuss how it felt not to be listened to.

4 Ask the students to invent other exercises involving *not* listening. Ask them, for homework, to watch how other people around them listen, or don't listen.

Listening

1 Ask for a volunteer to talk to you while you demonstrate Active Listening. Then ask the students what they noticed about what *you*, the listener, were doing.

2 Practise listening in a Round. The first person says something about the chosen topic, e.g. food. The second in the circle reflects what the first person says, and then turns to the third and says something about food. The third reflects that, and turns to the fourth, and so on. Discuss the process.

3 Divide into pairs and practise Active Listening. Partners give each other feedback.
4 Hold a class discussion on any topic, with each person reflecting the key phrases of what the last person said, before adding something of his own.
5 Try *Look and Listen* on p. 260.
6 Keep the listening skills going by practising and reminding, and try to remember to do a lot more listening yourself. The students can own the discussions and conversations, if you can get out of their way . . .

Problem solving

One of the best ways of handing responsibility to the students is to engage in the problem solving process with them, in regard to real problems which come up in the class.

A true story: In a class of 11-year-olds in California, we had an epidemic of stealing; things were disappearing from desks and cupboards during breaks and lunchtimes; the complaints were increasing every day. At our regular Friday classroom meeting, one of the boys brought the subject up for discussion in the group by putting it on the agenda, which was in the chairperson's possession.

First we discussed the ins and outs of the problem, who was affected by it (who *owned* the problem), how severe the problem was, how long it had been going on, how it was maintained by our policy of keeping the classroom doors open. The kids all felt that they owned the problem, and wanted to solve it. If the 'thief' was in the room at the time, he or she was certainly undetectable.

Next we brainstormed possible solutions, and then evaluated them. Some of the ideas were not acceptable, because they did not fit in with our established ground rules, such as the ones which said someone should hide in the classroom to be a spy and catch the thief in action, then punish him. Our ground rules, one of the students pointed out, did not allow punishment, and encouraged honesty, so those two were ruled out.

We looked at all the solutions and voted to try keeping the doors locked at breaktime for a week, after which we would re-evaluate the situation.

After only three days, the kids were fed up; they couldn't come in to get a ball or a coat or a sandwich, or to see me, or to work if they wanted. Besides, it made the room seem like a fortress.

At the next meeting, which they wanted brought forward to Wednesday, we re-evaluated our choice and decided it wasn't working. After much discussion, the students then decided to leave the doors open and take turns guarding the room during breaks. We then agreed to try that for a week.

On the following Friday, when we discussed it again, it was decided that the solution was good, and it was continued for another three weeks; after that they felt we could get along without the guard and there were no more thefts.

Perhaps the thief, having sat through all of this process, decided that crime was just too much trouble!

To draw out of this anecdote the steps in group problem solving, we can reduce them to four simple steps:

1 Discuss and *own* the problem.
2 Brainstorm solutions and select one.
3 Try out the chosen solution for an agreed length of time.
4 Re-evaluate, and start again if necessary.

Any of these steps could be done in small groups, or by secret ballots; there is no need to do all of them together. Also they can, of course, be adapted to your own use, as one teacher has done on the following pages.

Problem solving II

Last week I encountered Thomas Gordon's 'six-step problem-solving process', (Teacher Effectiveness Training 1974, p. 227–34) but I found it difficult to remember, and when I was trying to test the strategy later in the week I was unable to recall the order. Here is another strategy – similar to the first one, but one which I found much easier to remember. The initial idea was found in Edward de Bono's book entitled *The Thinking Course*, but I have adapted his idea.

1 Take the **P.I.S.**
PISCAE and add **CAE.**

2 Use each letter as a reminder:

P stands for *Purpose*
So define what is expected as the end product of the exercise. The shape of the letter can also help to remind you of what you are

supposed to be doing; e.g. when thinking of the purpose you need to circle or encompass the problem and identify its core feature.

3 I stands for *Information/Input*
Think about all the ingredients that need to go into your thinking. These need to be compartmentalised and clearly defined. You need to set perimeters, as the shape of the letter I indicates:

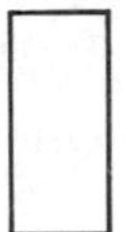

4 S stands for *Solution*
There are often many alternative solutions to a problem e.g.

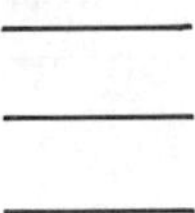

The letter S reminds us to think of linkages between solutions too, e.g.

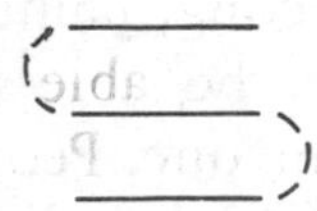

5 C stands for *Choice*
You must make a decision as to which solution you feel is most appropriate. The letter shape (if you are dyslexic!!) will remind you to focus down onto one solution.

6 **A** stands for *Action*
i.e. How is the plan to be put into operation? There are often different levels at this stage:

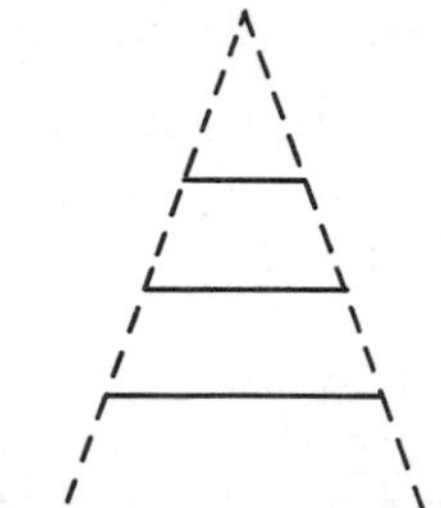

short term

medium term

long term

actions and implications

7 **E** – the last letter is the *Evaluation*
The letter shape reminds us of the pattern in the *Solutions* stage. It reminds us that we may need to go back to the solution stage after evaluation and choose a more appropriate solution if the one that was chosen was not satisfactory.

Role play

Mention the words 'role play' to a group of teachers, and you are very likely going to hear shudders and groans, and perhaps lose half of your group as they rush for the exits. From what people have told us in various training groups, this is because people often feel threatened by the idea of improvising in front of an audience. This is very understandable, because, as in the cases of art, poetry, singing and dancing, it often happens that people have been told in school that they are 'no good at it', and so they stop trying.

We feel that this is a very sad state of affairs, because song, dance, acting, painting, writing, are natural activities which people ought to be able to use for self-expression without interference from anyone. People have a right to play and enjoy themselves, without outside judgments.

So, every chance we get, we try to erase these old tapes about 'I can't do that!' by giving people the opportunity to express themselves in a safe and friendly atmosphere.

Role play, that is taking on a role for the purposes of exploring real life situations, is such a useful tool in the classroom that it seems a shame not to use it, and we have found that with some gentle exposure to the possibilities of it, teachers begin to lose their fears.

One way to introduce role play on a very light level without calling it that, is to play a few games which require a mild piece of acting, such as the Adverb Game, Courtroom, Toyshop etc. from the *Gamesters' Handbook*.

When people are going to take on roles, it is a good idea to spend a few minutes establishing and exploring the roles. So, for example, if you are doing assertiveness training and you want two people to be an aggressive driver and a meek policeman, take a few minutes to ask question like:

How old are you?
What are you wearing?
Where are you going?
Where do you come from?

In other words, just build up a picture of the characters.

Sometimes a person will be 'playing' herself, but the above questions can still apply and may allow the person a few moments to prepare by thinking about herself.

We would like to suggest that role play is supposed to be *fun*; it does not have to be deadly serious in order to provide learning. It is a lively, exciting, involving way of exploring ideas.

Use of role play in pastoral and guidance structures

Role play can be particularly effective as a teaching method in pastoral and guidance situations for the following reasons:

1 The choice of content can be decided entirely by the student. If 'titles' are suggested by the facilitator, they should be 'open' enough for the student to interpret freely.
2 The students can work through personal confusions and problematic situations without the pressure of reality, gaining experience from the reaction of others in role, so as to make informed decisions for themselves.
3 Role play can be a rehearsal for life, through which the young person gains in confidence by expressing his or her own needs but also experiences the needs of others.

Person-centred meetings

Almost everyone in business or the professions has direct experience of meetings. Meetings before work, during work, after work, lunchtimes, evenings, meetings, meetings, meetings. Sometimes they are very boring indeed. If you're a fly on the wall you can observe people with eyelids drooping, wrist watches receiving undue attention, doodles flourishing on notepads, and even long-delayed letters being written clandestinely. In other words, the people are *not* attending; they are not involved. The chairperson owns the agenda, the powers-that-be own the outcomes; why should the others pay attention?

The principles of ownership apply here as in the classroom. Meetings ought to belong to the people who are there, and if they were truly involved they would not be dozing.

We would suggest that Directors, Organisers, Perpetual Chairmen, who believe that the control of meetings ought always to remain in their hands, are woefully behind the times, and dangerously so. There are many examples of the trend towards networking and autonomy in all the major industrial powers.

> Looking around at the world it was clear to many that the problems of the day – a sagging economy, political unrest, and a litany of intractable social problems – were not solvable in a world organised according to the hierarchical principle . . . The failure of hierarchies to solve society's problems forced people to talk to each other and that was the beginning of networks. In a sense we clustered together among the ruins of the tumble-down pyramids to discuss what to do . . . that was the birth of the networking structure. (Naisbitt 1984)

Perhaps the most potent argument of all is that a meeting where everyone is actively involved produces *efficiency*. Things tend to get done, waffle is avoided, boredom is not a factor.

At any level of an organisation, the transformation does not happen overnight; people often become impatient while trying to master the new processes. An investment of time and rehearsal is required, and the methods need to be introduced by someone who is thoroughly versed in them.

So, how can this be accomplished in, say, a school, where all the staff are frantically, hectically busy?

We are offering a few, simple guidelines, which are appropriate for management or staff meetings, governors and PTA meetings, as well as for student council or classroom meetings.

Ground rules for meetings

1 Regular meetings at pre-agreed times, sticking closely to starting and finishing times.
2 Chairperson is rotated at each meeting, rota spelled out in advance. Chairperson is completely in charge each time, and collects the agenda in advance from colleagues. It is important that sanctions and interference are not imposed from above.
3 Every effort is made to save major policy decisions for those meetings, and not to have them decided elsewhere, so that everyone is *in reality* involved in problem solving, evaluating etc.
4 Talents and creativity of each person are valued, so that everyone pools their resources and does the thinking together.
5 Open, direct communication is encouraged, and sarcasm is discouraged, so that outside griping is not necessary. Listening to each other is a major ground rule.
6 When meetings are really effective, they take up less time, and people go away stimulated, not drained.
7 The chair's main tasks are to:

- see that people listen to each other
- prepare the agenda
- stick to the time limits and the ground rules
- see that people are appreciated and acknowledged for the work they do.

8 Matters which do not require everyone's attention may be delegated; however this can be done by outlining the issues and asking for volunteers. Thus, everyone knows that the issues belong to them and that they are not being manipulated.

Classroom meetings and student councils

Using the guidelines above, students can learn to run their own classroom meetings. The aims of such meetings are:

a To solve real problems of any kind which the group considers relevant.
b To provide all students with experience of debate, negotiation and chairing.
c To enhance communication and social skills.
d To place the ownership of problems squarely in the hands of the students.

'But', teachers will declaim, 'there is no time for all that!' Again, let us remind ourselves what we are all meant to be learning. In a self-contained classroom, an hour a week set aside for a regular meeting can pay off in terms of improved cooperation, solutions to worrying problems, more peaceful sleep for the teacher at night, and the feeling of ownership on the part of the students, as well as the enhanced skills mentioned above. We have seen seven-year-olds chairing such meetings.

In a secondary school, meetings could occur in form periods, in English, Drama, History classes, indeed, in any lesson where the teacher sees these skills as equally important to cognitive knowledge.

Within a school which wants to move towards a more student-centred ethos, one vital component of change is the Student Council. Many times we have seen a Puppet Council, where the students go through the motions of cloning staff meetings, and where lip service is paid to decision making, and everyone knows that the students have no real power to make decisions; in short, a farce, and just as boring as a badly run staff meeting.

We would sugest that students should own the discipline policy of the school. The discipline structure can be seen as comprising the rights and responsibilities of all citizens within the school, and can be jointly developed between students and staff. The Council could have a staff adviser, who would link with teachers and assist a process of negotiation, and otherwise interfere as little as possible. It could be agreed that any ideas or solutions produced by the Council could be implemented on a trial basis, and then evaluated and reconsidered if necessary.

It is a good idea to encourage open communication and direct feedback at all levels of the school; safety can be provided for people to talk to each other about what they are thinking and feeling. To aid understanding of the transitions that are being made, reading materials can be made available to teachers, students, parents, governors, councillors, to explain the changes in the atmosphere of the school, and to reassure people that academic standards will not slip because of the new ethos.

In some schools, student representatives attend staff meetings and vice versa; but then again, why not have joint meetings to begin with? Do we really need the barrier of secrecy and power?

Codes of behaviour v. ground rules

Codes of behaviour	Ground rules
Codes of behaviour, or the traditional School Rules, contain sanctions and threats of punishment. These are implied if not spelled out by words like *must*, *ought*, *should*, *will* and *do not*. They provide a basis for authoritarian control, with the headmaster and other managers responsible for their enforcement.	Ground Rules avoid referring to punishment or sanctions, because these two threats are not underlying the rules. Words like *can* and *may* and *desirable* replace the Musts and Oughts. They provide a basis for reminding people about their agreements.
School Rules spell out each piece of unwanted (negative) behaviour, and often refer to rules which are an invasion of personal privacy, e.g. 'Pupils *must* remove coats in school', or 'Pupils *must* not talk to staff with their hands in their pockets', 'Pupils will not normally be allowed out of lessons to go to the toilet. Pupils may go to the toilet between lessons, but should not loiter there longer than necessary'. (From a real but anonymous school in 1985)	Ground Rules are expressed positively, referring to the kind of behaviour that is agreed upon between staff and students. Trust is established as well, and we believe that human beings can be trusted to know when the toilet is the place to be, and when they are comfortable with their coats on or their hands in their pockets.
All orders and rules come from on High, usually no consultation is allowed, nor any negotiation. Likelihood of change in the rules is slim.	Rights and responsibilities are negotiated between students and staff, and are open to change. The ground rules apply to both students and staff alike. If they state 'In this school we listen to each other', then that works both ways.
The Powers at the top are 100% responsible for initiating and enforcing all School Rules. Enforcement means punishment, including suspension, which immediately puts the pupil in the position of being 'out' – of the school.	Each individual student and staff member is 100% responsible for his or her behaviour; this is a hard concept to grasp and needs time to be established. Ground Rules are developed over a long time, jointly. Sometimes responsible people make mistakes; they can learn from mistakes. Sometimes staff members forget that they are now working in a student-centred school and they shout or punish students. Their mistakes need forgiveness and *reminding* about, as well.

The school belongs to the students; their parents pay taxes so that they can be educated and cared for. We believe that we can assume an intrinsic right for students to stay in school, and not to be rejected or sent away, except in extreme circumstances. We would call very dangerous behaviour, use of weapons, heavy drugs, arson or injury of other students, extreme circumstances. We have a serious and inevitable responsibility to keep the students in the school and to provide for them. It would be ideal if a trained and skilled counsellor could be put in charge of a centre within the school for students who are having difficulty taking responsibility for their own behaviour, and could work with them on their social skills and behaviour until they were ready to take charge of themselves.

If the atmosphere of the school is *nourishing* rather than toxic, and if the school is organised for the comfort and caring of each person in it, behaviour problems tend to decrease. Sadly, some teachers tend to create discipline problems where none existed before.

ESPECIALLY FOR TEACHERS

What the teacher says

Introduction

In this section we want to forestall comments like:

'That's all very well for Drama, but what about Biology?'
'That's all very well for RE, but you can't do that in Science/Maths/Georgaphy/PE/Lanugages . . .'

We want to demonstrate that what the teacher *says* to the students, and does with them, makes the difference between traditional and student-centred methods. *Behind* what the teacher says are the teacher's *attitudes*:

Traditional Attitudes	Student-Centred Attitudes
I have all the information.	The syllabus, the exam, and the information are here for us to share; we own them together.
It is my job to transmit it to you.	I am not the fount of all knowledge.
I am responsible for your learning.	I am here to facilitate your learning by providing resources and support.
It is my job to make sure that you work.	I trust that you want to learn and will take responsibility for your own learning.
As the adult, and the professional, I have the expertise to make the right judgements and decisions about your learning.	

The following models are intended to illustrate the kinds of things that a traditional teacher and a student-centred teacher would be likely to say; we have deliberately included materials for several subjects in the curriculum. We hope you will notice that the student-centred lesson is neither unstructured nor permissive, nor has the teacher disappeared from the scene, nor abdicated responsibility. It is just that the structure is different, and there are different *kinds* of permission.

We have devised a 'key' to show where we think each lesson goes on a continuum from

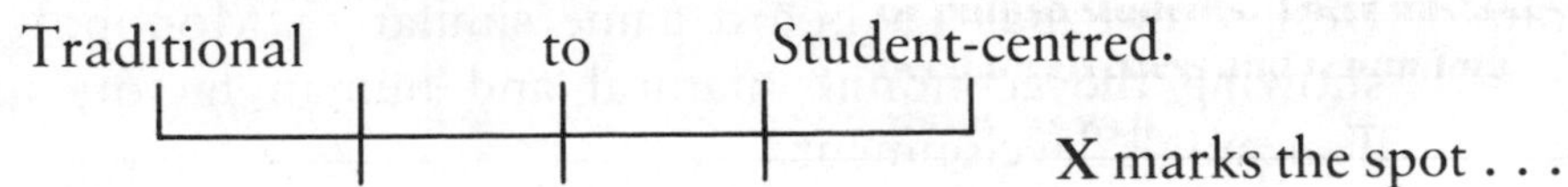

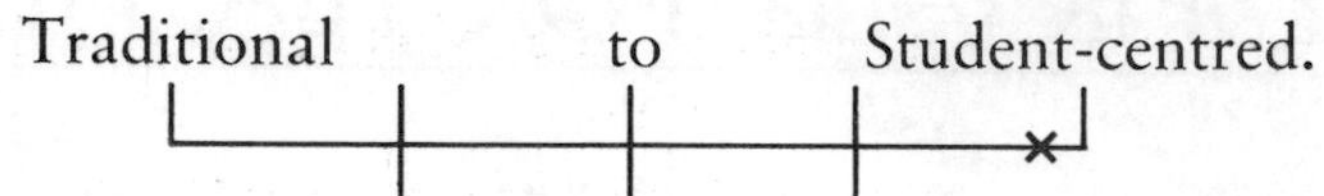

A Geography lesson: Tanzania

Traditional

Teacher gives out textbooks, exercise books and atlases.

Teacher introduces lesson: 'You remember last time we were studying world population and food supply. Ward, tell the class what we learned about Malthus' theory . . . Who can help him out? What about you Khan? . . . No. Worlock you try . . . Yes, that's right.

Now today we are going to learn about Tanzania's attempt to become self-sufficient. We will start with a video programme and these are the things I want you to notice: . . . Afterwards I will give you a worksheet on the film and you must finish it tonight for homework. So, pay very close attention to the programme.'

Student-centred

'I want to congratulate you on your projects about world population and food supply. I know you have all had a chance to look at and assess each other's work. Let's take another look at the syllabus and choose what we want to do next . . .

Now that we've each had a chance to say what we want, it seems like the majority have chosen Tanzania. So, how do we start? . . . OK, I'll see if I can get a video programme for next lesson. In the meantime start to think about who you want to work with.'

(Next lesson) 'Here's the video programme you asked for.

(Show video) Let's do a round of 'What I noticed' . . . There are lots of ideas there; let's review them. I'll put them on the board. . . . So, we've got a list of topics, now, how can we tackle them? . . . So, you're saying that you want to divide into five groups? When you've decided who you want to work with, go ahead into your groups and see if you can decide how to approach one of these topics in a way that will interest you.

(At the end of the lesson) Will you please come back into the circle for a few minutes so we can see what you've thought of. . . . So, we've heard from each group and what we have is:

Group 1 Design and make a board game similar to Monopoly, showing the economic, natural and human factors in Tanzania's development.

Group 2 A quiz show like Mastermind with questions on the Ujamaa system.
Group 3 A play on family life, bringing out the conflict between traditional and modern attitudes.
Group 4 A written report on President Nyrere.
Group 5 A set of visual displays, including posters, cuttings, maps and drawings.

Is everyone happy with what they have chosen? Before you go, I'd like each group to write up here what they're going to do by Thursday.

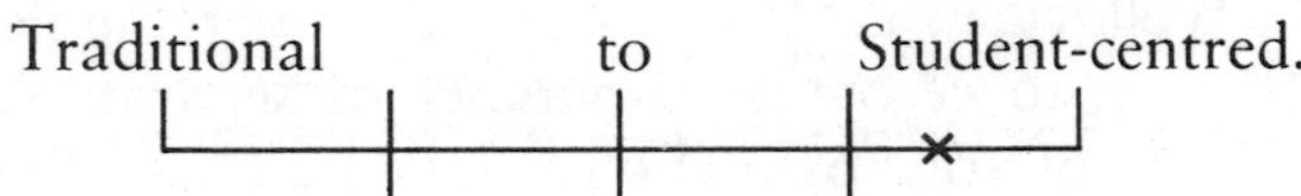

Social Education: Drugs

Traditional

'Line up quietly. Come in and stand behind your chairs. Now sit down, look at me and listen. Today we are going to start on drugs, and we are going to begin with a filmstrip. Simon and Davinder close the curtains, and Becky, you're in charge of lights. Stand by the switch so I know where you are. Williams, I told you last week you can't sit by Gordon – go and sit at the back.

Now you need to take detailed notes, so listen very carefully to the commentary. If there's any messing about when the lights are switched off, or any talking during the filmstrip, I'll dictate the notes instead.

Right, lights out . . .

(The filmstrip is got through without interruption. Little is seen, though, because everyone is writing.)

Yes, Arshed . . .

Stop there Arshed. I'm sure the rest of the class is not interested in your story about your brother's glue-sniffing. Anyway, we're running out of time and have this worksheet to do. Ruth, give them out – quietly.

Now, using the notes from the filmstrip, I want you to answer questions 1–10 on narcotics. You have got 15 minutes. If you don't get them done, you will have to finish them at home in addition to your other homework. Start now . . .

Homework: Write it down at the back of your book. Finish questions 1–10, then do questions 11–20 on socially acceptable drugs – alcohol and cigarettes. The work must be in tomorrow morning. Lennie Bradshaw and Richard Sattin will collect your books at registration and bring them to me – with a list of names of those who have not handed in.'

Student-Centred

'Let me remind you that last lesson the grup asked if we could move on to the topic of drugs today. So, let's have a circle . . . Now, if you'd like to throw out any ideas that the word 'drugs' sparks off in your minds, I'll record them on the flip chart . . .

(Group brainstorms theme)

Well, we've got a lot more ideas emerging now and I think you'll be able to recognise a number of separate subjects. Working in groups of your own choice – the numbers don't matter as long as you feel it will work – see if you can link together any of the words and phrases on the chart to make any subject areas. It would be a good idea to elect one of you to write things down and someone else to act as spokesperson . . .

(Groups work on ideas)

OK, have we all finished? Back to the circle. Now let's find out how we've grouped the ideas. Spokespeople, who'd be willing to start us off? Thanks Gary . . .

(Groups report back one by one)

You've all heard each other's ideas now and the main areas seem to be: heroin and cocaine; 'hash' or 'pot'; glue-sniffing; pills of various kinds; cigarettes and alcohol. There may, of course, be others we haven't mentioned yet, but for now we could pool ideas on *how* we could tackle these subjects. Shall we do a round? . . .

(The group does a round, followed by a general discussion on methods of exploration)

You now seem to have a great variety of ideas on how to go about this, so we should end up with a good mixture of facts, feelings, beliefs and experiences to try and present a total picture. You will now need to decide who you want to work with, and you need to choose together which subject you are going to do, or you can work alone if you prefer. I will provide any materials, books or other resources if you ask for them, but I don't want to answer any questions on what or how – you're all well able to make those decisions for yourselves, though of course I'll offer opinions if asked to. I can also give pointers on how to go about organising the various trips and visitors you suggested.

Well, that's enough chat from me. Shall we begin?'

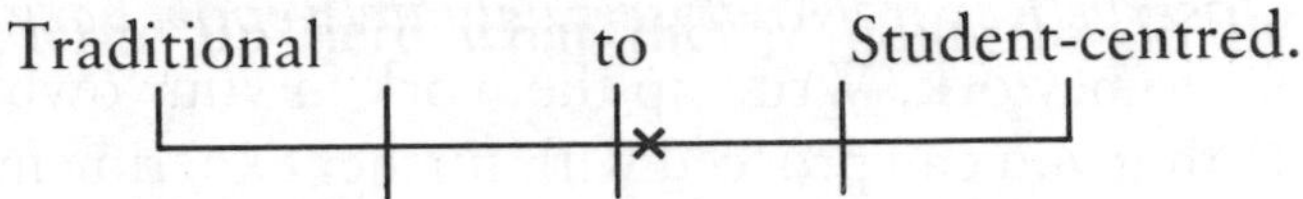

A Physics lesson

Traditional

Line up outside in silence.

Enter after teacher, remain standing.

Teacher greets class.

Coats off. Bags off bench. Sit.

Pay attention.

'Who can remember what we did last lesson?' Teacher asks the questions and individual pupils provide the answers to aid recall and set the scene for this lesson.

Instructions for experiment, possibly accompanied by worksheet.

Do it. No deviation allowed.

Complete the table of results.

'Yours didn't work – do it again.' or 'Here are the results you should have got.'

Label the diagram on the worksheet (or copy from board and label).

Class discussion of the results on a Q and A basis, leading to the formulation of the 'correct' conclusion, i.e. the one given in the book/expected by the Exam Board.

Homework: Answer questions from worksheet/copied from blackboard.

Student-Centred

Wait in an orderly but not a regimented group outside the room.

Teacher arrives and greets class.

Class follow teacher into room and sit where they wish.

Teacher positions self in the group but clearly and easily visible and audible to all.

If there is any reason for not starting the lesson, play the Waiting Game. 'Why are we not starting the lesson, David?' Discussion until the problem has been identified and resolved by group consensus.

Report-back session on the previous lesson by group reps selected at that time. Discussion leading to the identification of problem(s) generated by previous work.

Divide into groups and work on the problems using a problem solving approach. *(Brainstorm/Prioritise/Design Experiment/Do it/Observe/Record/Analyse/Evaluate/Report back.)*

Homework: Write up the work in your own words. Do research so that you can proceed with further experiments next time.

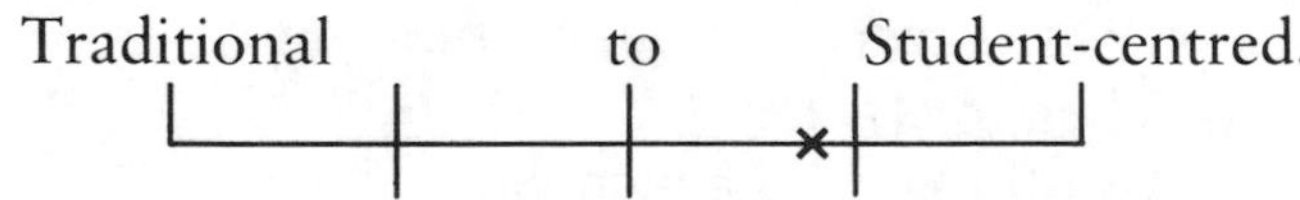

CDT: Picture frames

Traditional

'You are going to design a picture frame to fit a picture 150 mm × 70 mm. Your solution must be made in wood.'

Student-Centred

Homework set one week previously: Find a picture/drawing/poster/magazine cut out, of something you treasure or that means a lot to you.

Lesson 1

'Now we have the picture; in what way could it be displayed?' (After five/ten minutes discussion, the pupils decided on some kind of a picture frame.) What materials? Any available. Size? Within reason. Where is the frame to be displayed? Pupils decide on table or wall. A number of possible solutions are drawn and, for homework, pupils draw their choice to scale and make a list of materials.

N.B. If pupils cannot find a picture, ask them where, together, we could find one. (Only one pupil failed to bring a picture, but one was found in a magazine.)

N.B. Two pupils in the group showed no interest in the subject, but came up with an idea of their own. I allowed these to compiete their own idea.

Lesson 2
Working in adjoining workshops, pupils allowed to use any available material, work in either room with either member of staff.

Workrate and enthusiasm of pupils both excellent. Biggest problem turned out to be packing away; pupils did *not* want to.

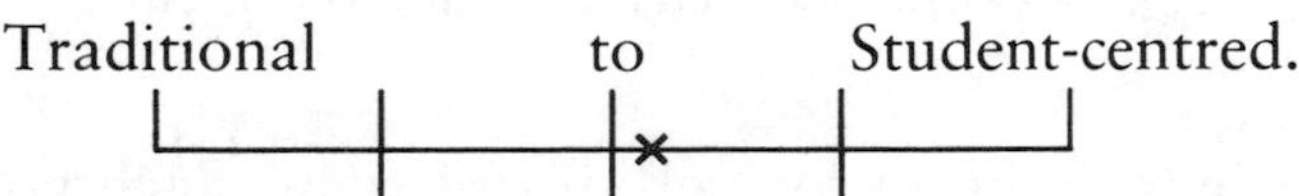

A Geography lesson: map reading

Traditional
Class have text book, exercise books, pens, etc.

'Turn to page 67 in text.

In your exercise book, put the date and a margin.

Now, look at the map on page 67.

(repeated four times)

This is an Ordnance Survey map. You can see that it is divided into squares with North at the top. The squares are there for . . .'

The Grid system is explained.

Class are then given a number of map references and told to identify a number of places on the map using the grid reference.

Student-Centred

Lesson 1
1 'Choose a partner who lives near you.
2 Either with your partner or by yourself, each draw on a sheet of A4 paper, using only half the page, a plan which shows your house in your road and your school. Show the way you go to school, and mark the names of the roads.
3 With your partner, compare and talk about your two plans. On the bottom half of the sheet of paper write down the ways your plans are the same and the ways they are different, e.g. bigger, smaller, careful, sketchy, etc.

With your partner and on a new piece of paper and still using half the page, draw another plan which shows both your houses, your roads, the school – in other words, put the two plans together.

4 Brainstorm:

a what were the problems *(pupils write on board)*

b how would you solve them? (taking one problem at a time)

or, instead of b above, give problems to pairs to come up with solutions.

5 In *fours* (two pairs). On another half sheet of A4 put together the two plans to make a new one which shows the school, where all four of you live and all the roads in between.'

Teacher photocopies (×4) each plan ready for next lesson.

Lesson 2
Class sitting in four groups of eight. Each group is supplied with eight copies of last lesson's work (as above), large sheets sugar paper, felt tips.

1 Task – put together the eight plans into one big master plan.
2 Teacher reverts to traditional method to discuss what might happen if we go on doing this – 16, 32, etc.
3 Demonstrate maps, pictures, models (cars, houses, dolls, etc.)
4 Put big plans on wall and give out small sheets of squared paper.
5 Class back in pairs. On small squared sheets, reproduce master plan. Use of squares may have emerged by this time. Discuss grid system and references.

Generating classroom activities for any topic

The following activities were invented by a group of teachers at a conference. We chose a topic which we considered to be fairly boring (as it is frequently taught), which was fractions in mathematics. We then brainstormed as many concepts as we could think of which related to fractions in any way.

We began inventing activities, and from each one we then drew out what we saw as skills which could be applied to any other topic.

Now we are inviting you to do this the other way round: pick a topic, get a friend or colleague to brainstorm with you around that topic. Then look at our list of skills which can apply to other topics. Now get your friend to help you think of activities which will illustrate or demonstrate those skills.

Activities in classroom	Skills which apply to other topics
Create a 'spray' on fractions in everyday life, i.e. brainstorm on the board in a pattern like this: Weights and Measures Interest rates Dividing things into equal shares Time *Fractions in everyday life* School timetable etc. etc. etc. etc. etc.	The teacher is 'selling' the topic, getting students involved, helping them appreciate how the topic is relevant to them.
Find out how they measured time and distance in the old days – see where fractions fit in.	It is useful to have an understanding of how present-day skills and processes were developed.
Make a video about fractions.	In order to film a topic, you have to have a clear understanding of it.
In groups of three–five, students devise a game about fractions, and get everyone to play it.	The best game of all is inventing games.
Invent a way to keep a pictorial record of their learning about fractions, e.g. a 'trail game', or a book, or a flow chart.	It is encouraging to see your own progress: ongoing evaluation, or assessment.
Take any information you have collected about fractions, and feed it to a computer.	A good skill is being able to relate the work you are doing to computers, word processors and other machines.
Use calculators to work with fractions.	A good skill is being able to relate the work you are doing to computers, word processors and other machines.
Use different machines; compete to see who completes the solution first.	A good skill is being able to relate the work you are doing to computers, word processors and other machines.
Make a nursery clock.	Use *real* problem solving exercises.
Have a charity tuck shop for one day: use fractions in the prices.	Raising money for a cause helps to create empathy; prices reflect real uses.

Activities in classroom	Skills which apply to other topics
Exchange places for a day with a teacher of a different age level.	It is helpful to have an appreciation of other teaching levels.
Interview someone much older about how they learned maths, especially fractions.	It is good to be aware of how times change.
Make a children's book about fractions. Show it to others.	A good way to really learn a topic is to share your learning with others.
Play the 'Star Power' simulation game – use fractions for points (adding).	One way to develop empathy is to have a real life experience of another person's 'shoes'.
Make a glossary of fraction terms. Use proverbs and sayings, e.g. 'half-wit'.	Every topic has its own jargon or technical terms. See the relationships between subjects.
When children have mastered a skill, e.g. adding fractions, get them to teach someone who hasn't.	A good way to really learn a topic is to share your learning with others.
Play mathematical 'Call My Bluff'.	You have to be very familiar with the specific technical language.
Interview a *sample* of people. Use graphs and charts to represent your results.	It is useful to apply what you learn in the classroom to outside, and vice versa.
Use mathematical skills in a simulated production line, working out, for example, estimated time and actual time, and fraction of time spent at each stage.	It is useful to be able to work to deadlines, and to have a finished product at the end.
Find other members of staff who use fractions in their lessons (even if they don't realise it), and join forces.	Team teaching uses people's strengths.
Find another member of staff to team-teach with. Exchange groups of students so that one teaches kids who are progressing fast (enrichment activities), and the other clears up gaps in the learning of students who are having difficulties.	Pooling talents, ideas and energies is often very rewarding.

Activities in classroom	Skills which apply to other topics
Collect magazine pictures; make a collage on 'Who Needs Fractions', e.g. a male nurse and a female doctor; a house-husband etc.	You can use your topic to break down sexual stereotypes.
Bring in food labels which break down ingredients. *Design* a label for a food product, using a pie chart to describe the fractions of each ingredient.	You can integrate communication skills, so that the topic is related to other topics.
Invent activities around Balance, Ratio, Proportion and Scales.	When students invent activities, they show that they understand the work they are doing.
Bring in real cakes of different shapes. Find as many ways as possible of dividing them equally (e.g. weight, measure, volume, etc.)	Problem solving with other people can be very enjoyable.
Decide how you would go about borrowing money to buy something you want, e.g. a motorbike, and how much you would pay in the end.	Being able to solve a practical problem for yourself is a useful skill.
Search the media for fractions, e.g. newspaper articles, statistics etc.	Use the media to help teach a topic.
Search the community for fractions.	To encourage understanding of links and relationships, tie the subject into surrounding stimuli.
Record one week's percentage of pupils attending school.	It is advisable to use every opportunity to link the topic with everyday life.
Measure the size of rooms, the height of pupils, the miles people walk in a week.	Using concrete objects to illustrate concepts makes things clearer.
Borrow cuisinaire rods and other objects used in junior schools for students to manipulate and experiment with.	It is sometimes a good idea to spend time clearing up misunderstandings and reinforcing learning from junior and infant schools.
Collect anonymous statements in a hat about how students feel about fractions or hold a Gripes Auction.	We want to encourage students to be more self-aware, and also to talk to us and each other about their feelings.

Activities in classroom	Skills which apply to other topics
Cut up cards into fractions; each child has a piece. Find out how many people have the same size piece as you, and create a whole, e.g. 4/4, 3/3.	One way of learning how something works is to understand the opposite function.

Develop your own activities to match the skills

	Skills which can apply to any topic
	The teacher is 'selling' the topic, getting students involved, helping them appreciate how the topic is relevant to them.
	It is useful to have an understanding of how present-day skills and processes were developed.
	In order to film a topic, you have to have a clear understanding of it.
	The best game of all is inventing games.
	It is encouraging to see your own progress: ongoing evaluation, or assessment.
	A good skill is being able to relate the work you are doing to computers, word processors and other machines.
	Use *real* problem solving exercises.
	Raising money for a cause helps to create empathy; prices reflect real uses.
	It is helpful to have an appreciaton of other teaching levels.
	It is good to be aware of how times change.

	Skills which can apply to any topic
	A good way to really learn a topic is to share your learning with others.
	One way to develop empathy is to have a real life experience of another person's 'shoes'
	Every topic has its own jargon or technical terms. See the relationships between subjects.
	You have to be very familiar with the specific technical language.
	It is useful to apply what you learn in the classroom to outside, and vice versa.
	It is useful to be able to work to deadlines, and to have a finished product at the end.
	Team teaching uses people's strengths.
	Pooling talents, ideas and energies is often very rewarding.
	You can use your topic to break down sexual stereotypes.
	You can integrate communication skills, so that the topic is related to other topics.
	When students invent activities, they show that they understand the work they are doing.
	Problem solving with other people can be very enjoyable.
	Being able to solve a practical problem for yourself is a useful skill.
	Use the media to help teach a topic.

	Skills which can apply to any topic
	To encourage understanding of links and relationships, tie the subject into surrounding stimuli.
	It is advisable to use every opportunity to link the topic with everyday life.
	Using concrete objects to illustrate concepts makes things clearer.
	It is sometimes a good idea to spend time clearing up misunderstandings and reinforcing learning from junior and infant schools.
	We want to encourage students to be more self-aware, and also to talk to us and each other about their feelings.
	One way of learning how something works is to understand the opposite function.

A parable retold

Once upon a time an old man sat by the side of the road, smoking his pipe, and gazing off into the distance, contemplating . . . who-knows-what? Along came a stranger who stopped to pass the time of day, putting down his bundle and taking out a ham sandwich and a bottle of wine, which he forgot to share with the old man. In the course of the conversation, the stranger pointed to the village nestled in the valley below, and asked, 'What are the people like in the town down there? I'm just moving to that village, you know.'

The old man puffed a puff on his pipe, and threw the question back 'What were they like in the town where you used to live, my friend?'

A thundercloud seemed to pass over the stranger's face: 'Oh, they were rogues and rascals of the worst sort. Liars, cheats, a pack of knaves they were. Never could get a kind word out of any of them.'

Smoke billowed from the old man's pipe, as he shook his head and spoke, 'Well then, that's what the people are like in that village down there, my son.'

The stranger heaved himself to his feet and walked sadly down the hill. The old man leaned back against the tree for his afternoon siesta.

Later, when he woke, he saw another stranger approaching. The newcomer smiled, and asked if he could share the shade of the stately tree. The old man shifted over to make room for him, and gratefully accepted the stranger's offer of an apple and some cheese.

As they chatted, the stranger pointed to the hamlet in the valley: 'What are the people like in that village?' he asked, 'I'm thinking of moving there soon.'

A twinkle, unobserved, appeared in the old man's eye, as once again he parried the question.

'What were they like where you've just come from, my son?' The stranger's face lit up. 'Oh, they're wonderful people, the salt of the earth, not a harsh word nor a dishonest act have I heard of these many years. I only wish I could stay, but it is time for me to move on.'

The old man hid his pleasure by lighting his pipe, as he responded, 'Well, I'm glad to say that that is exactly how you'll find those people in the village below.'

What are the people like? 1

Aims: Understanding human behaviour, looking at our own judgments and assumptions, exploring values, fun, stimulus to writing or drama, personal and social education

Materials: Paper, pens, blackboard, possibly other things later as activity develops

Procedure:

1 Read the story aloud, or have someone else read it.
2 In small groups, discuss the meaning and write a moral for the story.
3 Write all the possible meanings and morals on the board.
4 Discuss, with reference to a school context.

The activities can stop here, or lots more can follow:

5 Act out the story in small groups, expand it, adding other strangers, or adding the strangers' reactions to the old man's words of wisdom.
6 Devise a list of situations in which the central action could be interpreted in two widely differing ways. Act them out or discuss them.

or

Each person write on a piece of paper an action which he himself would condemn.

7 These are pooled, anonymously, and drawn out of a 'hat' one at a time, and read. For each one, think of situations in which those actions might be interpreted positively, or have a positive function. Discuss or act out.

N.B. Please beware of preaching, or of excluding people who may disagree with the consensus of the group. It is best if the leader takes a neutral role, and reminds people not to put each other down, even if values differ.

Variation: Point 6 could be limited to situations and actions involving students in school.

What are the people like? 2

Aims: Self-awareness, exploring human behaviour

Materials: None

Procedure:

1 Choose a partner, decide who is A and B.

2 A and B each make a statement about a student, e.g.

> 'George is someone who is always making excuses.'

3 Now each partner makes the same statement about himself, e.g.

> 'I am someone who is always making excuses.'

4 Now the two partners discuss whether the statements fit themselves, or not.

5 Talk with each other about how we pre-judge kids, and how these judgments may reflect our doubts and fears about ourselves . . .

N.B. Research shows that if teachers are told that a certain group of students, chosen at random, will achieve well in school, those particular students *will* achieve well. (Rosenthal and Jacobson 1968). With this in mind, we believe that we owe it to kids to greet them with open minds, and to assume that we will at least start out by liking each one and assuming that he or she will do well. Also, many times, the qualities we dislike or resent in other people are characteristics we don't want to own in ourselves. Thus the following activities for teachers . . .

School reports

Aims: Teacher's self-awareness about assumptions, judgments

Materials: Pens, paper

Procedure: Ask teachers to brainstorm, in small groups, a list of words which could be used in reports to describe individuals or classes of kids; first negative, then positive.

As a group, choose one of the words. For example, they might choose 'motivated' or 'lazy'. Each teacher then writes on his own paper all the other phrases and comments from the brainstorm which he would expect to appear with that word in a school report. The teachers then discuss, and compare notes about how they each use words, and what assumptions go along with those words.

Teacher-student fantasy

(A variation of this activity appears in *Gamesters' Handbook*)

Aims: Self-awareness, fun, trust-building, thinking about students

Materials: None

Procedure:
1. Choose a partner, and sit down facing her. Decide who is A and who is B.
2. Both close your eyes and think of the *worst* kid you ever had in class. (Each person has to define 'worst' for himself.)
3. A pretends that B is that student, and tells B what she thinks of him. Then it is B's turn to do the same.
4. Repeat the exercise with the *best* student you ever had.
5. Spend a few minutes talking to your partner about what has just happened.
6. The whole group brainstorm the qualities of the worst students and the best students. Discuss.

Variations: After the above is completed, then each person makes a list of the words which apply to herself from each set of adjectives. Each person then chooses one quality from the negative list, and makes a contract with his partner about how, when, where, he is going to work to change it.

The teacher's game

Aims: Self-awareness, empathy

Materials: Pens, paper, chairs or cushions

Procedure:
1. Close your eyes, think about what you were like when you were in school.
2. Now think of a student in your school who is similar to how you were.
3. Write a character description of each of the two people.
4. Get a partner, and a chair for each of you, plus one empty chair. Decide who is A and who is B.
5. A talks to the child in his school, imagining he/she is sitting on the empty chair, and saying 'You remind me of myself when I was your age, because . . .' A talks about how he feels towards that child. Then B has a turn.
6. The two partners talk about their feelings.

Focusing down

Aims: To enable concentration on and analysis of a particular problem into its component parts; self-assessment, problem solving, study skills

Materials: One plain piece of paper per person

Procedure: Draw a shape on one half of the paper like this:

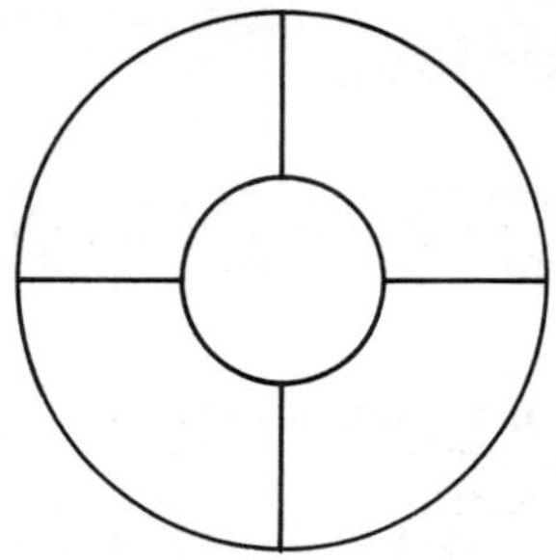

In the centre circle, write the subject/problem under scrutiny. In the outer rim, write aspects of the problem/subject, creating more segments as required. Draw the shape a second time and choose one of the entries in the segments to put in the centre circle. Sub-divide this again, using the segments. Discuss results.

Example

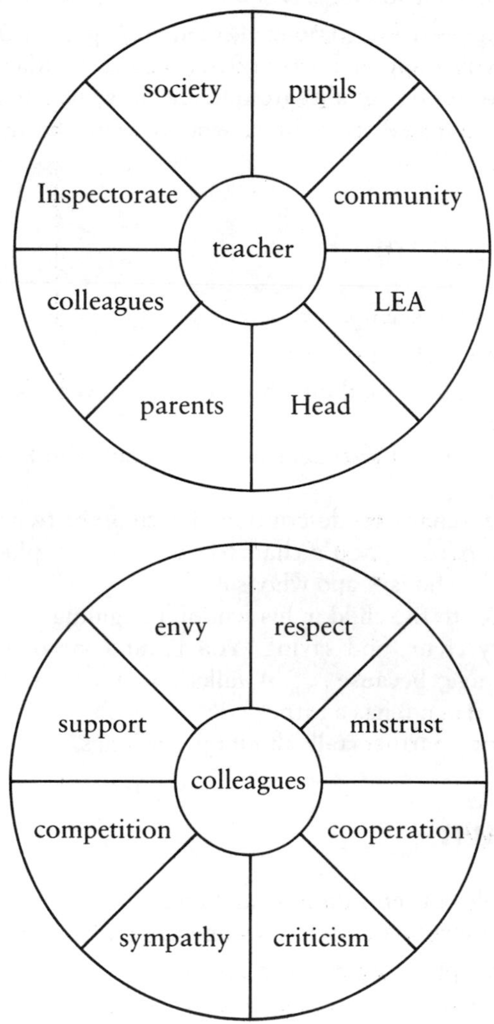

Feedback

Aims: Learning how to give feedback, how to handle difficult situations in groups

Materials: Pen and paper

Procedure:

1. Think of a training/teaching situation which you have encountered or might encounter, as a trainer/teacher. Describe it to your partner.
2. When you have each had a turn, exchange situations with another pair. Clarify and discuss if necessary (in about two minutes).
3. Choose one situation and plan with your partner how to approach it as the trainer. Other pair observes this planning session. Then the pairs switch over.
4. Give feedback to each pair from the observers.

N.B. When giving feedback, you may find the following guidelines helpful:

- People receiving feedback just listen, don't answer back or defend.
- Feedback is given in a supportive way.
- High quality feedback just describes what the observers noticed; it is not hurtful or degrading.
- Be aware of and discuss any areas of tension that were observed.

ACTIVITIES FOR SCHOOL SUBJECTS

A new way to get into small groups

Aim: Dividing a group into random smaller groups

Materials: None

Procedure:
1. Assign a number to everyone, by counting off around the circle.
2. Leader calls all prime numbers into one group, e.g. 2, 3, 5, 7, 11,
   Now all numbers divisible by 4
   Now all numbers divisible by 6
   Now any two numbers that add up to 25
   And so on . . .

Animal allsorts

Aim: Sorting animals into groups/classification

Materials: Paper/pins or sticky labels with name of a different animal on each one.

Procedure: An animal label is attached to everyone in the room. They have to sort themselves into groups and decide why they have put themselves in that group, e.g. because it has a tail, wings, no legs, etc. (This is another good way of getting them into groups.)

Definitions

Aims: To learn or reinforce technical vocabulary

Materials: Pen and paper

Procedure:
1. Work out definitions for parts first.
2. One person from each group/whole class calls out definitions.
3. Individuals write down correct word. Winner = first person with ten correct or team with the most points.

Variation: Could use above in teams, e.g. five teams of six. The front person in each team answers, and the first to answer correctly moves to the back. One rounder is completed each time the first person reaches the start. The first team to three rounders wins.

Making sense?

Aims: Concentration, observation, deduction. Introduction to sense organs

Materials: Blindfold/earplugs

Procedure: Sit or lie down. Close your eyes and concentrate on what you can sense/feel – think of as many things as possible. Open your eyes – what can be added to the list now? Brainstorm feelings.

Variation: Blindfold and/or earplug one person – they have to find their way from one end of the room to the other. Observations/deductions.

Human experiments

Aims: Demonstration and reinforcement of practical concepts

Materials: None

Procedure: Any process involving chemicals, components, materials, moving parts, observable changes – anything which involves interaction, mixing, contact, combination – can be represented by individuals or groups of students. They can act out what happens in a process, with all the necessary noises and movement.

e.g.

chemical experiments molecular structures	chemistry
bending and melting materials jointing wood	CDT
plant reproduction eating	biology
electricity light refraction	physics

Students can first find out about the properties and processes they wish to use and then do their own improvised experiments. They can see how the results of their 'human experiments' compare with the real thing.

Three examples of Human Experiments, in Physics and Biology, follow.

Conduction, convection and radiation

Concepts such as molecular movement, conduction, convection and radiation, radioactivity, are very difficult to comprehend because you are unable to see physically what is going on. This activity gives the pupils the experience of becoming a molecule/particle and can be used as a 'model' to show what happens in various situations.

Brainstorm or discuss with the students how a molecule moves, what happens when heat is added to a substance, how molecules are arranged in solids, liquids and gases. This may be done after several sessions of practical work showing these concepts, or after groups have carried out research, or as useful revision of an old topic.

After the brainstorm or discussion, a list of what the pupils understand by the above will have been obtained. Using the whole group, or volunteers, whatever space allows, students become molecules and arrange themselves in the form of a solid – a straight line packed tightly together may be a good idea. Heat is introduced at one end (for example, a chalk box with 'heat' written on it). This makes the first molecule vibrate vigorously; the box is passed down the line; each pupil who receives the box vibrates vigorously. This gives an impression of conduction.

By spreading the pupils out, it can be seen that one molecule must move to pass the heat onto the next; this shows a convection current.

By spreading out still further, a gas can be simulated; the 'heat' is thrown from pupil to pupil, simulating radiation.

Radioactivity

For this activity, you would need three benches, one marked 6 cm of air, one marked 3 mm of aluminium, one marked 10 cm of lead. The pupils divide into three groups – the alpha particles, the beta particles and the gamma-rays. A brainstorm or discussion after work on particles may be a good way to find out what is liable to happen to each group of particles/rays. The students then approach the benches en masse, the alpha particles stopping at the first bench, the beta stopping at the 2nd bench and the gamma-rays becoming tired and weary after they have passed through the lead.

I must stress that these activities were thought of by the students; they decided how they were going to behave and what props to use. I did not go in with any intention other than to form some sort of revision exercise using role play and I have included these only as examples of what can be achieved.

Using role play to revise the concepts of fertilisation and chemical messengers

This exercise took place after a series of lessons about sexual reproduction. After discussion, the students produced a list of what was necessary for sexual reproduction to take place. This was it:

Egg, sperm, chemical messengers and, with a little prompting from me, they added egg nucleus, sperm nucleus and sperm tail.

Then they decided that the way to show this was by some of them becoming an egg, some becoming sperm, some chemical messengers, and one the egg nucleus. After more discussion, it was decided that the sperm required two parts, the sperm nucleus and the tail.

They arranged themselves in the lab. like this:

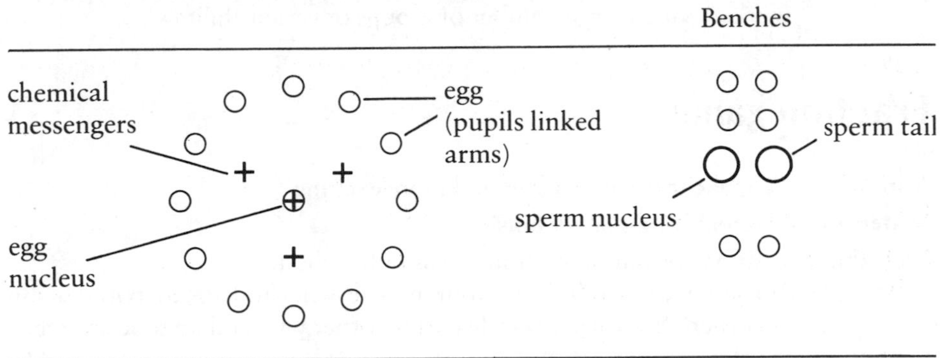

After more discussion, the chemical messengers were given two messages: one read 'come with me', the other read 'let no more sperm in'. The egg nucleus was also given an 'I'm fertilised' card to hold up at the end. The sperm moved about in random fashion, the nucleus allowing himself to be moved by the tail. Then the messengers came out and showed their messages to the sperm who followed them to the egg. The sperm milled around the egg. One sperm was allowed to enter and the messengers then took out 'let no more sperm in' messages to the outside of the egg. When the egg nucleus and the sperm nucleus had joined together, the sign 'I'm fertilised' was held up and the role play was over.

Discussion after this was very encouraging; all the students enjoyed the experience and found it a much more enjoyable and effective way of revising than by just reading their old notes.

The Standards game

Aim: To help students appreciate the need for British Standards and the standardisation of signs and symbols.

Materials: Drawing paper, boards and equipment

Procedure: Set the group to design a bungalow, including inside walls, outside walls, windows, doors and fixtures. When they have finished this, they swap with any other member of the group. They are not allowed to have any verbal communication and they imagine they are in Aberdeen and the designer in Birmingham. Each member of the group will need to work out sizes and what the fixtures are. The result of this is that each person has a different interpretation of the drawing in front of them.

This activity helps the group realise the need for standardisation and therefore the teaching becomes far easier. This activity has worked with a large number of groups of varied abilities.

Fraction game

Aim: To make fractions clearer and more exciting

Materials: Fraction cards, safety pins

Procedure:
1. Everyone pins a fraction on his or her chest.
2. Leader calls – 'I want four people who add up to two, in this corner'. 'I want six people in this corner who add up to four', etc.

Variation: Do the same with words, e.g. 'I want five people in this corner who make a complete sentence.'

Fizz

Aims: Table practice, reinforce number bonds, factors

Materials: None

Procedure:
1. Decide on which table to practise. Ask for volunteers (8›n›12) depending upon which table is chosen.
2. Volunteers form a circle within a larger circle. The volunteers start counting in turn from any point in any direction. The person who should say the multiple of the chosen table must say FIZZ instead. If any person gives an incorrect response on his turn, he/she can be challenged by anyone in the outside circle. If the challenge is successful, they change places and the game restarts from 1.

Variations:
1. As a 'round', with all students participating.
2. Introduce BUZZ by combining two tables e.g. fives and threes
   15 is FIZZ, BUZZ as it appears in both tables.

N.B. This game can be made infinitely difficult by combinations of tables.

Beat the computer

Aims: Practise speed and accuracy with number facts

Materials: One calculator; pens/pencils and paper

Procedure: 1 A volunteer 'becomes' a computer in a corner (a façade can be made in Art lessons) and is given a calculator.

2 Each class member writes down a simple addition sum. In turn they present their problem to the 'computer' by saying:

> 'The input for this calculation is *(gives problem)* . . . GO!'

The other pupils note the input and work out a solution.

3 The operator waits for a written output from the computer and says:

'STOP! The output from the computer is . . .' *(gives the computer's result)*, and asks two questions:

> 'Did you beat the computer?'
> 'Was the computer correct?'

This could lead to comparisons of other solutions and class discussion.

Variations: Level of difficulty is infinitely variable, according to:

a number of digits contained in input numbers
b the operations used.

Footprints

Aim: To introduce graphical representation of collected data

Materials: Scrap paper or newspaper; scissors; pens/pencils

Procedure: 1 Decide on source of data to be collected, e.g. shoe sizes.

2 Ask for one volunteer of each shoe size and space them along a line on the floor. Ask each one to make a label of his/her shoe size. Ask the remainder of the group to line up behind their shoe size label.

3 Discuss how this data could be displayed on the floor without people standing in lines. Do it.

4 Discuss how this data could be displayed on a wall. Display it.

Variation: Collect different data.

Filling bottles

Aims: Develop logical and sequential thought, reinforce number bonds

Materials: Chairs

Procedure: 1 Pose the problem: 'I have a container which holds five litres and another which holds three litres. How can I measure exactly one litre using only these containers.?'

2 Ask for a team of six volunteers to solve the problem, using five chairs in line as one container and three chairs in line as the other container. The remainder of the group will act as a reservoir which can be used to fill, empty or transfer from one container to the other.

Variations: 1 Vary the size of the bottles.
2 Vary the amount to be measured.

Definition snap

Aim: To reinforce knowledge of properties of geometrical shapes

Materials: Two identical sets of cards with geometrical definitions on and the names of the shapes

Procedure: Divide class into two equal groups. Issue cards at random to each group. Groups then intermingle to find a partner with the identical card by asking and answering questions:

Q 'Do you have the card which has these properties . . .?'
A 'No. I am not a . . .'
or
A 'Yes. I am a . . .'

Variation: Cards can carry definitions of any mathematical terminology or name.

Goesinto's

Aims: To reinforce knowledge of tables and factors, to introduce sets

Materials: A set of cards numbered 2–100, ten cards of each of the numbers 2, 3, 5, 7, 11

Procedure:
1 Group leader asks for five volunteers and issues cards numbered 2, 3, 5, 7, and 11.
2 Remainder of class select cards at random from pack. Class members then approach volunteers and ask if they are factors of their chosen number. If the answer is yes, they are given a card bearing the factor. After a set time, or when everyone is sure that they have collected all their factors, the group is brought together and each class member is asked to write on the blackboard what their number was and what factors they collected.
3 Discussion can then be centred around whether all the factors have been collected:

'What extra cards would you need to be sure that all the factors have been collected?'

4 Repeat the exercise as often as the group feel they would like.

Sort it

Aims: Sorting, develop logical thinking, introduction to set work

Materials: A collection of all sorts of items for sorting, based on two attributes, e.g. red items, plastic items. (Include items which are red *and* plastic as well as items which have neither attribute.)

Procedure: 1 Set aside two places; label one **red** and the other **plastic**.

2 Each class member is asked to choose one item from the collection (preferably unseen from a bag) and asked to put it in the right place. If there is no place to put it, then keep it.

3 Once every class member has had a turn, form a circle and discuss what would need to be done so that all the items chosen could be put somewhere, e.g.

Where would you put something that is **red** *and* **plastic**?
Where would you put something that is *neither* **red** *nor* **plastic**?

Variations: 1 Different collections of items can be used using two attributes only.

2 Three attribute sorting can be introduced.

Set it

Aims: Reinforce number bonds; set work

Materials: Cards, pens/pencils, chalk/rope

Procedure: 1 Using chalk or rope, establish three overlapping sets on the floor in the centre of a circle of class members.

2 Divide class into three equal groups and label them, e.g.

'even numbers less than 31'
'multiples of four'
'square numbers'.

3 Each group produces a set of cards which identify the members of their set. Each group then places the members of their set in the correct place on the floor.

4 Point out to class instances of numbers appearing more than once and discuss with them whether this is necessary or acceptable.

Variations: 1 Two set work if this exercise proves too difficult.

2 Any number of different set labels.

Fence it

Aim: To establish the link between area and perimeter for rectangles

Materials: Chalk

Procedure: 1 Ask for enough volunteers to leave 24 of the class uncommitted. Ask these 24 to line up facing the same direction.

2 Ask volunteers to view the arrangement from the front and record the number of 'bodies' long the line is. Repeat this from each end and from the back.

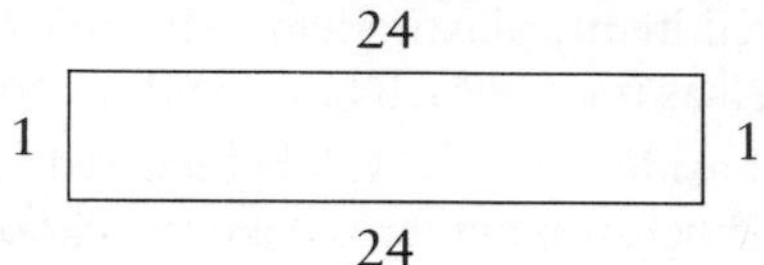

3 Record these details on the floor or on the blackboard. Record also the perimeter needed to fence them in (50).

4 Discuss the arrangement of the 24 and repeat the process for as many different arrangements as possible. Discuss the idea of a minimum perimeter for a maximum area enclosed.

Variation: Work in groups, using counters instead of 'bodies'.

Computer it

Aim: To identify the operations being performed by the 'computer'

Materials: Paper/card, pens/pencils, chairs

Procedures: 1 Choose or write any simple computer program, e.g.

```
10 INPUT n
20 LET n = n × 3
30 LET n = n + 5
40 PRINT n
50 GO TO 10
```

2 Ask for six volunteers. Give each volunteer a line number and the line details which must be kept secret. The sixth volunteer is the controller, who tells each line when to work. Arrange the program on chairs, sitting in line with arms folded.

3 Controller taps 10 on the shoulder, who holds out hands for input. Ask for a volunteer to write a smallish number on a piece of card or paper and give it to 10 and wait for a print out.

10 gives it to controller, who gives it to 20.

20 performs the operation, returns it to controller, who gives it to 30.

30 performs the operation, returns it to controller, who gives it to 40.

40 writes the answer on a piece of paper and gives the answer to the class member.

Controller moves to 50 who points to 10.

Controller activates 10 and asks for another input.

4 Class member writes both input and output on the blackboard. Input is continued until class can identify the operations being performed.

Variations: 1 Class members volunteer to change lines 20 or 30.

2 Extra lines can be added by discussion or by individuals.

Rituals

Aims: Enrichment for RE, fun, movement, trust and cooperation

Materials: Cannot tell in advance; students may need some art materials or costumes, if available

Procedure:

1 Discuss various rituals of different religious or national groups. Read about religious rituals in other countries.

2 Make up a ritual, with five or six other people, such as a ritual which will:

- bring rain
- banish disease
- make people happy
- celebrate marriage, birth, coming-of-age or death.

Variations:

1 Talk about rituals and traditions which exist in your family, e.g. locking all the doors before bed at night. Invent new ones.

2 Connect the invented ritual to an invented myth.

Poetry for fun

Many people feel that they haven't the confidence to write poetry, or have been told early on that their poems are no good. Simple structures such as the three below can often start people off on writing poetry, because these are almost always successful.

Cinquaines

Cinquaines are five-line poems, according to this structure:

1 (word)
2
3
2
1

Ask the class for a word (noun), then for two to describe it, and so on.
Example:

Love
Seeks response
Shrivels in vacuum
Blooms with
You

Septaines

Same as above, but the structure is

1
2
3
4
3
2
1

Example:

Peace
In tranquility
Yet violence threatens
As my mind erupts
Express these thoughts
Scream anger
Peace

Limericks

Five lines, according to this pattern:

A diner while dining at Crewe
Found a rather large mouse in his stew
Said the waiter, don't shout
And wave it about
Or the rest will be wanting one too.

Me – Poems

Aims: Enjoyment of writing poetry, self-awareness, trust building

Materials: Pens and paper

Procedure:
1. Think of a quality you have which you don't particularly like, or one that you're pleased with.
2. Write the word for that quality down the left side of your page, e.g.

S
H
Y
N
E
S
S

3. Use those letters to begin lines of poetry, and complete the poem. (It doesn't have to rhyme, although the example does.)

'Silence holds us all in chains,
How to break them lightly?
Young and tender, kids at risk
Need care to blossom rightly.
Even as we face each day,
So the children hide away,
So afraid to break the chains of
SHYNESS.'

Variations: Write your name down the left side instead.

D
A
V
I
D

Now complete the poem, as above.

Flock of words

Aims: Increased awareness of the meanings of the words we use

Materials: Paper, writing implement

Procedure: In pairs, A and B.
A tells B a favourite story.
B writes down every positive and negative word A uses.
Reverse process. B tells the story, A writes.
Analyse what was communicated by use of the words.

Variations: Instead of a favourite story, have a teacher's story about an incident with a child. Specify other types of stories.

Apostrophes

Aims: Creativity, drama skills, English punctuation skills, fun

Materials: Paper and pencils

Procedure:
1. A volunteer or group of volunteers is asked to perform two charades, one of which demonstrates the meaning of 'Dads' nose' and the other 'Dad's nose'. The whole class is given the word 'Dad' and then has to guess the meaning of the two charades.
2. The students then devise their own examples and rehearse and perform the charades which demonstrate them for the others to guess.

Language practice

Aim: To reduce anxiety in speaking a foreign language

Materials: None

Procedure:
1. Round of saying one word each in a foreign language.
2. Say a word across the circle to someone else, who says another to someone else, and so on.
3. Say a phrase to someone else in circle who responds in any language (preferably foreign) to the next person. If you cannot think of another phrase, repeat the previous one.

Information hunt

Aims: To enable all students to be actively involved in the lesson; to practise the language of any particular unit/topic

Materials: Cue-cards on any subject, e.g. way-finding, timetables, personal data

Procedure:
1. Cue-cards may have either questions or answers: information may be distributed throughout the whole class, or in smaller groups.

Example: train timetables
The task is to find out when all the trains leave. (There may be as many destinations as students in the class, or more, or fewer.)

Timetable

Destination	**Departure?**
Paris Lyon Bordeaux Marseilles Caen etc.	

Cue-cards

Paris 9.30	Lyon 13.25	etc. (one per student)

Each student has a copy of the blank timetable.

2 Distribute the cards around the class (one each). The students obtain the required information by asking questions, e.g. 'When does the train for Paris leave?'

Variation: All conversation must be in French, German, sign language etc.

Anonymity

Aim: In some 'sensitive' areas of personal growth and development, there may be a reluctance on the part of some students to discuss what their confusions or problems may be. In order to alleviate these extra pressures, but still allow for discussion, it may be helpful to use an anonymous starting point.

Materials: Squares of lined paper, pens

Area of work: Sex education or any sensitive topic or situation

Procedure:

1 Facilitator invites individual students to write on paper any confusions/problems they may have about the topic, adding that they need not sign their questions.
2 Papers folded when question has been written down, placed in a central pile.
3 Facilitator invites students to choose whom they would wish to work with and take one piece of paper from the pile.
4 Groups are requested to make a note of any suggestions they may have regarding the information on the paper.
5 Student from the group reports back to whole class with total group discussion in round.

Family game

Aims: To help children to realise that families are units of people who live together in cooperation and that different groupings of people are often quite acceptable. To illustrate actively that in different cultures and societies people do live together in different family structures. Group interaction.

Materials: None

Procedure:

1. Divide the class into four groups of approximately the same size by giving the students a number each from 1–4.
2. All number 1s need to think of an identity/role that would be appropriate for a mother figure. She can be aged anywhere between 16 to 80. Think of a name, job, favourite food, daily paper or magazine, hobby, etc. for the person so as to add a bit of life to 'her' character.
3. All number 2s need to think of a role that would be suitable for a father figure.
4. Numbers 3 and 4 think of a child's role.
5. Get students to mill about and explain their roles to others. Call out a number every now and again so they all have to join together in groups of that size (e.g. six or nine or three).
6. Keep changing the number.
7. When the final number has been called, the members of each group can create a story which justifies and explains thoroughly why they all live as a family. (You will be surprised at how original the stories are and how the students manage to think of reasons why this group of people live together as a family.) There will be plenty of follow-up discussion after they have explained their circumstances.

Robber

Aims: Encourage creativity, ingenuity and lateral thinking, cooperation

Materials: Blackboard or flip chart, paper and pen for each group

Procedure:

1. The leader asks the class to brainstorm onto the blackboard or flip chart what they would need in order to do a good piece of work. (This question could be related to the topic about to be studied, if there is one.)
2. Someone volunteers to be the robber and 'steals' the three things she feels to be most valuable and useful by rubbing or crossing them out.
3. The class then divides into groups of four or five and lists all the types of work they could produce using only the items left on the board.
4. Each group feeds back to the whole class.
5. A second brainstorm is done, like the first, on what the class could use to achieve good pieces of work.

Salesman

This game could be played whenever there are ideas to be discussed by the group, e.g. solutions to a problem, plans for a trip, concepts in a topic on the syllabus, experiments.

Aims: Group discussion and evaluation, decision-making, role play, communication, listening

Materials: Paper and pen for each group, 'salesman' badges

Procedure:

1. The class divides into groups of four or five.
2. Each group takes ownership of an idea, which they could generate themselves or which could be selected from a class brainstorm, on the theme in question.
3. A person in each group volunteers to be the salesman for the group and wears the badge.
4. Each group discusses its idea and decides how its salesman could convince other groups to 'buy' the idea.
5. After a previously agreed time, or when each group is ready, the salesmen go round trying to sell their ideas to other groups. Group members may only listen to what each salesman has to say; they may not ask questions or make comments. It may be helpful for each group to write down each suggestion as it is presented to them.
6. When the salesmen have been round to each group, they form their own group and listen to each other's ideas, then discuss their experiences as salesmen. At the same time, the other groups discuss and decide which idea they will buy.
7. Each group writes up or says which it has bought.

Variations:

1. Each group could have a sum of money and put a price on its own idea. It then tries to get good value for money in buying other ideas.
2. The game could be expanded to include advertising.

Obstacles

Aims: Consolidation or revision of a difficult topic, cooperation, support, communication

Materials: Five 'obstacles' which can be written on (could be pieces of card). Paper and pen for each group

Procedure:

1. Class divides into several groups.
2. Each group chooses a topic which it finds difficult to understand.
3. Each group brainstorms the difficulties which members have with the topic.
4. Five of these difficulties are chosen by each group and written on their 'obstacles'.
5. The class sits in a circle and the group which volunteers to begin sets up its 'obstacle course' by placing its 'obstacles' in a line across the circle.

6 A volunteer who feels able to run the course is then sought from the rest of the class. He goes to each obstacle in turn and overcomes it by explaining the answer to the difficulty clearly. When one course is successfully completed, another one is set up.

Variation: Relay race, if one volunteer cannot overcome all obstacles.

Memory board

Aims: To reinforce/revise a topic, working together

Materials: Blackboard or flip chart

Procedure:

1 Class divides into groups of four or five.

2 Leader or group choose a topic they wish to tackle.

3 Brainstorm all key facts, words or ideas about that topic onto board or flip chart.

4 When brainstorm is complete, leader gives one minute for people to memorise the facts, words or ideas, then rubs out or tears down the brainstorm.

5 Each group is given two minutes to reproduce the same facts, words or ideas by brainstorming onto their pieces of paper.

6 The game ends when a group has the full list. A new subject could then be chosen.

Rounders

Aims: Revision, light relief

Materials: None

Procedure: The students sit in teams in long rows. The ones at the front are 'batting'; a scorer and bowler/question person are nominated.

The people in front put up their hands to answer questions (e.g. in French, vocabulary, background information etc. – can be anything). The first one with hand up and correct answer moves to the *back* of his team. This is repeated until the first person in the team has returned to the front, i.e. one rounder scored.

Verbal football

Aims: Consolidation of topics, revision, concentration, fun

Materials: None

Procedure:

1 Class divides into two teams.

2 Teacher or student acts as referee.

3 Coin is tossed to decide which team has 'kickoff'.

4 The ball is passed by asking and answering questions.

5 Someone in the team with 'kickoff' asks a question.
6 If it is answered first by a member of his own team, the 'ball' has been passed. This player 'with the ball' asks a new question, and so on.
7 If a team puts together three passes, they have scored a goal.
8 A tackle is made if a member of the other team intercepts the 'ball' by answering the question first. He then asks a question, and so on.

GROUP ROLE PLAYS

(Involving adults other than teachers)

The following five games were developed separately yet have common aims, as follows:

1 Group decision making skills.
2 Relationships with other adults (not just teachers).
3 Discussion and team-work.
4 Widening of youngsters' perceptions of beyond-school environments.
5 Breakdown of stereotypes youngsters have of societal groups.
6 Enhance individual's awareness of how they operate in a group and of how they are perceived by others.

TV advertising

Procedure: 1 Divide a group of 15 into three. (Each group then, or previously, manufactures a product, e.g. a bottle of perfume; they will be marketing this using TV as a medium.)

2 Each group decides amongst themselves who takes which role:

Director
Performer
Technician
Make-up/Costume
Planner.

3 Each group then discusses its market target by brainstorm. Group planning takes place, writing a script in annotated cartoon as envisaged for recording by TV or video camera. A rehearsal is needed (timed), followed by production on video equipment.

4 Each group watches all the 'productions'.

5 Each group de-roles and assesses what it has learned, through discussion. This can then be drawn together in a main group through brainstorm or sub-group spokesperson using a flip chart.

N.B. A TV company employee gives valuable insight to the team concept and this media form.

Trade Union role play

Procedure: 1 Divide a group of 15 into three groups of five. One group are managers. One group are shop stewards or conveners. Third group are observers. Each group discusses how they perceive their role regarding characteristic behaviour, language, appearance, personality of individuals. Could brainstorm results.

2 Individuals pair off and act out role play along any theme, e.g. an unfair dismissal; wage negotiation; disciplinary hearing over a violent act, etc. An observer sits in on each and takes notes without participating.
3 Main group form a circle and feed back their reactions about **a** the process of negotiation, **b** how they perceived the other person. Observers have an important function in also feeding back.

N.B. The use of a real manager and a real trade unionist is valuable in *facilitating* each role-briefing, not directing. Once role play is complete, the manager and trade unionist have a vital role in clarifying youngsters' stereotypes and demonstrating how negotiation takes place in real situations.

A re-run can take place to consolidate pupils' learning.

Now get out of that

Procedure: 1 Divide a group of 15 into three groups of five. Provide each with a range of clues for a treasure hunt. Each group's clues lead to the same destination along four different routes in a park/forest/urban environment (a form of orienteering). A 4–5 km route is best.
2 Each group of five discuss with a flip chart what they liked; did not like; found difficult; learned about themselves as individuals; learned about their group.
3 Main group discussion (through brainstorm or discussion). Focus on:

a Leadership selection/group decision making.
b Leadership styles (control, responsibility and effectiveness).
c Group reaction/individual reaction to *b* above.
d Problem solving (did it work? How could it be improved?).
e Teamwork (was there any? Why/why not?).

Benefit: To enhance learning about leadership or group decision making (depending on whether a leader is allocated or nominated; depending on whether the group worked as a cooperative).

Family budgeting

Procedure: 1 Divide a group of 15 into three 'families'. Provide each family with five role cards. *They* decide who takes which role (father, teenage son, grannie, etc.). Each family is different in composition.
2 Provide key family members with a chequebook, deposit account book, and fixed income. Introduce chance cards in a series of 'rounds', each lasting 15 minutes. Provide a bank manager and bank cashier (preferably real volunteers from a commercial bank). Each family must handle the chance cards issued to them in each round and must plan/handle transactions accordingly, using the bank. Cheques can be written and posted into a postbox before the

end of each period. (A buzzer signals end of round and deadline.) A five minute period between rounds enables the bank to 'clear' transactions, and families to assess/plan/organise their affairs.

3 Break for ten minutes, then re-assemble, either in families or en masse, to discuss negatives and positives; what was learned; what came as a surprise. The learning acknowledged by youngsters can be written on flip charts.

N.B. The support of a real bank is useful for valid role play, materials and to act as an advisory service offering a perspective on reality.

Newspaper production

Procedure: 1 A group of 15 decide on roles:

1 editor 7 sub-editors 3 typists 3 sticking onto paper	} all individuals double up as journalists

2 All individuals collect their 'stories' from around the school/community in pairs with camera. Return to group and negotiate priorities for publication. The editor reads the stories and discusses with group the composition of the 'newspaper'. The sub-editors alter the stories to fit agreed format. Word processor used to type out articles. The pasting group arranges material ready for printing on offset litho.

3 After a ten minute break the group re-forms for a round discussion of **a** problems and **b** positives arising from the exercise. They split into pairs, each with a flip chart on which to write down 'What we learned from this'. Ideas shared in an open feedback or by brainstorming.

Aims:

1 Group decision making and discussion.
2 Understanding of newspaper organisation and functional roles.
3 Reporting (collection and production of an article).
4 Negotiation skills.
5 Understanding the viewpoints of others.

N.B. To acquire the neutral and advisory support of an employee from a real newspaper can provide a realism and perspective that gives insight into industry.

ASSESSMENT ACTIVITIES

DIY assessment quiz (For teachers)

These are not the usual questions that assessors ask; they are the 'secret' questions we ask when observing teachers.

1 Do you have the full attention of the kids, or are you alternately shouting and hushing and waiting for quiet?
2 Do you and the kids feel good at the end of a lesson?
3 Are the kids working together and supporting each other, or calling each other names, laughing at each other and putting each other down?
4 How much of your time is taken up with discipline problems?
5 Do people listen to each other in your classroom?
6 Is your seating arrangement promoting good communication?
7 Is the topic you are working on in any way relevant to the kids themselves?
8 How much choice do they have? (Every day, every hour.)
9 Are they involved in 'playing games' (e.g. trying to make you, themselves, or each other look like fools) or are they involved in the task at hand, whatever it is?
10 Can they have an interesting discussion for a few minutes without interruptions?
11 What do you want for yourself? What do you want for the kids?
12 What's the end of the lesson like?
13 Do you love coming to school, or dread it, or is it just your job?

Assessment of your own learning during in-service training

Some questions which might help

1 What things have I done that I am pleased with?
2 What range of feelings did I experience?
3 How open was I with the group?
4 What challenges did I take up?
5 What did I enjoy?
6 What questions have I that I didn't ask?
7 What have I learned about myself?
8 Is there a *specific example* of how I may be able to use something I have learned from the course at work?

Assessment questionnaire

Related to the introduction of student-centred methods in a class or group of students

Changes

1 How have the new lessons been different from the old ones?
2 What changes have you noticed in the teacher?
3 How have *you* changed since doing work the new way?
4 Has the class changed (e.g. unity, atmosphere, relationships, behaviour)?

Achievement

1 Did you get more work done this way than you would have done with the old methods?
2 How much interest and satisfaction have you felt doing this work?
3 What things have you learned from the work?
4 Did you think the way we assessed the work was fair? Were you satisfied with the assessment of your work?

The work

1 How easy was it to make decisions about your work (e.g. what to do, how to do it, how much to do at home)?
2 If you worked in a group, how did you get on with the others?
3 If you worked in a group, did everyone do their share?
4 How much homework did you set yourself/yourselves? Did you do it?
5 Wht problems did you face doing the work this way and how did you deal with them?
6 Did you get enough help from the teacher?

Assessment

1 What is good about this new way of working?
2 Is there anything you regret about what you/we have done?
3 If we were to do this again, how could it be improved?
4 How great a part do you want to play in making decisions and running lessons from now on?
5 What should we do next?

Subject assessment questionnaire

This is an example of a 'market research' questionnaire used to assess a second year Biology course. It led to negotiation between students and teacher.

Please complete the questionnaire below to help us improve the Biology course for next year's second years.

1 Name (fill this in if you want to) ....
2 How much have you enjoyed your Biology lessons this year ....
3 Have you found Biology

a Easy **b** About right **c** Difficult

4 You may feel that there were some bits of the work that you

A liked a lot
B felt were OK and worth keeping in next year
C felt were OK, but should miss them out next year
D did not like at all

Please fill in the questionnaire below by ticking the appropriate column.

Questionnaire

Topic	**A**	**B**	**C**	**D**	**Other comments** e.g. too advanced/useful/ relevant/already known
1 Comparing living and non-living things					
2 Measuring differences in human height and plotting bar graphs					
3 Using a hand lens and working out magnification					
4 Sorting animals into groups					
5 Using microscopes to look at cells					
6 Looking at single celled organisms under the microscope					
7 Studying yeast and amoeba					

Topic	A	B	C	D	**Other comments** e.g. too advanced/useful/ relevant/already known
8 Human sexual reproduction					
9 Studying butterflies					
10 Studying locusts and houseflies					
11 Studying birds/eggs hatching					
12 Studying development of frogs					
13 Dissecting flowers, e.g. buttercups					
14 Looking at pollen under the microscope					
15 Development of fruits and seeds					
16 Showing that plants make food by a process called photosynthesis					

Skills checklist

The following is a skills checklist used in part of a Social Education course.

	Week 1	2	3	4	5	6
Communiction 1 Can listen to advice and carry out instructions						
2 Can understand another's point of view						
3 Can talk with confidence to a small group						
4 Can talk with confidence to a large group						
5 Can understand and use non-verbal communication						
6 Can find information from different sources						
Social 7 Understand yourself better						
8 Can work with friends						
9 Can work with members of the opposite sex						
10 Can work with new people of your own age						
11 Can work with older/ younger people						
12 Work hard to make the group a success						
13 Reliable when something needs following through						

	Week 1	2	3	4	5	6
Decision making **14** Show a flexible, open mind						
15 Know when to ask for advice						
16 Can work by yourself when necessary						
17 Can accept a majority verdict						
18 Can plan your work						
19 Can judge your own performance and see ways of improving						
20 Can understand and use this checklist well						

What is the checklist?

Above are the things or 'skills' that we would like you to practise during this Social Education course. The reason for writing this checklist is to help us all to see

1 why we are playing some of the games
2 where we became more skilled over the six weeks or where we didn't change
3 what the teachers could change to make the course better.

How do I use it?

At the end of each session we will look at our checklist and see whether we have been trying any of the skills. When we have decided which skill we used, we have to decide how good we were at using it. To do this we choose a number between 0 and 5. Nought means no skill at all; 5 means highly skilled. This number is then written in the correct column. For example, if we played Tic-Toc and I thought I listened to instructions well, I might put a 3 in the column for Week 1. Maybe by week 6 I could feel skilled enough to put a 5 in the column. **Please Note:** This is designed to help you to see how *you* are improving *your* skills; it does not test you against anyone else in the group.

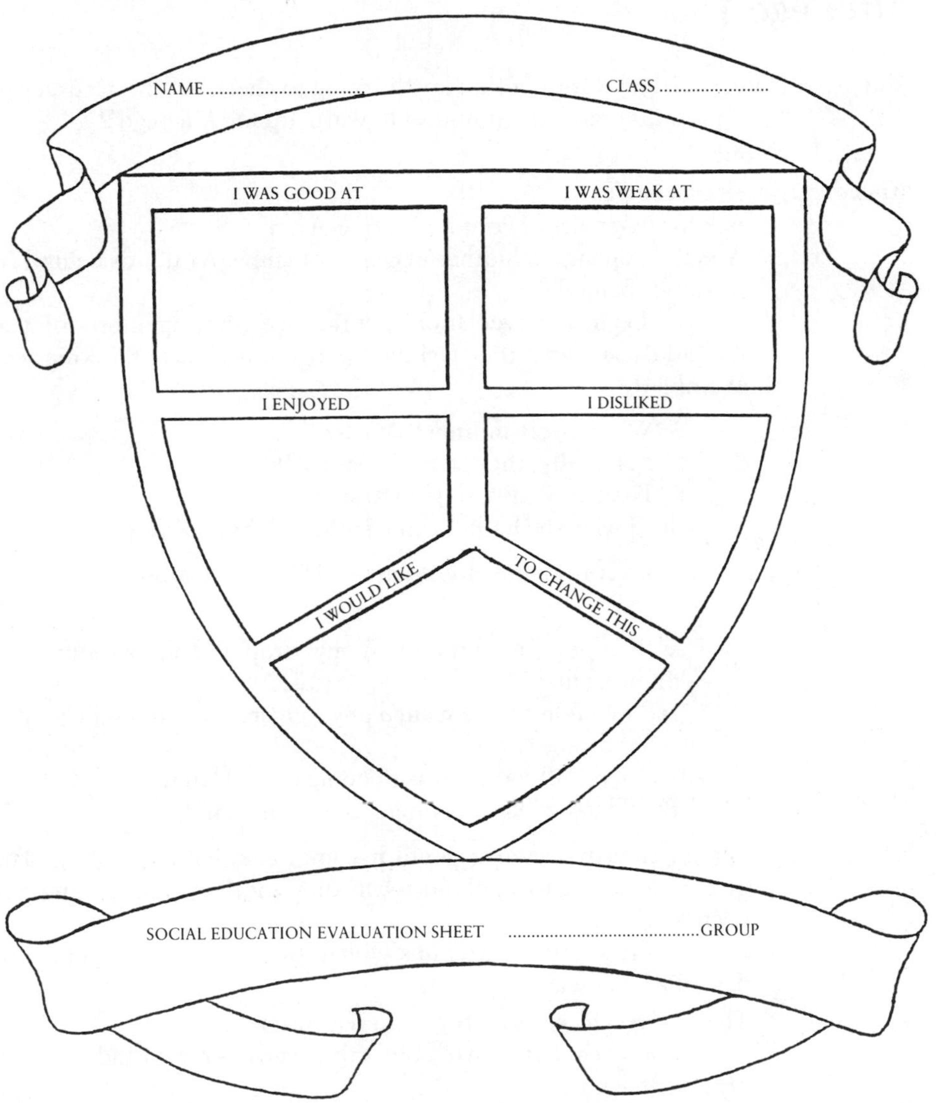
NAME..................................
CLASS ....
I WAS GOOD AT
I WAS WEAK AT
I ENJOYED
I DISLIKED
I WOULD LIKE
TO CHANGE THIS
SOCIAL EDUCATION EVALUATION SHEET
....GROUP

Alter ego 1

Aims: Fun, social education, role-play, learning to check out the accuracy of interpretations and assumptions, to warm up for Alter ego 2

Materials: None

Procedure:
1. Sit in a circle.
2. Ask for two pairs of volunteers, $A + A_1$, $B + B_1$.
3. A + B sit facing each other in centre of circle. A_1 stands behind A; B_1 stands behind B.
4. A and B begin a conversation as if they were having afternoon tea. A_1 and B_1 say what they feel their partners are really thinking. For example:

   A 'What lovely muffins!'
   (A_1 'Actually, they taste like straw.')
   B 'Thank you. I'm so glad to see you.'
   (B_1 'I wish she hadn't come without 'phoning first.')

   Not all secret thoughts are negative. The conversation may go like this:

   A 'I hope you don't mind my dropping in without 'phoning first.'
   (A_1 'I couldn't have waited any longer to see him – he's so handsome.')
   B 'Oh, it's all right, I wasn't going out till later.'
   (B_1 'I'd like to keep her here as long as I can.')

5. Let the improvisation go until it comes to a natural ending. The group can learn to applaud when they think a good ending has been reached.
6. Discuss the social interactions which took place. Invite people to describe what was happening.

Variations:
1. The group can choose lots of different situations.
2. A and B each have two conflicting egos, or two sides of an argument, e.g.:

   A 'I hope you don't mind my dropping in without 'phoning first.'
   B 'Oh that's OK; I'm pleased to see you.'
   (B_1 'Oh dear! This house is in a terrible mess; I'm so embarrassed, and what's more I should be doing my homework.')
   (B_2 'I don't care about the house or my homework; mybe I can ask her to come out with me this evening.')

Alter ego 2

This is the same as Alter ego 1, but is applied to a real classroom issue and is used as an evaluation or discussion activity.

Aims: Evaluation, changing politeness to honesty, self-awareness

Materials: None

Procedure:

1 Sit in a circle

2 Ask for two pairs of volunteers, A + A_1, B + B_1.

3 A and B sit facing each other in the centre of the circle. A_1 stands behind A; B_1 stands behind B.

4 The issue or activity to be evaluated is stated clearly and A + B begin a polite and tactful conversation about it.

A_1 and B_1 express what might be the real, underlying thoughts of A and B.

For example:

One of the small groups in the class has just finished making a video tape which the whole class has viewed.

> A 'What did you think of the video tape?'
> B 'Um, not bad.'
> (A_1 'I wonder if he means it?')
> (B_1 'Actually, I was pretty disappointed with the camera work.')
> A 'It's not as good as I thought it was going to be.'
> (A_1 'I'm really ashamed of the whole thing, but am afraid to say so.')
> and so on . . .

5 The four volunteers sit down and check out the accuracy of the secret thoughts.

6 The whole group is invited to join in the discussion.

Alter ego 3

Aims: Evaluation of the teacher's work, self-awareness

Materials: Willing colleague or student with pen and paper

Procedure:

1 Teacher invites a colleague or student whom he trusts to engage in an evaluation procedure.

2 Colleague or student comes in as an observer, watches the lesson and at various times writes down what he thinks are the teacher's non-verbalised thoughts.

3 After the lesson, the observer shows the teacher what he wrote and a discussion follows. This presupposes that a good deal of trust has already been established.

Variation: The observer could record what he thinks are the secret thoughts of a pupil, rather than the teacher. The discussion which follows could involve the observer, the student and the teacher.

Awareness continuum

Aims: Self-awareness, trust-building, self-disclosure

Materials: Pen and paper

Procedure:

1 Each person lists three strengths which they possess, and the opposite of that strength across from it, e.g.

Hardworking ______________________ Lazy
Enthusiastic ______________________ Indifferent

He marks where he thinks he is now on each continuum.

2 If people want to, they can share these thoughts with a partner or the group.

3 Each person lists three targets or goals for herself, and the opposite, e.g.

Loving ______________________ Loveless
Accepting ______________________ Intolerant

She then marks her present position on the continuum.

4 If desired, people can make contracts about how and where and when they are going to work to move towards the targets.

Variations: This game could be played with live people and chairs, setting up a Value continuum as in *Gamesters' Handbook*, P58

ACTIVITIES FOR ANY TIME

Introductory bingo

Aims: Fun, warm-up, getting-to-know-you
Materials: Card printed similar to below:

12	5	10	21
5	9	20	3
4	2	8	16
1	6	30	7

Procedure:
1 Each person has to move around the room talking to other people.
2 She can cross out a number when she finds a person to whom the number is in some way significant. She then moves on and talks to someone else, trying to find a reason why another number should be crossed out, e.g.

Person A lives at house number 7.
Person B has 5 children.
Person C has worked for 6 years at their present school, etc.

Remember to listen well – you may be asked to remember what the significance of certain numbers was!

Variations:
1 The length of the game may be determined by varying the number of squares on the card.
2 Blanks can be given out, and before the game begins participants are asked to fill them in with numbers which have some significance for them.

Name game

Aims: Learning names, concentration
Materials: One pen/pencil
Procedure:
1 Split into small groups (up to 15).
2 Hold a pencil/pen and say 'This is Peter, I'm Phyllis and who are you?' Hand pencil to the next person, who says 'This is Peter, you are Phyllis, I'm Bill, and who are you?' Each person adds his own name to the others around the circle.

Hello, I'm a scuba-diver

Aims: Getting to know each other, group interaction

Materials: None

Procedure:
1. Mingle freely amongst the group, swapping your name with six other people whom you may or may not know.
2. Choose six different people and shake hands when you greet them.
3. Choose another six people and when you give your name add one pertinent fact about yourself: e.g. I'm a scuba-diver; I grow cacti, etc.

Similarities and differences

Aims: Introductory, self awareness

Materials: Sheet of paper and pencil for each group

Procedure:
1. Draw these five shapes for the whole group to see

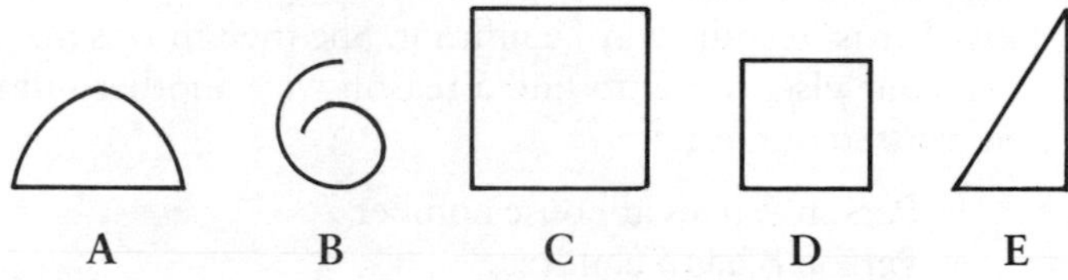

2. Ask the students to divide them into a group of two and a group of three according to similarities and differences. Ask them to explain their reasons for the groupings. A grouping of 4:1 is not allowed.
3. Ask students to split into groups of five and ask each group to divide itself into a two and a three, and to prepare their reasons.
4. Report back to whole group by demonstrating the divisions and then giving the reasons.

Variations:
1. Use objects instead of drawings.
2. Experiment with different group sizes and ratios.

N.B. Do not accept divisions of 3:1 or 4:1 unless you are confident about students' ability to accept isolation.

Rainstorm

Aims: Concentration, inspiration, group togetherness

Materials: None

Procedure: The leader starts off a series of sounds, each one passes around the circle and is sustained until it comes back to the leader, who starts the next one going round. Each person keeps one sound going until the next one is received. The sounds:

1 rub hands together quickly
2 snap fingers
3 clap hands on knees
4 stamp feet

Repeat in reverse order: 4, 3, 2, 1.

Community sneezing

Aims: Fun, making a break in a boring meeting, lightening the atmosphere

Materials: None

Procedure: 1 Leader says 'Decide which one of you is a number one, a number two or a number three.'
2 Number ones say 'Hatchoo', number twos say 'Histchoo', number threes 'Hotschoo'.
3 After that, anyone can say 'one, two, three, Sneeze!' at any time, and each group does their own version.

Maze

Aims: Trust-building, eye contact, warm-up, relax, two-minutes-before-the-bell-rings

Materials: None

Procedure: 1 The group divides into fours, and then into pairs within these fours.
2 The first pair stand still (arm's length) apart, looking at each other.
3 The other pair walk around them very fast, trying to avoid each other. If and when they collide, they then stand still and the other pair start moving round them.

Variations: 1 Double up and work in fours and eights.
2 Get the group to invent new variations, adding objects, or adding different movements.

The plank

Aims: Warm-up, learning names, getting to know each other, physical contact

Materials: Two drama rostra (wooden blocks), a strong plank, imaginary piranhas

Procedure: The plank is supported at each end by a rostrum. Group memebers stand on the plank. Leader says 'You are on a bridge over the

Amazon River. The water is full of piranhas; if you fall in you will be eaten. Get yourselves into alphabetical order according to first names.'

Variation: Instead of the plank, a piece of string can be laid out on the floor. The group members are standing on the string, spread out along its length. Procedure as for The plank.

Trusty trains

Aims: Trust building, fun

Materials: Blindfolds (optional)

Procedure: Group divides into fours, one person behind the other, with hands on the shoulders of the person in front. All close their eyes except the last person, who guides the train with signals, such as toots, whistles, screaming brakes, etc.

Variations:
1 Longer trains, maybe eight or 16.
2 All close eyes except person in front.
3 *All* close eyes.

Finding the distance

Aims: Exploring how people feel about physical contact, trust building, fun

Materials: None

Procedure:
1 Form into two lines, facing each other across the room.
2 This game is to be done non-verbally!
3 Become a partner to the person opposite you in the line.
4 Move towards your partner until you come too close for comfort; move away until you are comfortable.
5 Move back further; try to make eye contact. Move closer until eye contact is comfortable.
6 Experiment with standing nose-to-nose, back-to-back, shoulder-to-shoulder, and other variations.
7 Share your feelings about the exercise with your partner.
8 Share feedback in the big group.

Feeling hands

Aims: Getting to know each other, group interaction

Materials: None

Procedure:
1 Form two concentric circles, each consisting of six to ten people standing. Players face each other. Inner circle feel the hands of each of the people in the outer circle in turn.
2 Inner circle now close their eyes. The outer circle moves round until told to stop at random. Each person in the inner circle, eyes

still closed, takes the hands of the person opposite and tries to guess their identity.

3 Repeat the process as often as desired.

4 At an appropriate moment switch inner and outer circles.

Golem

A golem is a piece of malleable clay.

Aims: Trust, group cohesion, sensitivity

Materials: None

Procedure:

1 One member of a group of six or so is the golem. The golem can be moved to any position, which it retains until moved, but can make no move on its own, not even to retain its balance.

2 The other members of the group make it walk, supporting and manoeuvring it. Remember, it can make *no* movement of its own: feet must be lifted, legs flexed by the team.

3 Discuss how it felt.

Variations: The golem is made to fly, supported by the team. The golem flies, changing its shape, as if able to dance in the air.

To bluff or not to bluff?

Aims: To encourage the individual to be more open, to provide an opportunity to share sensitive issues in a secure framework, to encourage the listener to be caring and supportive

Materials: Card or paper for making notes

Procedure:

1 Ask group to sit with an inner and an outer circle facing each other, i.e. partners.

2 Ask each person to think about people that they have known, have felt at ease with, and with whom they felt they could share some of their innermost thoughts and feelings. It may be helpful to jot down some of the qualities that spring to mind that these 'special people' possess.

3 Each group member is going to be asked to share something with your partner that you have *usually kept to yourself*. You may want to choose something from this list, or you may think of something else. Here are some suggestions:

Your biggest fear.
Your worst habit.
Your most embarrassing moment.
Your secret desire.
Your biggest worry.
A personality trait that you have difficulty in controlling.

4 Decide which of these you feel able and willing to share, but do make an effort to share something that is usually kept private. Choose something that is true and real to you. It may help you to jot down a few points about what you are going to say, e.g. why or how the problem started, how you have tried to deal with it, etc.
5 Now think of another example but, rather than this example being true, you can make up a fictitious or 'bluff' story.
6 Take turns in relating the true and fictitious stories to your listening partner. You may do these in any order so that the other person has no way of knowing which is true and which is false. It is not necessary for the listener to guess which is true. Make sure the listener is supportive and encouraging during both accounts. (They may wish to hold your hand, put hand on shoulder, etc., but only do this if you feel it is appropriate.)
7 The listener should respond to both accounts as if they were both true. If the person giving the account wishes to share which is true/false, they may do so of their *own accord*, but must not be asked.
8 At the end of the exercise, share with each other how supportive they felt you were. How secure they feel. Did they offer helpful suggestions/advice? Did you feel differently when telling them true/false accounts?

Swap shop

Aims: Empathy, self-awareness

Materials: None

Procedure:

1 Ask each member of the class to find a partner whom she or he knows well, and to go and sit next to that partner.
2 Spend an agreed length of time, say five minutes, talking, sitting, walking around with your partner, observing carefully your partner's mannerisms.
3 Ask partners to swap identities for the rest of the lesson, so each person takes her partner's name, and mannerisms, works in her partner's book, using his pen, imitating her partner's speech. All interactions during the lesson should be 'in role'. The teacher should refer to people in role.
4 Carry on the lesson in the usual way.
5 Allow time at the end of the lesson for partners to talk to each other about the experience and for the class to say what they got out of the exercise.

Variation: The group leader/teacher could also swap with a student.

Trading places

Aims: Empathy, trust building, understanding, breaking down barriers and hierarchies

Materials: None

Procedure:
1. Choose, with the students, any classroom activity; a lesson, a planning session, an evaluation.
2. Ask for a volunteer to trade places with you (the teacher) for ten minutes. Be sure to stay in role for the whole time, and let the student handle whatever might happen.
3. When the time is up, discuss the experience with the student and the class.
4. Try it many times, with different students.

Skills auction

Aims: Trust building, confidence building, self-assessment, acquiring new skills

Materials: Pens, paper, hat, gavel (optional), play money or counters, flip chart/blackboard

Procedure:
1. On a small piece of paper, write one specific skill that you would very much like to have (anonymously). Examples might be:

   I would like to be able to hammer a nail in straight.
   I would like to be able to remember people's names.

2. Put all the papers in a hat.
3. Someone reads out all the papers, and the leader writes them up on the blackboard or flip chart.
4. Everyone is given £100 to spend at the auction, either in play money or counters, or clothespegs, or even bits of paper. Each person is responsible for keeping track of her own bidding.
5. Someone plays Auctioneer, and the auction is held. Each person can bid for as many skills as they want until they have spent their £100. When a skill has been sold, the new owner keeps the piece of paper.
6. Either use the skills which exist in the group, or bring in outside experts, and allow people to master the skills for which they have been bidding.

Masks

Aims: To help establish three forms of non-verbal expression: body movements, especially hands and arms; facial expression; eye contact

Materials: A mask which has eye holes that can be closed

Procedure: 1 This activity can be done in threes or as a group activity. In threes, one person wears the mask and the other two observe his reactions and comment on them afterwards. Working as a whole group, one person wears the mask and sits in the centre; a round elicits reactions afterwards.

2 The person wearing the mask must try to express a feeling, e.g. aggression, submission, assertion, using only the parts uncovered. Wearing the mask with the eyeholes closed, he can only use his body to express the feeling (i.e. body language). By opening the eye holes, this allows him to use his eyes to express the feeling (i.e. eye contact). Removing the mask altogether allows the use of all three: body language, eye contact and facial expression.

It's a secret

Aims: Feel comfortable with self-disclosure, trust

Materials: Piece of paper

Procedure:
1 Write a sentence beginning 'Not many people know that I . . .'
2 Put it in the middle of the group, pick one out.
3 Guess whose it is but don't say *what* it is.
4 Give it to who you think it belongs to. If you have a piece and you don't know who to give it to, pile it back in the middle.
5 Go around the circle. You can:

read it out
challenge
pass.

6 Do a round – own the secret or pass.

The layering game

Aims: Social education, self awareness, role play, English, Drama

Materials: Pencil and paper

Procedure:
1 Get a small group together, three or four people.
2 Write some simple dialogue, as bland as possible, e.g.

A Did you get the eggs in town today?
B No, they were sold out by the time I got there.
A Did you try the new supermarket?
B I couldn't find it.
C I hear it's more expensive anyway.
D I bought some eggs at the corner shop . . . here they are.
A It's a good thing you did because I was planning to make a cake.

3 Decide who is A, B, C, D. Each person writes the thoughts that underlie the statements of your character. For example, B's line, 'I couldn't find it', could be said ashamedly, definatly, neutrally, etc., with the thinking that would lie behind such a tone.
4 Practise the scene, using body language and eyes, voices and positions to show the underlying thoughts.
5 Each person writes the investment or attitude that is determining how the person responds. So, B's line could be determined by an earlier experience with A and B could be feeling 'I didn't try very hard because I wanted to get even with you for forgetting the chocolate yesterday'.
6 Do the scene again, this time letting other groups watch it. Ask for feedback on what they saw, and how the characters were interacting.

Quick on the draw

The standard version of the game below is an introduction to the process of the game. The variation explains how the game can be applied to various topics within the curriculum.

Aims: Fun, group cooperation, concentration, reviewing

Materials: Sheets of drawing paper and a felt pen for each group. A list of subjects or objects to be drawn

Procedure:
1 Group divides into smaller groups of four or five, each group with paper and pen, and at equal distances from the leader.
2 The leader (could be anyone) has a list of subjects such as song/book/film titles or pub signs.
3 When the leader says 'Go', someone in each group runs to the leader, reads the first title off the list, returns to her group and draws the subject for the rest to guess. No words may be written. As soon as the group has the answer, another person runs with it to the leader and reads the second item on the list.
4 The procedure is repeated until a group has guessed correctly all the subjects on the list.

Variation: Apply the above game to any topic within any subject on the curriculum. For example:

> Revising the Second World War for O Level History:
>
> The leader has a list of questions, each group has to record its answers on the paper. The game ends when one group has completed its list correctly. The groups then devise lists of questions for revision so they can play the game again.

Fisherman's ring

Aims: To encourage standpoint-taking, to discourage 'ownership' of ideas, to encourage active listening

Materials: One copy of an incident where a character is under stress or two characters are in conflict

Procedure:
1. Form two concentric circles of up to 15 people seated on chairs facing each other, i.e. partners. Read out or tell the incident in as much convincing clear detail as possible.
2. Inner circle A are to adopt one character's argument and expound it clearly. Outer circle B to adopt antagonistic viewpoint and argue equally clearly.
3. Outer circle move two or three places to the right. Outer circle to switch arguments and, instead of B, argue A's case. Inner circle likewise. Continue moving and switching arguments to suit.
4. Get the whole group together to share the results.

Look and listen

Aims: Concentration, listening skills

Materials: None

Procedure:
1. The group sits in a circle and each member has a number from one onwards round the circle.
2. The group decides on a subject about which to tell a story, e.g. Going to a football match, Dave's first day at school.
3. Someone volunteers to start and everyone in the group looks at him. The volunteer creates the first sentence of the story, then calls a number.
4. The person with that number sums up what the previous person said, then adds a second sentence while everyone looks at him. When he has finished his sentence, he calls another number. All eyes turn to this person who sums up *only what the previous person said*, adds a third sentence, then calls a new number. And so on.
5. And so on until the story is finished.

Variations:
1. Each person waits until everyone is looking at her before she begins.
2. The 'story' could be a new topic to be studied or an old one to be revised in any subject in the curriculum.

The token game

Aims: Deal with over-dominant group members, equalise participation, listening skills

Materials: Tokens, toothpicks or pennies

Procedure:
1. Choose a topic to discuss in the circle. Agree on a time limit and see that each person has five tokens at the start.
2. Every time a person talks, he throws in a token. When his tokens are gone, he must remain silent. Meanwhile, everyone is looking at and listening to the speaker.
3. When the time is up, discuss how people feel if they have all their tokens left, and how people feel who ran out. Discuss participation, and how to equalise it in the group, if people think that is desirable.

Pass the charisma

Aims: To define charisma, examine how people act when they have it, help to equalise the participation in the group

Materials: Small cushions, or cuddly toys, or other soft objects (these may seem like non-standard classroom equipment, and they are; you will find that they are very useful in a student-centred setting)

Procedure:
1. Sit in a circle, choose a topic to discuss, like popularity, or happiness. (This game is probably more suited to subjects in the personal and social education areas, but could be adapted.)
2. Each person has a soft object or cushion.
3. The topic is discussed, and at any given moment, people may throw the cushions all to one person, who then has to hold forth on the topic in an extremely charismatic manner.
4. After she has been applauded, she throws the topic, as well as the cushions, to someone else.
5. Discuss charisma, how do we get it, how do we learn it, are we born with it?

Variations: After the discussion, draw, paint or write about charisma, or make a play about it.

APPENDIX

The background to the student-centred learning programme within The Birmingham Initiative

History is made at a pace in education these days. The shock to the secondary system generated through TVEI is still at work. The underlying commitment of all involved can be traced to a conviction that our schools and colleges have not been meeting the needs of students – especially as they reach the age of self-determination and a role in adult society.

TVEI is all about curriculum change – change with a purpose; change with momentum – but the lessons of previous curriculum initiatives are clear. Curriculum change is not the same as curriculum development and this awareness has been exposed increasingly with the progress of the Initiative in Birmingham. Development of the curriculum is essentially about the personal development of learners and teachers, and less about structures, systems and resources. Harmonising these themes of development has been a fascinating exercise for all of us and continues to be a challenge.

Our first priorities in the Birmingham Initiative were designing a successful submission to meet MSC criteria and using this as a foundation for the creation of curriculum programmes in our eight schools. Our next step was the appointment of teams of teachers to work from 1 September 1983. In the space of five weeks 22 teachers were appointed and then we signed our contract . . !

Our initial in-service work was an exercise in survival! Teacher workshops were set up and specialist teams learned new technical skills, developed profiles, planned work observation and experience programmes, and began to design and adapt syllabuses. The late summer of 1983 saw remarkable progress by teachers and curriculum advisers in coping with the requirements of new classroom and workshop practice with unknown equipment and fresh teaching schemes. Schools continued to be adapted and equipped, but teachers and learners were often frustrated about delays in supplying the necessary hardware.

The next phase of development early in 1984 was the establishment of support structures to facilitate the work of teachers. Advisory teachers were appointed for specialist curriculum areas and panels of teachers, heads, inspectors and industrialists were set up to steer aspects of TVEI. All of these panels began to reflect the experience and needs of learners and teachers. The Staff Development Panel was chaired by David Settle, newly apponted Director of Professional Support Services for the city. The panel rapidly facilitated full expression of the feelings of teachers about the support they needed to adopt the wider range of strategies and roles that they were being expected to use. Small group work, negotiated learning, profiling of student abilities, partnership with industrial tutors – *all of these innovations and others were challenging the traditional role of the teacher across the curriculum.*

The powerful force of this awareness, born of tough experience rather than dreamed up in theory, was increasingly influential in TVEI. Our use of co-ordinators in schools to lead teams of teachers gave us an important channel of communication and action. Nonetheless David Settle recognised the need for a catalytic influence in Birmingham if we were to challenge traditional attitudes and processes. He gave us a lead in finding the right person to develop practical policies of in-service training for student-centred learning, and we decided to concentrate on the development of our teachers.

Donna Brandes, an acknowledged expert in the field, had worked on Tyneside with David in the previous four years. She came to Birmingham on a limited term contract to initiate a staff development programme. We started preliminary planning in August 1984 and Donna was with us from December 1984 until the following June. This book includes the story of her work with a self-selected group of teachers and on a negotiated programme with TVEI schools. Her compelling influence has triggered the forces for change and development through the expressed needs of teachers drawn from schools and colleges who were given the chance and the leadership to interact with each other; and who now are prepared to carry the work forward without her.

Professor Ted Wragg stressed the crucial significance of teacher development to the overall success of TVEI when he spoke to TVEI co-ordinators in July 1984. I think that we listened well then and that we have acted with this priority at the forefront of the Initiative ever since. We have got something going in this city which is immensely exciting and powerful . . .

Chris Lea,
Project Director,
Birmingham TVEI

The seven steps in Birmingham

Motivation

The initial motivation in Birmingham was detected by the TVEI Staff Development Panel. They heard teachers expressing a need for training which would be school based, useful to all specialised subjects, and would concentrate on techniques for group work, all founded on the basis of a negotiated curriculum.

Further motivation came from David Settle, who told Chris Lea about his previous work with Donna, she, in turn, was excited about the opportunity to spread student-centred learning methods. The MSC was happy to fund the consultancy, for a student-centred approach to learning is central to the philosophy of TVEI.

On coming to Birmingham, Donna looked for a teaching partner for long-term development, and met Paul, who, dissatisfied with his own traditional teaching style, expressed a strong motivation to take on the 'new' methods. Also at this time teachers were invited to commit themselves to intensive training and the Core Group was formed with the following aims:

a To develop a group of highly skilled trainers who could continue to work with teachers at the end of the 28 weeks.

b To produce materials for future training.

c To develop skills in participatory learning methods for *all* areas of the curriculum; negotiating skills; sharing responsibility; personal growth; counselling and listening; communication; problem solving.

d To provide an opportunity to try out the 'new' methods in school and come back to the Core Group for support and sharing.

Establishing trust

We worked to establish trust and credibility by meeting and talking to: the Chief Education Officer; all of the heads and staff members of the TVEI schools; Councillors; the Inspectorate; Advisory Teachers; various TVEI panels; and in some schools groups of parents, governors and students, and occasionally industrialists. Informal contact was as important as attending scheduled meetings.

At the same time trust was beginning to grow among the members of the Core Group as communication and honesty improved; people were encouraged to take risks, and activities which deliberately aimed to increase trust were done. Donna and Paul began to develop a close and trusting teaching partnership; TVEI and Core Group residential weekends provided powerful trust-building experiences. Students, too, were beginning to accept the alternative methods. Also, we had an open classroom, and received a fairly constant stream of visitors, ranging from fellow teachers to HMI.

Towards the end of the project, more staff from TVEI and non-TVEI schools, and from TVEI projects in other authorities, were showing interest in student-centred learning. Contacts were made, training sessions held and credibility was expanded and increased.

Assessment

With each new group of staff members, students, or other educators, the first task was always to take account of the present state of people's knowledge about, or practice of, student-centred learning. Within each group there was always a vast range of information, and a wide spread from acceptance to non-acceptance. The method had to be flexible enough to deal with all variations of response. Evaluation was a constant theme of our teaching parntership, of the Core Group's progress, and of the students' activities. Assessment was considered to be a key element of growth.

Resistance

Vive La Resistance! It added some pepper to the stew of self-congratulation and complacency; it was predominant in some of the groups we worked with. At times, learning to stay centred while the cynical cyclone raged around us was the biggest challenge of all. It was important to make time for people to express their doubts and fears in informal conversation and in group sessions. It was helpful to think of three stages in the introduction of student-centred learning methods:

1 an explanation of the principles;
2 the expression of doubts, questions and resistance;
3 a willingness to learn and practise the necessary skills and strategies.

With most groups, stage three was not achieved without allowing stage two to take place first. On one or two occasions, groups with very limited time were asked if they would be willing to miss out stage two; they agreed and stage three proceeded successfully.

Awareness

Awareness was achieved progressively in the Core Group; a high degree of self-awareness was one of the goals of the group, and it grew at varying rates, to varying degrees, in different people. One of the most gratifying experiences we had in the project was to work with the students, staff members, educators and managers, as their awareness and ours was developing.

Problem solving

Problem solving, in one form or another, characterised our activities with every group; it was almost the life-blood of the process, the means by which various groups at every level of the project were able to exercise their responsibility. Through problem solving, groups experienced participatory methods for themselves, and so it was a way of *demonstrating* how ownership could be transferred successfully. It was a feature, for example, of the management and governors' meetings Donna attended. Interested groups were not given lectures about student-centred methodology, but were invited to participate in the methods as they applied to each group. In all groups, including the Core Group, learning was by doing.

Problem solving was also the means by which Donna, as the change agent, could become increasingly redundant. It was important for this to become an established way of life, in order for the groups to become independent, and for the innovation to continue without the central facilitator.

Contracts

The consultancy contract with the LEA was for seven months, and it was agreed that during this time Donna would carry forth the work in three main ways:

a the Core Group;
b the work with Paul and two groups of students, over seven months, at Queensbridge School;
c the intention to work in as many of the TVEI schools as possible (in the end this included five of the eight schools).

Of course, many other mini-contracts appeared throughout the project, notably the Core Group's commitment to a three-hour session each week, a very demanding discipline, which most of the

30 initial members maintained faithfully. From time to time members were also encouraged to make personal contracts as an aid to professional growth. In lessons, the idea of contracts began to develop, within student groups, concerning the completion of work.

Multi-level innovation

At Queensbridge School, where Donna worked over the seven months, she was able to work in a participatory way with the following people:

The Board of Governors
The Joint Management Committee
The full staff
A working party for PSME
A self-selected group of staff for in-service training in student-centred methods
Alongside a dozen individual teachers in their classrooms
5-B (once a week) and Tech One (twice a week) with Paul.

In general, then, the work proceeded on many levels, including informal conversations with teachers in the staff room, with the Head and Deputy Head, with year tutors, and of course with students.

The multi-level approach did not only exist at Queensbridge. It was a feature of the Core Group, which comprised teachers, administrators, managers, inspectors and advisory teachers. Beyond the Core Group, there was a concerted effort to stimulate interest in student-centred learning at many levels in the Authority.

Networks

As this is being written (June 1985), many networks have been established across Birmingham, which include educators who were not involved when the project began. Various members of the Core Group have been leading, or helping to lead, in-service training sessions for other teachers. Chris Lea and David Settle have been at the initial hub of networks all over the city, the region, and the country, spreading the lessons learned through TVEI, and the philosophy of student-centred learning.

A vision for the future

In the year in which this book was written, the MSC issued guidelines to LEAs inviting them to use available money to develop their in-service programmes. Within these guidelines appears the phrase: 'The emphasis should be on pupil-centred learning, non-didactic teaching methods, problem solving, and practical relevant experience.'

Throughout the country, thousands of teachers have been slowly moving in this direction. Their paths have often been blocked by those who feel that they stand to lose by what they see as a release of control. The MSC's words will be heartening. It is up to those who believe in student-centred learning to make it work.

If we succeed, then I believe the future in education to be very exciting. Schools and colleges will be healthy places to be. Learners and teachers alike will be giving and taking support and trust from one another. Making mistakes in this enviroment will be acceptable; taking risks will be the norm. Cooperation will complement competition. Outcomes will be decided and measured by learners as well as teachers. Everyone will have a stake in owning the action.

My children are now 12 and 14 years of age. Before they leave the system, I want them to experience these changes, so that their children will have a real chance of growing up in a new world.

David Settle,
Director of Professional Support Services,
Birmingham LEA

Members of the Core Group

Colin Baldyga
Peter Beckhelling
Julie Boden
Rhoma Bowdler
Martyn Briggs
Graham Burrows
Kay Chaffer
Peter Connah
Keith Dennis
Paul Ginnis
David Greer
Jean Grigg
Roy Hamer
Yvonne Hanson
Keith Hardwick
Diana Harrap
Carol-Ann Heeks
Tim Jones
Ali Kalsheker
Chris Lea
Marian McFall
Tony Parker
Malcolm Peters
Eric Sant
Laurie Scullard
Chris Traxson
Jacky West

The following were members of the Core Group for a substantial period, but were unable to complete the course:

Chris Giudici
Peter Hewitt
Charles O'Brien

Members of Tech 1

Amjid Ali
Imran Arif
Paul Cameron
Stephen Ellis
Arshed Kadir
Kurshid Rehman
Mark Robinson
Jasvinder Singh
Matthew Taylor
George Webb

Members of 5-B

Nasreen Kahnum
Hyacinth McDonald
Vina Sangani
Haqiqat Ali
Pervez Azam
Mark Balfour
Jamil Bashir
Simon Brown
Anthony Dada
David Galil
Faizul Haq
Javid Hussain
Anil Jagatia
Shoketh Khan
Abdul Mannon
Habib Rehman
Tarac Sarwar
Paul Shipley
Malkeat Singh
Shahnawaz Walayat

Reading list for student-centred learning

If this book list were being written from the student-centred end of the continuum of teaching styles, it would say 'Go to the bookshop and look for books which interest you about this subject', or, even further along the scale, 'What is it you want to know, and where could you find it?' Most of these books are American; they can be ordered from Changes Bookshop in London.

*****

Any book by (or about):

Carl Rogers	Virginia Satir
John Holt	Werner Erhard
Thomas Gordon	Dorothy Heathcote
Sidney Simon	Gavin Bolton
Postman and Weingartner	Leslie Button
Herbet Kohl	David Hargreaves
George Brown	Donna Brandes
George Leonard	Gaie Houston

Examples of recommended texts

Client-Centred Therapy	Carl Rogers
Values Clarification	Sidney Simon
How to Survive in Your Native Land	James Herndon
Teacher Effectiveness Training	Thomas Gordon
Parent Effectiveness Training	Thomas Gordon
Leader Effectiveness Training	Thomas Gordon
TA for Managers	Ron Clements
Games People Play	Eric Berne
I'm OK, You're OK	Thomas Harris
On Becoming a Person	Carl Rogers
Confluent Education	Aaron Hillman
Will the Real Teacher Please Stand Up?	Greer and Rubenstein

BIBLIOGRAPHY

Abercrombie, M.L.J. 1979: *Aims and Techniques of Group Teaching*. Society for Research into Higher Education, University of Surrey.

Alschuler, Alfred S. 1980: *School Discipline: A Socially Literate Solution*. McGraw–Hill, New York.

Amidon, E.J. and Flanders, N.A. 1967: *The Role of the Teacher in the Classroom*. Association for Productive Teaching.

Argyris, C. 1960: *Understanding Organizational Behavior*. Tavistock.

Argyris, C. and Schön, D.A. 1978: *Theory in Practice: Increasing Professional Effectiveness*. Jossey–Bass Publishers, San Francisco.

Ashton, F. 1982: Teacher Education: A Critical View of Skills Training. *Journal of In-Service Education*, Vol. 8, No. 3, Summer.

Ausubel, D., Novak, J.D. and Hanesian, H. 1968: *Educational Psychology. A Cognitive View*. Holt, Rinehart & Winston, New York.

Bannister, D. and Fransella, Fay 1971: *Inquiring Man. The Theory of Personal Constructs*. Penguin Books Ltd., Harmondsworth, Middlesex.

Batten, Thomas R. 1967: *The Non-directive Approach in Group and Community Work*. Oxford University Press.

Bennett, Neville 1976: *Teaching Styles and Pupil Progress*. Open Books, London.

Bligh, Donald A. 1972: *What's the Use of Lectures?* Penguin Books Ltd., Harmondsworth, Middlesex.

Brammer, Lawrence M. and Shostrom, Everett L. 1977: *Therapeutic Psychology: Fundamentals of Counselling and Psycho-Therapy*. Prentice–Hall Inc., New Jersey.

Brandes, Donna and Phillips, Howard 1978: *Gamesters' Handbook*. Hutchinson, London.

Brandes, Donna 1983: *Gamesters Two*. Hutchinson, London.

Brown, George I. 1971: *Human Teaching for Human Learning: An Introduction to Confluent Education*. Esalen/Penguin Books Ltd.

Brown, George I. et al. 1976: *Getting It All Together: Confluent Education*. Phi Delta Kappa, Bloomington, Indiana.

Bruner, Jerome S. 1971: *The Relevance of Education*. Norton & Co., New York.

Cohen, S. 1972: *Folk Devils and Moral Panics*.

Colman, Andrew 1982: *Game Theory and Experimental Games: The Study of Strategic Interaction*. Pergamon.

Cox, C.B. and Dyson, A.E. 1971: *The Black Papers on Education*. Davis–Poynter Ltd., London

Curwin,Richard L. and Fuhrmann, Barbara S. 1975: *Discovering Your Teaching Self: Humanistic Approaches to Effective Teaching*. Prentice–Hall, New Jersey.

de Bono, Edward 1972: *About Think*. Jonathan Cape, London.

Dellinger, Dixie G. 1982: *Out of the Heart: How to design writing assignments for High School courses*. Berkeley University, California.

Dewey, John 1938: *Education and Experience*. Collier Macmillan, New York.

Douglas, Mary 1982: *In the Active Voice*. Routledge & Kegan Paul, London.

Egan, G. 1982: *The Skilled Helper, Model, Skills and Methods for Effective Helping*. 2nd Edition, Brooks, Cole, Monterey, California.

Esland, Geoff; Dale, Roger and Sadler, J. 1972: *The Social Organization of Teaching and Learning*. Open University Press, Milton Keynes.

Evans, M. and Satow, A. 1983: *Working with Groups*. HEC/TACADE.

Fagan, J. and Shepherd, I.L. 1970: *What is Gestalt Therapy?* Harper and Row, New York.

Fagan, J. and Shepherd, I.L. 1970: *Gestalt Therapy Now*. Harper Colophon Books, 1970.

Fantini, Mario D. 1976: *Alternative Education: A Source Book for Parents, Teachers, Students and Administrators*. Doubleday, New York.

Faure, Edgar et al. 1972: *Learning To Be. The World of Education Today and Tomorrow*. UNESCO, Paris

Ferguson, M. 1982: *The Aquarian Conspiracy. Personal and Social Transformation in the 1980s*. Granada, London.

Festinger, Leon 1957: *A Theory of Cognitive Dissonance*. Stanford University Press, California.

Froebel, Friederich 1899: *Education by Development*. Appleton, New York.

Glaser, Barney and Strauss, Anselm L. 1967: *The Discovery of Grounded Theory: Strategies for Qualitative Research*. Aldine Publishing Co., Chicago.

Glasser, William 1969: *Schools Without Failure*. Harper Colophon, New York.

Gordon, Thomas 1974: *Teacher Effectiveness Training*. Peter H. Wyden, New York.

Goulding, M.M. and Goulding, R.L. 1979: *Changing Lives Through Redicision Therapy*. Grove Press, New York.

Hamilton, David 1976: *Curriculum Evaluation*. Open Books, London.

Handy, C. 1976: *Understanding Organisations*. Penguin, Middlesex.

Handy, C. 1979: *Gods of Management, Who They Are, How They Work and Why They Fail*. Pan Books, London.

Hargreaves, David H. 1972: *Interpersonal Relations and Education*. Routledge & Kegan Paul, London.

Hargreaves, David H. 1982: *The Challenge for the Comprehensive School: Culture, Curriculum and Community*. Routledge & Kegan Paul, London.

Harré, Romano and Secord, Paul F. 1972: *The Explanation of Social Behaviour*. Blackwell, Oxford.

Hart, Harold H. (Ed.) 1970: *Summerhill: For and Against*. Hart Publishing Co., New York.

Herndon, James 1971: *How to Survive in Your Native Land*. Simon & Schuster, New York.

Hills, Philip, J. 1976: *The Self-Teaching Process in Higher Education*. Croom Helm, London.

Holt, John 1972: *Freedom and Beyond*. Dell, New York.

Holt, John 1977: *How Children Fail*. Penguin Books Ltd., Middlesex.

Houston, G. 1982: *The Relative-Sized Red Book of Gestalt Therapy*. Rochester Foundation, London

Howgate, Lynn 1982: *Building Self-Esteem Through the Writing Process*. Berkeley University, California.

Hubley, John 1982: *The Notion of Felt Needs*. Leeds Health Education Diploma Course.

Hudson, K. 1978: *The Jargon of the Professions*. Macmillan, London.

Illich, Ivan 1971: *Deschooling Society*. Harper & Row.

Jackson, P.W. and Messick, S. 1971: The person, the product, and the response: conceptual problems in the assessment of creativity. *Personality Growth and Learning. A Source Book*, p. 89. Longman.

Janis, Irving and Mann, Leon 1977: *Decision Making*. Free Press, New York.

Knowles, Malcolm 1970: *The Modern Practice of Adult Education: Andragogy versus Pedagogy*. Follett Publishing Co., Chicago.

Knowles, Malcolm 1978: *The Adult Learner: A Neglected Species*. Gulf Publishing Co., Houston.

Lindeman, E.C. 1926: *The Meaning of Adult Education*. New Republic, New York.

MacDonald, Barry and Walker, Rob 1976: *Changing the Curriculum*. Open Books, London.

MacDonald, Barry 1978: *The Experience of Innovation*. Centre for Applied Research in Education, University of East Anglia.

McGregor, Douglas 1960: *The Human Side of Experience*. McGraw–Hill, New York.

McGuiness, John 1982: *Planned Pastoral Care: A Guide for Teachers*. McGraw–Hill, New York.

McLeish, John Matheson and Park, James 1973: *The Psychology of the Learning Group*. Hutchinson University Library, London.

Magee, Bryan 1982: *Popper*. Fontana Paperbacks, Glasgow.

Margulies, Newton and Wallace, J. 1973: *Organisational Change Techniques and Application*. Scott Foresman, Glenview, Illinois.

Marsh, Peter; Rosser, R. and Hane, R. 1980: *The Rules of Disorder*. Routledge & Kegan Paul, London.

Marshall, Judi and McLean, Adrian 1983: *Intervening in Cultures*. University of Bath, Centre for the Study of Organizational Change and Development.

Maslow, Abraham 1966: *The Psychology of Science*. Harper and Row, New York.

Maslow, Abraham 1969: *Toward a Psychology of Being*. Van Nostrand Reinhold.

Maslow, A. 1970, rev. ed.: *Motivation and Personality*. Hayser & Bros., New York.

Maslow, A. 1976: *The Farther Reaches of Human Nature*. Penguin Books.

Morris, Lynn and Fitz-Gibbon, Carol 1978: *How to Measure Program Implementation*. Sage Publications, Beverley Hills.

Moustakas, Clark 1956: *The Teacher and the Child*. McGraw–Hill, New York.

Naisbitt, John 1984: *Megatrends*. MacDonald & Co., London.

Neill, A.S. 1962: *Summerhill*. Victor Gollancz Ltd., London.

Nisbet, John 1975: Innovation – Bandwagon or Hearse?. *Curriculum Innovation*. Croom Helm, London.

Parlett, Malcolm and King, J. 1971: *Concentrated Study: A Pedagogic Innovation Observed*. Society for Research into Higher Education, London.

Parlett, M. and Hamilton, D. 1972: *Evaluation as Illumination: A New Approach to the Study of Innovatory Programmes*. Occasional Paper 9, Centre for the Research in Educational Sciences, University of Edinburgh.

Parlett, Malcolm and Dearden, Garry 1977: *Introduction to Illuminative Evaluation: Studies in Higher Education*. Pacific Soundings Press, California.

Parlett, Malcolm 1981: *Illuminative Evaluation*. Wiley and Sons Ltd., Chichester.

Parlett, Malcolm 1983: *Experiential Knowledge*. (Unpublished chapter).

Parlett, Malcolm undated: Illuminative Evaluation, in *International Encyclopedia of Education: Research and Studies.* (Article No. 035/90698) to be published by Pergamon.

Parrott, A. and Flude, R. 1983: 'A Curriculum Fit for Adults?' *Adult Education*, Vol. 56, No. 2, pp. 117–21.

Passons, W. 1975: *Gestalt Approaches to Counselling.* Holt, Rinehart and Winston, New York.

Pearson, Geoffrey 1975: *The Deviant Imagination.* Macmillan, London.

Perls, F.S., Hefferline, R.F. and Goodman, P. 1951: *Gestalt Therapy.* Crown Publishers, New York.

Perls, F.S., Hefferline, R.F. and Goodman, P. 1973: *Gestalt Therapy, Excitement and Growth in the Human Personality.* Penguin, London.

Peters, Richard 1959: *Authority, Responsibility and Education.* Allen & Unwin Ltd., London.

Postman, Neil and Weingartner, Charles 1969: *Teaching as a Subversive Activity.* Delacorte, New York.

Reason, Peter and Rowan, John (Eds) 1981: *Human Inquiry. A Sourcebook of the New Paradigm Research.* John Wiley & Sons, Chichester.

Revans, Reg. 1982: 'Action Learning: Its Origins and Nature'. *Higher Education Review*, p. 20.

Rico, Gabriele and Claggett, Mary 1980: *Balancing the Hemispheres: Brain Research and the Teaching of Writing.* Berkeley University, California.

Rhinehart, L. 1976: *The Book of est.* Holt, Rinehart, New York.

Rogers, Carl 1961: *On Becoming a Person.* Houghton Mifflin Co., Boston.

Rogers, Carl 1965: *Client-Centred Therapy.* Houghton Mifflin Co., Boston.

Rogers, Carl 1969: *Freedom to Learn.* Merrill, Ohio.

Rosenthal, R. and Jacobson, L. 1968: *Pygmalion in the Classroom: Teacher Expectation and Pupils' Intellectual Development.* Holt, Rinehart & Winston.

Rothschild, Lord 1977: *Meditations of a Broomstick.* Collins, London.

Rutter, Michael et al. 1979: *Fifteen Thousand Hours: Secondary Schools and their effects on Children.* Open Books, London.

Samples, Bob; Charles, Cheryl and Barnhart, Dick 1977: *The Wholeschool Book. Teaching and Learning late in the 20th Century.* Addison–Wesley Publishing Co., Reading, Massachusetts.

Schmuck, R.A.; Runkel, P.J.; Arends, J.H. and Arends, R.I. 1977: *The Second Handbook of Organisational Development in Schools.* Mayfield Publishing Co., Palo Alto, California.

Schön, D.A.: *The Reflective Practitioner.*

School of Education, University of Exeter 1984: *The Hargreaves Challenge: A Response.* Perspectives No. 13.

Settle D. 1984: *Ownership.* Unpublished paper, Birmingham LEA.

Silberman, Melvin; Allender, Jerome and Yanoff, Jay 1972: *The Psychology of Open Teaching and Learning.*

Simons, Helen (Ed.) 1980: *Towards a Science of the Singular.* Centre for Applied Research in Education, University of East Anglia.

Smith, Peter B. 1973: *Groups within Organisations. Applications of Social Psychology to Organisational Behaviour.* Harper and Row, London.

Smith, Peter B. 1980: *Group Process and Personal Change.* Harper and Row, London.

Spooner, R. 1983: What it takes to be a real teacher. *Education*, Vol. 162, No. 4, p. 270.

Spradley, James 1980: *Participant Observation*. Holt, Rinehart and Winston, New York.

Stenhouse, Lawrence 1967: *Culture and Education*. Nelson, London.

Stenhouse, Lawrence 1975: *An Introduction to Curriculum Research and Development*. Heinemann Ed. Books Ltd., London.

Szasz, Thomas 1962: *The Myth of Mental Illness: Foundations of a Theory of Personal Conduct*. Secker & Warburg, London.

Van De Riet, V.; Korb, M.P. and Gorrell, J.J. 1980: *Gestalt Therapy: An Introduction*. Pergamon Press, New York.

Watzlawick, P.; Beavin, J.H. and Jackson, D.D. 1967: *Pragmatics of Human Communication: A Study of Interactional Patterns, Pathologies and Paradoxes*. W.W. Norton, New York.

Watzlawick, P.; Weakland, T. and Fisch, R. 1974: *Change: Principles of Problem Formation and Problem Resolution*. W.W. Norton, New York.

Weinstein, Gerald and Fantini, Mario (Eds) 1970: *Toward Humanistic Education: A Curriculum of Affect*. Praeger, New York.

Wilkinson, R. 1983: Are You Fit to Train Others? *Education and Training*, July, p. 30.

Williamson, Bill 1982: *Class, Culture and Community. A Biographical Study of Social Change in Mining*. Routledge & Kegan Paul, London.

Zimbardo, Philip G.; Ebbesen, Ebbe and Maslach, Christina 1977: *Influencing Attitudes and Changing Behaviour*. Addison–Wesley Publishing Co.

Zinker, J. 1977: *Creative Process in Gestalt Therapy*. Brunner, Mazel.